DR BARRETT

Dedicated

To my mom, Lorene Hopkins Barrett

SOS Life Enhancement
SOS Self Improvement
Let us help you climb your mountain
Copyright © 2015 Dr. John C. Barrett Jr. PH-D
SOS Publications West Plains, Missouri U.S.A. Printed in U.S.A.

Dr. John C. Barrett Jr. is the coordinator of Support Outreach Services = SOS. Dr. Barrett is dedicated to publishing books on helping you help yourself. It is our hope that this book will help you discover truths for your own life and help you meet the needs of others.

All Scripture quotations, unless otherwise noted, are taken from the NKJV are taken from the Holy Bible, New King James Version, copyright © 1979, 1980, 1982 by Thomas Nelson, Inc. Used by permission.

All rights reserved. Except for brief quotations in critical publications or reviews, no part of this book may be reproduced in any manner without prior written permission from the publisher. Requests for permissions should be addressed to:

Support Outreach Services (SOS) LLC West Plains, MO 65775
(417) 204-8022 – drbarrettphd@yahoo.com
www.sosselfhelpbooks.info

ISBN-10 0692574018
ISBN-13 9780692574010

Cover Design: Lisa Narodowski – WiredNDesign Book Design: Lisa Narodowski – WircdNDc

SOS NEW BEGINNINGS
Analytical Study Guide
Dr. John Barrett
B.S/M.A/PH-D
Clinical Psychologist
Counselor / Analysis
Group Sessions

Support Outreach Services =
SOS Publications
Author: John C. Barrett Jr. B.S/ M.A/PH-D

To participate in any of our services are free. When you order our books, and the study materials and DVD's, there is an expense:
One book $15.00
Two Books $25.00
Three Books $35.00
Study materials $10.00
Shipping costs $ 10.00

What you do will enable us to carry out some of these programs and services.

Our information network will give you a list of study guides, newsletters are on the link, and some booklets are free. There is so much information out there and there are all kinds of help.

Our processing center is an independent processing center. One of the links is called: "Gems for Jams." This is a community service bulletin board, but really it is much more than that.

ALWAYS LOOK FOR THE LIGHT HOUSE BECAUSE IT LEADS THE SHIPS SAFELY INTO THE HARBOR

Preparing for New Beginning
Poem: {1}

By John O'Donohue
In out-of-the-way places of the heart,
Where your thoughts never think to wander,
This beginning has been quietly forming,
Waiting until you were ready to emerge.
For a long time it has watched your desire,
Feeling the emptiness growing inside you,
Noticing how you willed yourself on,
Still unable to leave what you had outgrown.
It watched you play with the seduction of safety
And the gray promises that sameness whispered,
Heard the waves of turmoil rise and relent,
Wondered would you always live like this.
Then the delight, when your courage kindled,
And out you stepped onto new ground,
Your eyes young again with energy and dream,
A path of plenitude opening before you.
Though your destination is not yet clear
You can trust the promise of this opening;
Unfurl yourself into the grace of beginning
That is at one with your life's desire.
Awaken your spirit to adventure;
Hold nothing back, learn to find ease in risk;
Soon you will be home in a new rhythm,
For your soul senses the world that awaits you.
John O'Donohue

Table of Contents

Publications by Support Outreach Services   P. 1
Subjects: Profiles, Charts Axioms, & Questionnaires   P. 3
INDEX   P. 5
PREFACE   P. 10
Chapters 1 – 6   New Beginnings I, Preparing for Dating & Marriage
Chapter 7   New Beginnings II, Preparing for The effects of Divorce
Chapters 8 - 10   New Beginnings III, Preparing for Single Parenting
Chapters 11 - 12   New Beginnings IV, Preparing for Addictions & Treatments
Chapter 13, New beginnings V, Health & Fitness Program & Workout

Chapter 1   P. 14
New Beginnings I, Dating & Marriage
PREPARING FOR PERSONAL RELATIONSHIPS

Chapter 2   P. 72
PREPARE YOUR HEART AND MIND FOR MARRIAGE AND FAMILY

Chapter 3   P. 90
DEFINING THE RELATIONSHIP, MARRIAGE AND HAVING CHILDREN

Chapter 4   P. 104
The QUITE BEFORE and AFTER THE STORM.

Chapter 5   P. 124
THE WARNING SIGNS IN RELATIONSHIPS & MARRIAGE

Chapter 6   P. 148
PREPARING FOR SEX IN THE MARRIAGE

New Beginnings II,
The effects of Divorce

Chapter 7   P. 190

MARRIAGE – FAMILY & ADDICTIONS

PARPARING YOURSELF BEFORE AND AFTER DIVORCE
New Beginnings III,
Single Parenting, Adoption, & Blinded Families

Chapter 8   P. 226
SINGLE PARENTING

Chapter9   P. 260
STEPPARENTS AND ADOPTED PARENTS ROLE

Chapter 10   P. 272
BLENDED FAMILIES

New Beginnings IV,
Addictions& Treatments

Chapter 11   P. 282
ADDICTIONS AS IT RELATES TO FAMILIES

Chapter 12   P. 326
TREATMENTS FOR ADDICTIONS

New Beginnings V,
Health & Fitness Program & Workout

Chapter 13   P. 370
MY SECRETS TO A
HEALTHY HEART & FITNESS!

Chapter 14   P. 380
SUPPORT OUTREACH SERVICES

Appendix *i*
Résumé of Studies   P. 391

Appendix *ii*
Definitions: P. 394

Appendix *iii*
Web References   P. 396

Appendix *iiii*
Poems & Charts References   P. 399

Appendix *iiiii*
Bible References   P. 400

Subjects: Profiles, Charts / Axioms, & Questionnaires

Chapter 1
Dating and preparing before marriage?
Let me profile how the (Genogram) works and why it will be helpful in understand the genetic ties in a family?

Chapter 2
What is the acid test in a relationship and marriage, it is "LOVE"
Self-Awareness is a key in understanding happiness in a relationship.

Chapter 3
Love and Marriage in Relation to Your Identity
Describing the different power struggles
The role children play in marriage

Chapter 4
Describing the different power struggles and how each affects a relationship and marriage.
Formula for marriage and family problems
The questionnaire on love.

Chapter 5
Assessment of the relationship
Self-Awareness is a key in understanding happiness in a relationship.
How to maintain a good relationship is being able to communicate with each other?
Know your communications' Skills
Normal and abnormal is defined by good and poor emotional control:
11 Principles for a better marriage

Chapter 6
Sexual problems in the marriage.
I Corinthians 7: 1-40
Ephesians 5:21-33
Sexual-attractions / affairs
Sexual Addictions & Desires Sexuality
Concluding with rising children
Summary of marriage

Chapter 7
The Real Hurt & Pain:
Divorce: the Real Hurt & Pain:
*1 kissed A (Prince or Princess) & they turned out to be a __?
In our real world, we don't always get A (Prince or Princess).
Mixed Marriages a. Blended Families, b. Stepchildren & others.
The 10 Most Common Causes of Divorce / Marriage and Separation Advice
There are some miss conceptions about divorce.
Why do people get divorced?
Drugs and Alcoholism
Infidelity/Adultery / Abuse
Divorce Planning & Preparedness do you need to get a lawyer?
Healing Your Heart after Divorce

Chapter 8
Children of divorced parents are more likely to end their own marriage.
Questionnaire II. 14 Critical Situations?
The effects on divorced children
Preparing for Divorce, Single Parenting, &
    Blended family's Study Guide
The results of addictions in the family

Chapter 9
My personal profile as a stepparent
A Stepparent's Role

Chapter 10
Profile of emotional involvement in the children of blinded families
Step Children

Chapter 11
 1) Substance abuse
 2) Talking and dealing with teens and young adults about addictions

Help and healing Addiction center and group theory

Alcoholism-Drugs-Pills-Smoking
Drugs, Brain, and Behavior – The Science of Addiction – Addiction and Health
Four personal examples of alcoholism by the author.
Is alcoholism a social issue or a disease?

Chapter 12
Teen Drinking Statics a Family Guide.
Alcoholism
Evaluation of Addictions
The effects of parental exposure on Executive Functions
Mental disorders / illness / disease and their treatment

Chapter 13
Rehabilitation & Maintenance)
It starts with Health-Awareness!

Chapter 14
Review of our services

Review of Marriage and Family Stages.
The identity crisis (New married couples)
Stage 1
Parenting children crisis (Adolescent and teens)
Stage 2
Empty nest crisis (New adjustments, and changes)
The mid-life crisis (Burn out and unfulfillment)
Stage 3
Families who deal crisis (with addictions)

PREFACE

Self-Help Book

We are going to profile each book and each book has its own identity and helpful in the different aspects of person's life. This is the third in a series of books **SOS New Beginnings, Analytical Study Guide** we deal with these personal situations that helps a person acquire a better understanding of what a person is going through in their **Relationships, Marriage** and **Family.** I deal with **Divorce, Single Parenting,** and **Blended Families**. I have centered this study around young adults, singles and young couples. I find that age regardless is relevant when a person is dealing with any situation I think it will be helpful because there are different stages in life and in relationships of any kind. Weather its dating or marriage; everyone faces any number of problems throughout life. I draw from a vast number of sources and you can pick any one or all of these situations. These studies will help anyone who wants help in these areas.

Preparing a person's heart and mind for dating, marriage / family & children, in chapters 1-6 "New Beginnings preparing before and after divorce", "I did not kiss a princess". Single Parenting, Blended Families, and Addictions in the family chapters 7-10. Addictions, Alcoholism-Drugs-Pills-Smoking an evaluation of the addictions; we unlock information about treatments and the different kinds of help, we make an analysis of Alcoholism-Drugs-Pills/Medications-Smoking-etc. = Co-dependency, chapters 11 & 12 & other information on Health Awareness & Support outreach Services chapters in 13 & 14.

Self Help Book: SOS LIFE ENHANCEMENT, The Functions of the brain, (*who is that person in your mirror?*). Cognitive Behavior Identity in chapters 1-7 and Cognitive Modification in chapters 7-10, check-ups (Evaluations, Assessments, Analysis in the form of questionnaires.

Self Help Book: "SOS SELF-IMPROVEMENT, *Self-Image, Self-Esteem & Self-Worth".* The assessments of a person are based on self-concepts there are two terms we will deal with throughout that study:

Meta Cognition Awareness and the aspect of Intelligence and how they fit into the psychology of one's self. We deal with three basic areas: (Identity) "self-image, self-esteem, and self-worth" as I deal with a person there are no two people alike.

My biography is about my family and me it sets the stage for my studies, *"Facing the real me, Run John Run, The real hurt and pain, and the real cry for help, the real world and me."* The reasons for these studies are unique because of my perception of what happened to me. I have personal feeling that go into these studies.

Self-Help Books HAVE VALUE BECAUSE:
WE NEVER KNOW WHAT WILL HAPPEN!
I DON'T RECOMMEND READING ANY ONE OF THESE STUDIES IN ONE SETTING!

I want people who read any of my books to take time stop at any point; because you need to let the information help you, come back when you feel the need for more information about the study. You may not need this book now, but likely, there is someone in your family who will need the information in this study, some may wait until they feel the need the study and how they can help a person.

Support **O**utreach Services

Support-**network** is to find help when dealing with any circumstances and problems. It does not mean there are not answers and/or maybe there are multiple answers or solutions in some cases, I will look at each study from different points of view, and in some cases none of the choices are good ones.

Outreach **Network, we** call this our **o**utreach program**.**

Surveys, Evaluations, and Matching Profiles
Conferences, Seminars, & Retreats, Work Shops and Manuals.

Are *you* hitting the bulls-eye in *your life*?

I use different Methods and Case Studies!
Illustrations, personal experiences & examples!
Personal profiles relating to the different subjects in each book!

We believe **Health-Awareness** is a vital part of *your* make-up.
Services Network Links & Hot Topics

My mission as the coordinator of Support Outreach Services LLC will be to help a person feel they can do something to help themselves. I know there is a lot of information in these studies, the important thing is to go at your pace and that is why I have different chapters and subjects headings relating to different kinds of problems in our books and booklets. This is my burden Gal. 6:1-3, "Bearing one another's burdens"….

Dr. John C Barrett Jr. B.S /M.A / in Counseling, & PH-D in Psychology

DR BARRETT

NEW BEGINNING I, DATING & MARRIAGE

Chapter 1

PREPARING FOR PERSONAL RELATIONSHIPS

Opening Statement

If you have not read any of my books I would like to take a few minutes to get acquainted with you the reader. This book is different because of the way we present the problems in relationships and each of these subjects have become a problem in our society. I will let you know how a person or couple gets to know themselves in relation frame work of the subjects we cover. I will start with dating & the engagement period, there is much more to be learned as we deal with your past and present relationships and the marriage.

The key is choosing the right marriage partner and that is great, but it may be difficult because a person can be attracted to a person for the wrong reasons and the consequences are usually devastating to the person and it will affect the relationship sooner or later. The marriage has a much better chance in developing and growing if you find things in common opposites do make good marriage if they complement each other's personalities, getting it right between each other, if don't you agree on things. If you didn't that does not mean you can't have a great relationship we want to help you get the relationship and marriage on tract.

Now, I hope we can help you in making your relationship and/or marriage better, we will go back through the problems you have had or if any during dating and during the engagement stage, and preparing for the wedding. We think it is important to go through the marriage stages. Learn from what is affecting your relationship (the good & bad) and learn how to solve problems and develop new communication skills. Do you know at this point what you want in a relationship, you need to stop & listen as I profile relationships.

Personal relationships

This part study will help in any **personal relationships**; I will spend a great deal of time dealing with the **personal situations in relationships** as I look at each **profile** and **references** in this study.

Now let's look at personal relationships, they are complex in nature because people are complex beings, within a person is the love, relationships are based on love, and how does the brain interrupts the love into what a person thinks of someone else, that will be a part of this study on relationships and raising a family. What if your marriage doesn't work and you have to deal with a divorce, single parenting, and blended families. There are other problems such as addictions in marriages.

Let me profile how the Genogram works and why it will be helpful in understanding the genetic pasted on in a family?

There are two ways I use the Genogram in my counseling, I know there is no way I can explain how the genogram works in this book, you will have to email me if you want or we can do this on the phone or in person. For now I want to explain how important it is for you to understand the need for a genetic profile and how the temperament analysis can help you it will tell us a lot about a person by knowing their parents and grandparents. The more you know about them will be helpful in helping you know *who you are*? There is a lot to be learned from a person's birth order and the number of children, the oldest to youngest, we will deal with this later in our study guide.

The genogram will help us by going back at least one generation or more if the person knows anything about their family history for several generations. It allows one to clearly diagram the general and complex information about a family. It organizes the basic relationships among family members, their names, important dates, and the characteristics of each person (personality, health, vocation, addictions etc.) of individual family members.

I have not read any of my books I would like to take a few minutes to get acquainted with you the reader. This book is different because of the way we present the problems in relationships and each of these subjects have become a problem in our society. I will let you know how a person or couple gets to know themselves in relation frame work of the subjects we cover. I will start with dating & the engagement period, there is much more to be learned as we deal with your past and present relationships and the marriage.

The key is choosing the right marriage partner and that is great, but it may be difficult because a person can be attracted to a person for the wrong reasons and the consequences are usually devastating to the person and it will affect the relationship sooner or later. The marriage has a much better chance in developing and growing if you find things in common opposites do make good marriage if they complement each other's personalities, getting it right between each other, if don't you agree on things. If you didn't that does not mean you can't have a great relationship we want to help you get the relationship and marriage on tract.

Now, I hope we can help you in making your relationship and/or marriage better, we will go back through the problems you have had or if any during dating and during the engagement stage, and preparing for the wedding. We think it is important to go through the marriage stages. Learn from what is affecting your relationship (the good & bad) and learn how to solve problems and develop new communication skills. Do you know at this point what you want in a relationship, you need to stop& listen as I profile relationships, and I will prepare you for a loving relationship in your marriage; this is our goal in these studies.

We are going to help you develop a good relationship and marriage; there are three stages in a relationship and then marriage. I want to make it very clear as we go through each stage how important each stage will be in your relationship. I believe in a concept of looking at courting and dating it does not stop when you get married you still need to date and court your wife.

This part study will help in any **personal relationships**; I will spend a great deal of time dealing with the **personal situations in relationships** as I look at each **profile** and **references** in this study.

Now let's look at personal relationships, they are complex in nature because people are complex beings, within a person is the love, relationships are based on love, and how does the brain interrupts the love into what a person thinks of someone else, that will be a part of this study on relationships and raising a family. What if your marriage doesn't work and you have to deal with a divorce, single parenting, and blended families. There are other problems such as addictions in marriages.

Let me profile how the Genogram works and why it will be helpful in understanding the genetic pasted on in a family?

There are two ways I use the Genogram in my counseling, I know there is no way I can explain how the genogram works in this book, you will have to email me if you want or we can do this on the phone or in person. For now I want to explain how important it is for you to understand the need for a genetic profile and how the temperament analysis can help you it will tell us a lot about a person by knowing their parents and grandparents. The more you know about them will be helpful in helping you know *who you are*? There is a lot to be learned from a person's birth order and the number of children, the oldest to youngest, we will deal with this later in our study guide.

The genogram will help us by going back at least one generation or more if the person knows anything about their family history for several generations. It allows one to clearly diagram the general and complex information about a family. It organizes the basic relationships among family members, their names, important dates, and the characteristics of each person (personality, health, vocation, addictions etc.) of individual family members.

The genogram gives a person ways to study the family based on the assumption that some basic patterns come from one or both the mother, father and their children, problems from past generations and may wellbe repeated in future generations. These repeated patterns may include relationship factors, personality characteristics, specific illnesses, etc. For example, one family may be typified by female dominate personality over several generations. Another family may have members with exceptional musical talent. A family may have a history of diabetes such information is easily profiled in a genogram.

By creating a careful history with knowledge of these details that relate to the present generation, it is possible to reconstruct many important aspects of the way individuals and family has reacted in the pasted generations and that makes it predictable in future generations.

Uses for the genogram:

1) It is helpful to see the family as a group of individuals who are connected to each other in important ways. There is interdependence among family members. What occurs with one family member may affect the other members of the family?

2) The individual members of the family see commonalties and uniqueness within the family members. This can facilitate the development in a sense of identity.

3) Clarifying the available options for change in the family. For example, a given family may come to see itself as too hard on their children, how it affects teen and young adults, and a desire to create a little more discipline as a parent.

4) What happens when one member of the family is known as the "escape goat" (we will give more details later) or person "with the problem" independent of the total family structure.

5) Provide both simple information (dates, births, marriages, deaths) and complex information (triangles, power struggles, family

issues, scripts) for making decisions and seeing what needs to be done in the further.

6) People may better understand their own strengths and weaknesses and how these may affect them as an individual, couple, or family.

Names, nicknames, family titles for each person.

1) Dates of birth, death, severe illness, marriages, separations, divorces, other rites of passage.

2) Physical locations and dates of important moves.

3) Genetic characteristics between members of the extended family or their strengths, and the type of relationship. Double lines may illustrate frequent contact and close relationships. Dashed lines may illustrate distant relationships and infrequent contact. Lines with slashes may illustrate conflict in different relationships.

4) Emotional problems. What was the issue or event? When?

5) Ethnicity, occupation, socioeconomic level, religious affiliation and participation.

6) Affairs, power struggles, alcoholism and/or drugs problems.

7) Important health problems and behavioral characteristics.

By seeing family patterns will show up, you fill in the information you want to help you or a family member as we go through the genogram. Individuals may realize their personal identity more fully by seeing themselves as a part of a family network, and by observing family values passed down over the generations. As you learn more about your family members, you will begin to appreciate the role your ancestors played in your life, and each of us have a responsibility to them to do the same for our children, thus giving a link between the past and future generations.

You may need more than one genogram to get all the information you want for each generation, go as far back as you can, the two things I look for and trace are addictions, drugs, and alcoholism, by any family members, the second is behavior patterns depression, anxiety, and anger problems. (Use a color for addicted family members, a different color for behaviors, the third color maybe for illnesses like cancer, or diseases).

Say for instance there is three generation of depression in your family on one side, but not the other what is likely to happen to all of the children, some will have more depression than others, why? More than likely one or more will have server depression because it goes back three generations. To break that genetic tie it will take two to three generations to break it, the same goes for drugs and it can skip a generation. If a person's mother has been on drugs the child comes into the world with the addiction from the mother, and it can result from a father if they have the same blood type.

That is why it is so important to understand where your emotions or drug problems came from and which parent it comes from. Our goal is to help you solve the previous problems, and not carry any excess baggage if possible. When there is damage in a relationship a person needs to look at their own personal baggage before they go any farther and cause any more damage to the relationship or family members.

Now I want you to try and fill out the family genogram it will help you as you go on with this study, or you may need to do some more study before you are ready to finish and complete the genetic and behavior genogram. You may want it to go back three generations with aunts and uncles as you see the genogram below. This is a part of the introduction, so you will know what to look for in the rest of this study. Email drbarrettphd@yahoo.com or phone 417 204-8022

Profiling our studies

Let me give you some back ground for these studies I have been doing groups sessions for over ten years personal, family, and addictions. I have done them in churches because they care and want to help people, and another reason they have the space, we have never done them during a service at the church, it is usually before the service because some like to go to their own church and some don't go to church at all. Let me tell some of these life stories of men who were on drugs and alcohol for over 20 years, each one will tell you they were at the end of their road and the next trip to the hospital could have been their last, all of them started in their early teens.

The thing that changed their life was being in a rehab center, more than that they wanted to quit, all of them will tell you they could not have done it without Gods help. Two of them went Bible College and one of them had a relapse later and realized he needed more help, one is a preacher and another works in a rehab program, the other one does Bible studies in a prison. The one thing they have in common they replaced the addiction with something constructive in their life. I am the coordinator of a "relapse program" and they are mentors to those who come to our group sessions. We probably have three out ten that really changes their life, but all of them have moderate success and most have two or three relapse during recovery, each time they say I will never do it again.

I also do counseling at the Masters Ranch & Christian Academy. I have boys who have had family problems with aggressive behaviors at home, school, and others who have had addictions as early as 12 years of age. The ones with bad addictions come from parents who have been on drugs and alcohol during and before the birth of a child. I have some that the mother was on drugs and alcohol during the time of birth. The adopted parents take them because they want to help them not realizing what the addictions came due to the child because of addictions, most of them come from great homes while others come from alcohol and drug homes. The point I want make they raised them in a good environment and they still got on drugs, what does that tell us the environment is not enough, I want to make it very clear the addictions can be traced if you use the genetic genogram and include it in your family genogram. It is very predictable when we know the history of the addictions in your family. For most alcoholics and drug addiction people live a life of broken promises to themselves and their family.

At the ranch we have good kids and you wouldn't know they've had problems they do very good because they are in a controlled home they stay at least one year others stay for two years, and some are there until they reach the age of 18. The boys, again most of the boys have problems when they go back into society and their home. I have known of some who came back three times, the success rate is around 70% and there are a number who really turn their life around and we are proud of them because we had a part in their life.

I will deal with addictions in the family/children and treatments in chapters 11 & 12, but now you can go on with the study or have you start work on your genogram. \

I would like to take a few minutes to get acquainted with you the reader. This book is different because of the way we present the problems in relationships and each of these subjects have become a problem in our society. I will let you know how a person or couple gets to know themselves in relation frame work of the subjects we cover. I will start with dating & the engagement period, there is much more to be learned as we deal with your past and present relationships and the marriage.

The key is choosing the right marriage partner and that is great, but it may be difficult because a person can be attracted to a person for the wrong reasons and the consequences are usually devastating to the person and it will affect the relationship sooner or later. The marriage has a much better chance in developing and growing if you find things in common opposites do make good marriage if they complement each other's personalities, getting it right between each other, if don't you agree on things. If you didn't that does not mean you can't have a great relationship we want to help you get the relationship and marriage on tract.

Now, I hope we can help you in making your relationship and/or marriage better, we will go back through the problems you have had or if any during dating and during the engagement stage, and preparing for the wedding. We think it is important to go through the marriage stages. Learn from what is affecting your relationship (the good & bad) and learn how to solve problems and develop new communication skills. Do you know at this point what you want in a relationship, you need to stop& listen as I profile relationships, and I will prepare you for a loving relationship in your marriage; this is our goal in these studies.

We are going to help you develop a good relationship and marriage; there are three stages in a relationship and then marriage. I want to make it very clear as we go through each stage how important each stage will be in your relationship. I believe in a concept of looking at courting and dating it does not stop when you get married you need to date and court your wife.

Dating   Courtship   Wedding

Personal relationships

This part study will help in any **personal relationships**; I will spend a great deal of time dealing with the **personal situations in relationships** as I look at each **profile** and **references** in this study.

Now let's look at personal relationships, they are complex in nature because people are complex beings, within a person is the love, relationships are based on love, and how does the brain interrupts the love into what a person thinks of someone else, that will be a part of this study on relationships and raising a family. What if your marriage doesn't work and you have to deal with a divorce, single parenting, and blended families. There are other problems such as addictions in marriages.

Let me profile how the Genogram works and why it will be helpful in understanding the genetic pasted on in a family?

There are two ways I use the Genogram in my counseling, I know there is no way I can explain how the genogram works in this book, you will have to email me if you want or we can do this on the phone or in person. For now I want to explain how important it is for you to understand the need for a genetic profile and how the temperament analysis can help you it will tell us a lot about a person by knowing their parents and grandparents. The more you know about them will be helpful in helping you know *who you are*? There is a lot to be learned from a person's birth order and the number of children, the oldest to youngest, we will deal with this later in our study guide.

The genogram will help us by going back at least one generation or more if the person knows anything about their family history for several generations. It allows one to clearly diagram the general and complex information about a family. It organizes the basic relationships among family members, their names, important dates, and the characteristics of each person (personality, health, vocation, addictions etc.) of individual family members.

The genogram gives a person ways to study the family based on the assumption that some basic patterns come from one or both the mother, father and their children, problems from past generations and may well be repeated in future generations. These repeated patterns may include relationship factors, personality characteristics, specific illnesses, etc. For example, one family may be typified by female dominate personality over several generations. Another family may have members with exceptional musical talent. A family may have a history of diabetes such information is easily profiled in a genogram.

By creating a careful history with knowledge of these details that relate to the present generation, it is possible to reconstruct many important aspects of the way individuals and family has reacted in the past generations and that makes it predictable in future generations.

Uses for the genogram:

7) It is helpful to see the family as a group of individuals who are connected to each other in important ways. There is interdependence among family members. What occurs with one family member may affect the other members of the family?

8) The individual members of the family see commonalties and uniqueness within the family members. This can facilitate the development in a sense of identity.

9) Clarifying the available options for change in the family. For example, a given family may come to see itself as too hard on their children, how it affects teen and young adults, and a desire to create a little more discipline as a parent.

10) What happens when one member of the family is known as the "escape goat" (we will give more details later) or person "with the problem" independent of the total family structure.

11) Provide both simple information (dates, births, marriages, deaths) and complex information (triangles, power struggles, family issues, scripts) for making decisions and seeing what needs to be done in the further.

12) People may better understand their own strengths and weaknesses and how these may affect them as an individual, couple, or family.

Names, nicknames, family titles for each person.

1) Dates of birth, death, severe illness, marriages, separations, divorces, other rites of passage.

2) Physical locations and dates of important moves.

3) Genetic characteristics between members of the extended family or their strengths, and the type of relationship. Double lines may illustrate frequent contact and close relationships. Dashed lines may illustrate distant relationships and infrequent contact. Lines with slashes may illustrate conflict in different relationships.

4) Emotional problems. What was the issue or event? When?

5) Ethnicity, occupation, socioeconomic level, religious affiliation and participation.

6) Affairs, power struggles, alcoholism and/or drugs problems.

7) Important health problems and behavioral characteristics.

By seeing family patterns will show up, you fill in the information you want to help you or a family member as we go through the genogram. Individuals may realize their personal identity more fully by seeing themselves as a part of a family network, and by observing family values passed down over the generations. As you learn more about your family members, you will begin to appreciate the role your ancestors played in your life, and each of us have a responsibility to them to do the same for our children, thus giving a link between the past and future generations.

You may need more than one genogram to get all the information you want for each generation, go as far back as you can, the two things I look for and trace are addictions, drugs, and alcoholism, by any family members, the second is behavior patterns depression, anxiety, and anger problems. (Use a color for addicted family members, a different color for behaviors, the third color maybe for illnesses like cancer, or diseases). Say for instance there is three generation of depression in your family on one side, but not the other what is likely to happen to all of the children, some will have more depression than others, why? More than likely one or more will have server depression because it goes back three generations. To break that genetic tie it will take two to three generations to break it, the same goes for drugs and it can skip a generation. If a person's mother has been on drugs the child comes into the world with the addiction from the mother, and it can result from a father if they have the same blood type.

That is why it is so important to understand where your emotions or drug problems came from and which parent it comes from. Our goal is to help you solve the previous problems, and not carry any excess baggage if possible. When there is damage in a relationship a person needs to look at their own personal baggage before they go any farther and cause any more damage to the relationship or family members.

Now I want you to try and fill out the family genogram it will help you as you go on with this study, or you may need to do some more study before you are ready to finish and complete the genetic and behavior genogram. You may want it to go back three generations with aunts and uncles as you see the genogram below. This is a part of the introduction, so you will know what to look for in the rest of this study. Email drbarrettphd@yahoo.com or phone 417 204-8022

Let me give you some back ground for these studies I have been doing groups sessions for over ten years personal, family, and addictions. I have done them in churches because they care and want to help people, and another reason they have the space, we have never done them during a service at the church, it is usually before the service because some like to go to their own church and some don't go to church at all. Let me tell some of these life stories of men who were on drugs and alcohol for over 20 years, each one will tell you they were at the end of their road and the next trip to the hospital could have been their last, all of them started in their early teens.

The thing that changed their life was being in a rehab center, more than that they wanted to quit, all of them will tell you they could not have done without Gods help. Two of them went Bible College and one of them had a relapse later and realized he needed more help, one is a preacher and another works in a rehab program, the other one does Bible studies in a prison. The one thing they have in common they replaced the addiction with something constructive in their life. I am the coordinator of a "relapse program" and they are mentors to those who come to our group sessions. We probably have three out ten that really changes their life, but all of them have moderate success and most have two or three relapse during recovery, each time they say I will never do it again.

I also do counseling at the Masters Ranch & Christian Academy. I have boys who have had family problems with aggressive behaviors at home, school, and others who have had addictions as early as 12 years of age. The ones with bad addictions come from parents who have been on drugs and alcohol during and before the birth of a child. I have some that the mother was on drugs and alcohol during the time of birth. The adopted parents take them because they want to help them not realizing what the addictions came due to the child because of addictions, most of them come from great homes while others come from alcohol and drug homes. The point I want make they raised them in a good environment and they still got on drugs, what does that tell us the environment is not enough, I want to make it very clear the addictions can be traced if you use the genetic genogram and include it in your family genogram. It is very predictable when we know the history of the addictions in your family. For most alcoholics and drug addiction people live a life of broken promises to themselves and their family.

At the ranch we have good kids and you wouldn't know they've had problems they do very good because they are in a controlled home they stay at least one year others stay for two years, and some are there until they reach the age of 18. The boys, again most of the boys have problems when they go back into society and their home. I have known of some who came back three times, the success rate is around 70% and there are a number who really turn their life around and we are proud of them because we had a part in their life.

I will deal with addictions in the family/children and treatments in chapters 11 & 12, but now you can go on with the study or have you start work on your genogram.

MARRIAGE – FAMILY & ADDICTIONS

Family Genogram

Genetic & Temperament Analysis

Use X in a circle or square and write in information

Name _____ Your

Age_____

Date _____

Female ◯
Male ☐ Your Date of Birth _____
What City _____ State ____ Urban _____ Enter City_____
Rural _____
Genetic Father's Name Married ( ) Divorced ( )
_____
Genetic Mother's Name Married ( ) Divorced ( ) _____ Her
Maiden Name_____
Genetic birth order ( )
Genetic # Brothers ( ) & # Sisters ( )
Their birth order 1. ( ) name _____ Sex M   F
Their birth order 2. ( ) name _____ Sex M   F
Their birth order 3. ( ) name _____ Sex M   F
Their birth order 4. ( ) name _____ Sex M   F
Adopted Dad Married ( ) Divorced ( )
Adopted Mother Married ( ) Divorced ( )
Adopted Family order ( ) # of Brothers ( ) # of Sisters ( )
Single Parent order   ( ) # of Brothers ( ) # of Sisters ( )
Second Family order ( ) # of Brothers ___ # of Sisters ( )

Genetic & Temperament Analysis
Birth Oder in Each Generation

Grand Father   Dads side   Grand Mother

Grand Father   Mother side   Grand Mother

# of Bothers ( )   # of Sisters ( )   # of Bothers ( ) # of Sisters ( )
Father – Mother's name   Father
Mother

Ants – Uncle   How many Ants   # of children
How many Uncles # of children
How many Cousins

Only One Your Husband's Name
(Others)
Only One Your Wife's Name
_____ (Others)
Children by: 1. _____ 2. _____ 3. _____
4. _____ 5. _____
Family Children's Name _____ Age _____
Birth order ____ Temperament _____
_____ Age _____ Birth order _____
Temperament _____
_____ Age _____ Birth order _____
Temperament _____
_____ Age _____ Birth order _____
Temperament _____

Let's look at *your* personal relationships; do *you have any say* in the decisions being made? Is it a totalitarian relationship or marriage? That is not a good factor does *your* vote count and does what *you* have to say contribute to the decisions being made? *You* should have a unilateral part in the decisions being made; do your suggestions mean something? That does not mean two people agree on everything, but can they come to an agreement on some points of the disagreement.

Let me be honest I would not consider anyone who I have not known less than a year and dated for at least six months, and would tell anyone who came to me for counseling and teach them about good relationships, I would tell them the same thing. I believe *you* should wait a year or more, because people need to get know each other's good and bad points, they need to know each other's different moods, dislikes, and temperaments in all kinds of situations they may get into as they are dealing with their relationship. That is why it is so important to able communicate with each other, in a way this helps the relationship grow, I find many of these relationships go to fast and end up in separation, unhappiness, and even divorce. I know of people who have had a short relationship and the marriage lasted for years.

This is another reason why it is even harder to define *who you are in a relationship*, a person can lose their identity in a relationship, and they don't know what works because of their past relationships. Now it's time to add to what is **"Personal-Relationships"** everyone has to deal with the impact of personal relationships they need to learn how to deal with the present relationship and what they want and expect of themselves and the other person. Why would they even want the relationship?

I put a major emphasis on the person because they have to live with their circumstances and relationships. It is important to know who you are and then your attitude toward relationships and how you feel in the relationship is very important. Of course the impact of these studies has a great deal to do with how a person relates to their problems in a relationship.

Now, how has a person dealt with their relationships in the past this will shed some light on the present relationship? A person has their emotions to deal with; each person's pride and ego can affect their love for someone else. In this study we deal with the interactions within the relationship, but on the other hand a person may fell alone whether they are married or single.

Then dealing with the relationship when things go wrong, and how it affects the person regardless of what is going on in the relationship. Every person has (needs, wants, and desires), and they may vary with the individual. However, how are those needs being met? How to deal with those wants in a relationship is important regardless of which sex they are. This study guide will deal with how to solve different problems in relationships. How can we help a person understand their personal (needs, wants, and desires), and still have good relationships.

MARRIAGE – FAMILY & ADDICTIONS

Questionnaire I on Your Marriage Relationship

The Life Cycle (Age + Stage) enters the picture as we look at marriage, family, and situation! (Each person will fill out a profile separately)

Name _____
Spouses Name _____
   Age _____ **Spouses Age** _____

   Single _____ How long have *you* been married _____ (years)

The Life Cycle (Age + Stage) enters the picture as we look at the person in the marriage,
   Family, and situation!

- *WHO am I?* Who is the person *you* see the mirror?

  _____

- *WHAT are you dealing with?* What are you dealing with in your relationship?

- *WHERE am I Going?* What is *your* destiny in a marriage relationship?

  _____

- *WHO is that person?* Personal characteristics of *you* bring to the relationship.

  _____

- *WHY am I acting this way*, or how am I reacting to the other person in my life? _____

   Age + Stage + (4) X-Factors personality, temperament, behavior, &
Patterns = Character!

_____
   Personality
_____
   Temperament
_____
   Behavior
_____

Patterns

Age + Stage + Circumstances + (3) X-Factors + Stress/Demands = Pressure

Stress

Demands

= Pressure

No. of children _____ **ages** _____, **married or single** _____ **Divorced** _____

Signature _____

Pre marriage choosing the right person.

One of the most important decisions a person makes is getting to know the person they are going to spend the rest of their life with (marriage), I like the part in the marriage vole where it says "until death" in many cases it is until they get a divorce or separate.

Is this the RIGHT person for you?
- Physical attraction plays a big part?
- Personal-appearance?
- Their personality?
- Their attitude?

There is that physical attraction that governs the fleshly desires. That can be one the greatest motives and one of the weakest arguments in defense of any **relationship**, another I can't find any one any better, some can be so choosy that no one is good enough for them.

Look at your **relationship** real close before marriage and why you would want to marry that person. That can solve a lot of problems, not after the fact. If there is a problem solve it before marriage, not after. If it can't be solved before the marriage, it won't likely get solved after the marriage and if you're married what problems still exist.

Look for:
1. a good wholesome attitude.
2. how much love can they give?
3. what do they think of you?

Lookout for:
1. a negative attitude.
2. for a shallow person and personality.
3. for their personal bad habits.

Advice on Marriage Relationship, Inspirational quotes
Page 1 of 3 [1]
"It is better to light the candle, than chase away the darkness"
Qualities of a good marriage
By Maria Fontaine

"So much has been said and written about marriage—much of it rather complicated or seemingly contradictory—that I was curious as to what Jesus would have to say on the subject. He has such a wonderful way of explaining things simply, clearly, and positively that I was sure He could put things in perspective. So I asked Him to summarize some of the main qualities of a good marriage, and He did. Here's the message He gave:

Marriage wasn't meant to be so complicated or difficult that only a few could do it successfully. It's within the reach of nearly everyone. It's also what will make most people happiest and their lives most meaningful, productive, and satisfying, because it's a basic part of God's plan for mankind. No one excels in all of the following areas, of course, so don't be discouraged if you feel you fall short in some. Just do your best and ask me or someone to help you find your way.

Putting me first. It's a spiritual law that when you put your time with me first, both alone and with your husband or wife, everything else falls into place. "Seek first the kingdom of God and His righteousness, and all these [other] things shall be added to you" (Matthew 6:33).

Unselfishness. Selfishness is at the root of most marriage problems. For a marriage to work, both partners need to put the happiness of the other before their own. That's real love—the kind that lasts.

I want to see you succeed in marriage and as individuals, and I'm the Answer Man. I can make mountains of problems melt away.

Willingness to recognize and work on problems. Most of the problems that sink marriages start small but grow out of hand because the couple fails to deal with the problems soon enough. Often they tell themselves that the problem will go away if they ignore it or when circumstances change, but that passive approach seldom works. Those with the strongest marriages are those who learn to face their problems head-on and take active steps to overcome them together.

Good communication. In order to understand and meet each other's needs, as well as to unite to overcome problems, good communication is a must.

Forgiveness. A readiness to forgive is a key to a solid, secure marriage. Be quick to apologize for any hurtful words or actions you may have directed at your wife or husband.

Being supportive. To make your marriage all it can be, dwell on each other's good qualities and always look for ways to bring out the best in each other, rather than belittle, criticize, or nag.

Teamwork. Discuss and agree on goals and priorities, and learn to tackle problems together. "Two are better than one, because they have a good reward for their labor. For if they fall, one will lift up his companion" (Ecclesiastes 4:9-10).

Consideration. Being considerate of each other's feelings, likes and dislikes, time, and energy not only says "I love you" in a most convincing and endearing way, but it also relieves stress, prevents friction, and keeps lots of little problems from ever happening.

Affection. You'd be surprised at how many marriages fall short because of a lack of outward affection. Vocal expressions of your love for one another are also important, but sometimes touching, kissing, and hugging can convey love and reassurance even better. They are physical manifestations of inward feelings.

Equality. Equality means involving each other in decisions, parenting your children together, and sharing financial and household responsibilities, but it goes deeper than that. It's not just a matter of scheduling or dividing the workload equally, but of valuing and respecting each other so each one's strengths can come to the fore.

Admiration. Few things boost self-esteem or make people want to succeed in the truly important things of life more than hearing that their good qualities are noticed and admired. Sharpen your appreciation of the wonderful person you married, and watch him or her become even more wonderful.

Reaching out to others. Even if you seem to be the most compatible couple in the world and feel completely satisfied and secure in each other's company, in order for your marriage to thrive, you both need other friends. Others can help you grow in ways that your husband or wife can't, so your marriage will actually be strengthened as you each spend time and do things with others.

A sense of humor. "A merry heart does good, like medicine" (Proverbs 17:22). Lighten up a little and you'll find that most of the everyday inconveniences, annoyances, and problems you face aren't so bad after all.

Optimism. Optimism—the tendency to believe and expect the best—linked to faith in me nearly always pays off big, because I love to reward faith. Conversely, few things can drag down a marriage faster than pessimism—expecting the worst and complaining about the downside of situations.

Including Me. I want to see you succeed in marriage and as individuals, and I'm the Answer Man. I can make mountains of problems melt away, and I can make your dreams come true, but there's one condition: Include Me. You'll be amazed at what the three of us can accomplish together!"
http://www.wordofloveforyou.com/advicemarriage.html 1/ 19 / 2012

I'm saying a person is not likely to change because of their preexisting problems, I know no one is perfect, if there are things WRONG in the previous **relationships** work them out talk about them with the present partner or relationship and come to understanding of what went WRONG. You are the only one that can know your heart and feelings. How you deal with your heart is the next question and how do you know what is best for you. That can be tough to deal with because there needs to be a give and take in a relationship.

I advocate looking for the <u>warning signs</u> before marriage not after. <u>Be careful</u>! The love you give is the most important gift you have to give; the need to love someone is a basic need and desire. The <u>root of the</u>

problem can lie in a person's basic needs and desires if they are not the same that will cause problems. Is their heart and motives in proper prospective? Is it wrong when a person thinks no one else will love them? That is no way to feel about *yourself*, but this can cause a person to get into and stay in a **bad relationship**.

They will have a tendency to stick it out, and go as far as they can because they think no one else will have them. This is the bad part of that **relationship**, and they need help. Both parties are to blame to a degree, but usually one party is taking advantage of the other person's need for love. They both need to understand what is happening and where this is **relationship** going. This is a very basic need in every person's life, and when someone takes advantages of that love it is **WRONG**. But, even worse when it leads to abuse and infidelity. They have violated the other person's love. This relationship is in real trouble something needs to be done to help them.

How far is a person willing to go in a **relationship** will determine whether you will want to save the relationship, but on the other hand is the other person willing to meet the challenge of making it work? Let me remind you a person can only go as far as the other person will let them. It can get to the point of danger, but to the damage to a person can affect the whole family, friends, and co-workers.

The extent of the damage in a personal relationship can bring about a lot of heartaches and pain. The next question can the damage be repaired of course it can in most cases, but how much damage is very important, and how far should a person be willing to go in solving their problems, no unsolved problem is good. That is where problems add to the different circumstances in the **relationship**.

The future is not *ours* to see, but the (past and now) are very relevant, and what a person has been dealing with along the way and believe me, **"a person *will have to someday*". A person will know** that when a relationship is goes bad.

Also, there is another relevant aspect to deal with, when the age & stage in the relationship doesn't match is another problem. There are miss-matches to deal with when people don't agree, and when it causes problems in the relationship.

Example, being married, not having children by 30. This is more likely to put more pressure on the female gender, but what if the male doesn't want children it will have its influence on the female as will because it becomes a priority for the female, it can affect their relationship. When a couple feels pressure they are more likely to get in hurry, stressed-out, or make wrong choices.

Men are more likely to be job oriented by the age of 30, and even women feel this pressure.

What about people that never seem to grow-up, and never take on the changes in their life. A person may say that's not for me, but one day all this will catch-up with them if it has not already done so, and then what happens?

It wasn't just one day, and then BAM a problem happened it usually has been coming on over a period of time, but usually there is something that triggers the reaction.

Preparing for marriage

In this study I am going to try and prepare you for marriage. There is some good information for couples who are planning to get married. I want you to talk about sharing in the household duties, and helping each other in other ways. I believe two people should have equal responsibility in major decisions with respect for each other's (wants, needs and desires), and what is best for each other must come first, then the children.
Illustration, two men were taking about their wife's and one said "we've not had an argument in months; he said my wife came up with a plan. They would talk things over when there was a major decisions to be made, it is funny we haven't had a major decision during that time."

I am concerned if a person does not spend the time needed to make the other person feel wanted and loved. They will need to do a lot to fulfill that promise, can you be happy with *your* own interests while the other person fulfills their own at the same time, but a person or couple should never be too busy to have fun, go to events, and travel.

There are some things that happen and some things cannot be helped and *there* are choices, talk about these things when they happen, *you* can do more or you need to take time to know more about *them* tell them how *you* feel. <u>One</u> can *you* honestly love someone without fear, or has *your* heart been so damaged that *your* love for that person has put your love in jeopardy, and the most important thing is love and why do *you* want someone to love *you*?

That is why a (man and woman) make a good team in marriage, and this can be a good combination in marriage. The two opposite elements go together real will if they recognize each other as being important in all things, but it does not grantee success in a marriage or relationship. The things you have in common maybe just as important.

Stage 1 Dating and Teen sex

I want to spend time on dating and why teens need to know more about the dating process. In the past few years adults and teens have become sexually active during dating. Adults have the same view before marriage and because there are so many divorces I want each person to look at the negatives premarital sex.

Dating and the influences before marriage?
Why Teens Have Sex   Pages 1 &2 [2]
WHY TEENS HAVE SEX

"**Inner drives**. Normal adolescents — even yours — have sexual interests and feelings. They also deeply need love and affirmation. As a result, they can become emotionally and sexually attracted to others around them and drawn toward physical intimacy. Sadly, our culture

practically drowns kids in sexual-temptation.
Seductive messages. Virtually all popular media (movies, TV, videos, music, the Internet) as well as educational, healthcare and governmental organizations have been influenced by the sexual revolution of the 1960s. As a result, unless they live in complete isolation, adolescents are regularly exposed to sexually provocative material that expresses immoral viewpoints, fires up sexual desires and wears down resistance to physical intimacy. Even in the "safe" confines of the classroom, a teenager's natural modesty may be dismantled during explicit presentations about sexual matters in mixed company.

Lack of supervision. Because of fragmented families, complex parental work schedules, easier access to transportation and at times, carelessness among adults who should know better, adolescents today are more likely to find opportunities to be alone together for long stretches of time. In such circumstances, nature is likely to take its course, even when a commitment has been made to wait until the wedding night for sex.

Overbearing, overprotective supervision. Adolescents who are smothered in a controlling, micromanaging, suspicious environment are strong candidates for rebellion once the opportunity arises. Ironically, a big (and dangerous) rebellion may represent an effort to break loose from an overabundance of trivial constraints. Parents can set appropriate boundaries while still entrusting adolescents with increasing responsibility to manage themselves and their sexuality.

Peer pressure. This ever-present influence comes in three powerful forms:

- A general sense that "everyone is doing it except me."
- Personal comments from friends and acquaintances — including disparaging remarks like "Hey, check out Jason, the last American virgin!"
- Direct pressure from another person who wants a sexual experience or an invitation from a willing potential partner. Come-ons, smooth talk and outright coercion by men who want sex with a woman are timeworn negative behaviors. Resistance to them may be lowered by a need for closeness and acceptance and the mistaken belief that

physical intimacy will secure a man's love. In recent years a turnabout has become common: A young man is informed by his girlfriend that she wants to have sex with him. In a situation like this, personal convictions that sex is intended for marriage will be put to the ultimate test.

- **Lack of reasons (and desire) to wait.** The majority of teenagers keep an informal mental tally of reasons for and against premarital sex. Inner longings and external pressure pull them toward it, while standards taught at home and church, medical warnings and commonsense-restraints-put-on-the-brakes.

For many teenagers (even those who intend to abstain until marriage), decisions about sex tend to be made based on the drift of this internal "vote count." When the moment of truth arrives, the tally may be close — or a landslide in the wrong direction. Adolescents with a shaky or negative self-concept may be particularly vulnerable to sexual involvement when one of the reasons is the possibility of winning approval from their peers. Therefore, without being overbearing or obsessive, make an effort to have ongoing dialogues with your teenager about the many compelling reasons to postpone sex until the wedding night. (It should go without saying that you should be talking to your teenager about many things besides areas of concern and danger. If your communication is smooth in other less volatile areas, it will likely flow more easily with a sensitive topic such as sexuality.) The following list of reasons to wait may help you formulate and express you're like this, personal convictions that sex is intended for marriage will be put to the ultimate test.

Lack of reasons (and desire) to wait. The majority of teenagers keep an informal mental tally of reasons for and against premarital sex. Inner longings and external pressure pull them toward it, while standards taught at home and church, medical warnings and commonsense restraints-put-on-the-brakes.

For many teenagers (even those who intend to abstain until marriage), decisions about sex tend to be made based on the drift of this internal 'vote count.' When the moment of truth arrives, the tally may be close — or a landslide in the wrong direction. Adolescents with a shaky or negative self-concept may be particularly vulnerable to sexual involvement when one of the reasons is the possibility of winning approval from their peers. Therefore, without being overbearing or obsessive, make an effort to have ongoing dialogues with your teenager about the many compelling reasons to postpone sex until the wedding night. (It should go without saying that you should be talking to your teenager about many things besides areas of concern and danger. If your communication is smooth in other less volatile areas, it will likely flow more easily with a sensitive topic such as sexuality.) The following list of reasons to wait may help you formulate and express your thoughts during these important conversations:

- **The incidence of sexually transmitted diseases** (STDs) has reached epidemic proportions. Several of these diseases are incurable, some are fatal, and many have long-term physical and emotional consequences.
- **Sex is how babies get started**. Each year one million teenagers will become pregnant, resulting in more than 400,000 abortions and nearly a half million births. 1. Whatever the circumstances of the sexual encounter that began it, a pregnancy cannot be ignored, and whatever follows, it will have a permanent impact on the young mother's life.
- **Infertility**. An estimated 10 to 15 percent of couples (about 10 million people) have difficulty conceiving. A significant number (but not all) of these infertility problems arise as a consequence of sexually transmitted diseases and thus could have been avoided if both husband and wife had postponed sex until marriage.
- **"Safe sex"**. Many people believe that teens will avoid the physical consequences of sex if they take certain precautions, including:
  1) limiting their number of sexual partners,
  2) knowing their potential partner's sexual history and avoiding having sex with someone who has had many partners,
  3) using a condom. Unfortunately, scientific study and experience have shown that safer sex is not foolproof, and the results can be devastating.

- **Devaluation**. Sex outside of the commitment of a marital relationship devalues the act and the individuals involved.
- **Sex never enhances a teenage romance**. It almost always overwhelms and stifles the relationship. Condoms can't prevent a broken heart, and antibiotics can't cure one.
- **The "damaged goods" self-concept**. Early sexual experiences never enhance self-esteem but usually leave a strong feeling of having been used, violated and devalued.
- Despite the rising tide of sexual anarchy in our society, a great **many people still believe the words right and wrong apply to sexual behavior**. Even someone with a casual exposure to traditional Judeo-Christian values should pick up an important message: The Designer of sex cares a lot about when it's done and with whom. Sex outside of marriage can be dangerous to one's physical, emotional and spiritual health. Even for those who do not follow specific religious precepts, basic decency and concern for the wellbeing of others should curtail the vast majority of sexual adventures, which so often are loaded with selfish agendas.

What lowers the risk for teen sex:
- Studies have shown that religious commitment consistently lowers the likelihood of adolescent sexual behavior.
- Educational accomplishment/commitment to school.
- Friends who have a similar commitment to abstinence.
- Presence of both parents in the home, especially the biological father. Positive involvement of a father with his teenage offspring has been shown
to be an effective deterrent to early sexual activity.
- Parental and community values that support sexual abstinence until marriage and making them clearly known.
- A host of other interesting activities and passions. Adolescents who have other burning interests — such as earning academic honors; starting on a certain career path; participating in ministry or excelling

in music, drama, sports or other areas — will be less likely to allow premature sexual involvement to derail their plans and dreams.

Be a role model for the kinds of relationships you want your kids to develop-with-members of the-opposite-sex.

Parents should make every effort to keep their marriage intact and to nourish, enrich and celebrate it, demonstrating respect and affection for each other on an ongoing basis. This gives adolescents a sense of security and a strong attachment to your values. Fathers have a particularly important role to play. A boy who sees his father treat his mother with physical and verbal courtesies and is taught to do likewise will be more likely to carry this behavior and attitude into his own relationships with women. Girls who are consistently affirmed, cherished and treated respectfully by their fathers aren't as likely to begin a desperate search for male affection that could lead to sexual involvement. Furthermore, they will expect appropriate behavior from the other men in their lives. Single parents who are bringing up teenagers must repeatedly affirm them and create as stable a home life as possible. Values concerning non-marital sex should be practiced as well as preached. A sexually active single parent or one who has a live-in partner is proclaiming in no uncertain terms that this activity is all right for teenagers as well."

1. R. M. Cavanaugh, "Anticipatory Guidance for the Adolescent: Has It Come of Age?"
Pediatrics in Review (1994): 15.

2. Excerpted from the *Complete Book of Baby & Child Care*, published by Tyndale House Publishers, Inc. Copyright © 1999 Focus on the Family. All rights reserved. International copyright secured.

TroubledWith.com is a service of Focus on the Family. It is intended as a practical reference, and should not be considered as a substitute for advice from medical, mental health or legal professionals."
http://www.troubledwith.com/stellent/groups/puublic/%5C@fort_troubled with/documents/art...   3/7/06

Profile on why people get into premarital sex.

By that (I) mean there are the basic needs and desires, motivated by some there is an emotional involvement in the relationships, (according to the Primary and Secondary needs and desires).

Here is a very elementary profile in human-nature. This could happen and does all of the time, sometimes the primary needs and desires are taken over by lustful intentions or they are over shadowed by the desire for another person, in this case by the secondary desires, it could be a person is motivated by a simple (whim or impulse). Sorting this out is complicated to say-the-least and most of the time a person doesn't even think about it while they are doing it or know why it is happening, the mind and conscious does it every day things, but when the flesh takes over it over rules the heart.

Now let's take an example much more complicated by the human desire for sex. Take for instance the sexual desire and need is normal. Now we use the same primes for a person's secondary needs becomes a desire as it takes over their thoughts and they are influenced by the desire for another person, another example, when a person gives into those sexual needs and desires, (which is a wonderful experience if it is right time and right person, for some it becomes a sexual addiction) which is filling a secondary need at the same time. It can take many different forms of pleasure, but never-the-less it can drive a person to do the wrong thing.

Now let's break this analogy down a little farther. What has a person done to the relationship in this case they could be causing irreparable damage especially if they are married and they are involved with physical relationship out the marriage or relationship, and emotionally action controls that relationship. The physical aspects are usually co-existent, but the emotional aspects are much more complicated because the commitment to each other may not be the same afterwards, one may feel they have to put up with it to keep the relationship.

The primary needs of the relationship have been over showed by the desire of one person's desire for sex outside the marriage; usually this causes problems in the relationship to one's self and causes problems in the total concept of the relationship. This is just one example of a bad sexual relationship.

Examining premarital sex while dating.
Sex Smarts for Teens   Pages 1 – 3 [3]

"After all of the effort and progress that has been made to bring about equality for boys and girls, one would think that the two genders would appear equal in attitudes and actions on most topics. Well, it seems that's not the case when it comes to sex. The Kaiser Family Foundation and *Seventeen Magazine* conducted a survey exploring perceptions of gender roles among teens. The findings may motivate you to help your teen understand and live out God's standard for purity.

Out of 517 teenagers surveyed 15 out 17 more than a third said there is a double standard for boys and girls. In addition to the everyday madness of a hormone-raging, emotion-flaring, body-changing teenager, your teens have to decipher and deal with many mixed messages about sex. They sense differences in sexual attitudes, expectations, and rules between genders, and as you will see, it isn't really fair.

According to the survey, 9 in 10 teens said that it is good for a girl to be a virgin. About the same number (91 percent) of teens said girls get bad reputations for having sex. However, 78 percent of teens said that girls often lose their boyfriends because they won't have sex.

Attitudes about boys tell a different story. About 77 percent of teens thought that it is good for a boy to be a virgin. But only about half said that a boy would lose a girlfriend because he says no to sex. When a boy does have sex, only 4 out of 10 teens said that he would get a bad reputation.

These double standards and confusing messages about sex add to the pressure of your teen's decision making. Consider that 87 percent of teens said girls feel a lot or some pressure from boys to have sex, while only about half of the teens said boys feel pressured by girls to have sex. However, 67 percent of boys said they are feeling pressure from other boys to have sex with girls.

The study found that 69 percent of teens agreed that it is the girl who usually says no to sex. Most teens said it is usually the boy who brings up the idea of having sex. This may be a result of differing expectations of boys and girls in relationships. When asked how long teens usually date someone before having sex, 28 percent of boys said a month or less! (This was the highest percentage out of the five time frames.) Girls seem to think it doesn't happen that fast, since most of them said teens date someone between two and six months before having sex.

Seventeen published an article in January 2003 reporting some of the results from the study. One interesting fact from the study was omitted from the Seventeen article— 91 percent of the teens said that most people have sex before they are really ready. I guess that is a message they didn't want teens to hear.

Set Higher Standards for Teen

You're challenge as a parent is to set a higher standard for your teen—one that is the same for boys and girls. You'll want to set a standard that they will adhere to above any other—God's standard of morality.

Equip them at home so they can be prepared to ignore the world's standards outside your home. Our society is telling them that abstinence is unrealistic, sex is recreation, oral sex is no big deal, relationships are unnecessary, and morality is relative; but when your teens encounter those false messages with a Christian worldview, they will see how far from God's standard our society really is.

The article in Seventeen quotes a psychologist who said, 'The key is to develop a set of standards for yourself.' It sounds like good instruction at first; but, as you take a closer look, you see that this advice echoes the voice of moral relativism. This doctor is telling teens to 'just do what works for you.' This approach is based upon the idea that right and wrong depends on the situation and feelings. Let your teens know that God's standards are not customizable.

Take a stand with your teenager by teaching expectations about sex and purity. Make these expectations consistent with all teenagers in your home. The study found that 85 percent of the teens agreed that parents' expectations differ for boys and girls. Avoid the trap of only stressing purity to your teen daughter! Please don't have the attitude of 'boys will be boys' with your teen son.

Parents must model purity and morality at home. Fathers, model for your son how to treat a girl by serving, honoring, and loving your wife. This will also influence your daughter's expectations of how she should be treated by a guy. Mothers, talk with your daughter about how to dress and act. Model for her a respectful, encouraging, and loving attitude toward your husband.

Josh McDowell, internationally known speaker and author of the book *Why True Love Waits*, says 'One of the greatest securities of a child comes from the love of the parents for each other. Young people today are longing for relationships that will last. They are crying out for role models of men and women who have it together—in love, marriage, sex, and family.... One of the greatest things parents can do for their children is to love one another and let their children know it.'

Have you seen those television commercials about the anti-drug? They say, 'Talk. Know. Ask. Parents: the anti-drug.' The same applies to sex. McDowell writes that if he had to narrow it down to just one reason why kids get involved in premarital sex, it would be this: inattentive parents. He writes, 'Adolescents who receive warmth, love, and caring from parents, and whose parents openly disapprove of adolescent premarital sex and contraception, are less likely to become sexually active.'

Some parents have 'the talk' with their teenager and assume all is then settled with sexual issues. Your teenager needs more than a one-time lecture; she needs open communication. He needs to feel comfortable asking you any question. She needs her parents to listen to her. He needs his folks to stand with him during his struggles with purity. Continuous communication about what is going on in your teenager's life is a great way to show your support. Another idea is to have special moments or dates with your teen to talk about or to honor his/her commitment to purity.

Parents Win Over Peer Pressure

Although peer pressure about sex is strong among teenagers, according to a *Gallup Survey*, parents seem to have more influence than friends on a teen's decision whether or not to have sex with someone. Ask your teenager about the sexual messages he sees and hears and the pressures he faces that are contrary to a Christian worldview. (Prepare for a shock!) Talk through these issues with him and influence him for good.

When teens are faced with such double standards and immorality, they need to know where to go to figure it all out. That is when you can point them to the truth. Teenagers need to adopt a biblical worldview. When your teen looks at everything through the lens of Scripture, he will be able to recognize godly behavior versus ungodly. He will identify the reasons behind the rules. Instead of just telling you're teen, 'Don't have premarital sex because God says so,' instill in him a love for God's Word and plan for marriage.

Your teaching could sound more like, 'God says to flee sexual immorality because He created sex for a marriage relationship and most of what we see in our world today has distorted this ideal. Sex within marriage is a wonderful thing, but outside marriage it can be disastrous. God knows this! He also knows how much we struggle with sexual temptation. That is why Paul tells us to flee from sexual immorality. Run, and run fast! He doesn't say this to ruin our good time...but quite the opposite. Think about it. These boundaries are for our own protection. Jesus said that He came to give abundant life. He told us to be holy like He is holy. The Bible tells us to keep the marriage bed pure. Paul writes that our sanctification is God's will that we abstain from sexual immorality.'

God's plan for purity is a high standard, but it is one with great rewards. You won't be able to change the double standard your teens face, but you can help them reach for God's standard of purity in a culture that is undoubtedly against it."

Kristi Cherry *is a copy editor in Student Ministry Publishing at Life Way Christian Resources. She is the contact person for True Love Waits and the producer for*
www.truelovewaits.com
http://www.lifeway.com/lwc/article_main_page/0,1703,A%253D158381%2526M%253M%50hmtl   3/7/06

Facts about Living Together Before Marriage Pages 1–3 [4]
Living Together Before Marriage

"Some social commentators and young people have suggested living together before marriage is a good idea. There is, however, an ever-growing collection of data that sheds an unfavorable light on the arrangement once called 'living in sin.'

The prevailing theory is that couples can strengthen their relationships by living together before getting married. Instead of strengthening marriages, however, living together damages future marriages dramatically.

For example, if a woman lives with a man before marriage, she is more likely to cheat on him after marriage. In a recent study published in the *Journal of Marriage and the Family* researchers analyzed reported sexual relationships of 1,235 women, ages 20 to 37, and found that it was 3.3 times more likely that a woman who had cohabited before marriage would have a secondary sex partner after marriage. The study also found that married women were 'five times less likely to have a secondary sex partner than cohabiting women' and that 'cohabiting relationships appear to be more similar to dating relationships than to marriage.'

A recent study at Johns Hopkins University found that when couples choose to live together outside of wedlock, their relationship is something quite different from and significantly weaker than marriage. Researchers found specifically that most cohabitations end within two years and that 'cohabitations are not informal marriages, but relationships formed by a looser bond. 'The Johns Hopkins' study went on to show that men and women looking for someone with whom to cohabit look for 'characteristics such as education which can reflect a short-term ability to contribute to the relationship. 'In contrast, men and women looking for a spouse pay more attention to 'ascribed characteristics (such as age and religion) that reflect long-term considerations.' The researchers concluded, 'While cohabiters anticipate time together, married persons anticipate a lifetime.'

Couples who live together before their wedding day will likely be setting a court date for a divorce not long thereafter. In a study at the University of Western Ontario, sociologists investigated the relationship between cohabitation and divorce among Canadian couples. Through analysis of a national representative sample of over 8,000 ever-married men and women, the sociologists established that 'premarital cohabitors in Canada have over twice the risk of divorce...when compared with noncohabitors.' It is possible, the researchers acknowledge, that living in a nonmarital union 'can have a direct negative impact on subsequent marital stability,' perhaps because living in such a union 'undermine[s] the legitimacy of formal marriage" and so "reduces commitment to marriage.' The researchers also see something more than coincidental in the parallel rise in premarital cohabitation and marital instability. [3]

In an article in *Family Therapy*, sociologists at Northern State University uncovered in their study of college students that cohabitation puts women in a perilous position, often at the mercy of men who regard rape with a disturbing indifference. The study also found that those who are most likely to cohabit indicate 'Lower levels of religiosity, more liberal attitudes toward sexual behavior, less traditional views of marriage, and less traditional views of sex roles.' All of these findings were expected and unsurprising. What the authors of the study did not expect to find, however, was that 'those males who had cohabited displayed the most accepting views of rape.' Previous studies have found that men typically cohabit because of the "convenience" of the relationship, whereas women cohabit with 'the expectation that cohabitation will lead to marriage'–thus creating a relationship in which men are likely to 'hold a position of power' over women who expect much more from the relationship than they do. No wonder that 'cohabiting couples report greater tension in the relationship' than do married couples'.

In a recent study published in the *Journal of Social and Personal Relationships*, researchers found that only 30 percent of the sample cohabiting couples ultimately married, casting doubt on the value of so-called 'trial marriages.' The study also showed that those couples who had cohabited before marriage were more likely to have led lives marked by promiscuity than couples who had never cohabited. Cohabitors broke with tradition in other ways, too. Husbands who had cohabited before wedlock were less likely to be employed full time and more likely to have "lower occupational status" than their counterparts who had not cohabited before marriage. Also, wives who had cohabited were more likely to be employed full time than their counterparts who had not. This pattern of employment may explain why married couples who had first cohabited report 'less traditional division of domestic labor,' with husbands performing more 'feminine chores' and wives performing more 'masculine chores,' than couples who had not cohabited. The *Journal of Social and Personal Relationships* article also agreed with earlier findings that couples who have cohabited are more likely to divorce than married couples who have never cohabited."

Endnotes

As reported in *The Family in America: New Research*, June 1996, p. 3; (Renata Forste and KorayTanfer, 'Sexual Exclusivity Among Dating, Cohabiting and Married Women," *Journal of Marriage and the Family* 58 [1996]: 33-47 .)

Robert Schoen and Robin M. Weinick, "Partner Choice in Marriages and Cohabitations," *Journal of Marriage and the Family* 55 [1993]: 408-414.

David R. Hall and John Z. Zhoa, "Cohabitation and Divorce in Canada: Testing the Selectivity Hypothesis," *Journal of Marriage and the Family* 57 (1995): 421-427.

Terry Huffman et al., "Gender Differences and Factors Related to the Disposition Toward Cohabitation," *Family Therapy* 21 (1994): 171-184.

John D. Cunningham and John K. Antill "Cohabitation and Marriage: Retrospective and Predictive Comparisons," *Journal of Social and Personal Relationships* 11 (1994): 77-93.

This resource may be reprinted without change and in its entirely for non-commercial purposes without prior permission from the Rocky Mountain Family Council.

http://www.rmfc.org/fs/fs0064.htm　　　　　　　　3/7/06

Pregnancy is another reason for marring
Women Aged 15 – 29 Are Increasingly Having First Child Before Marriage　　　　　　　　Page 1of 3 [5]
Women Aged 15-29 Are Increasingly Having Children Before Marriage

"The proportion of first births to 15-29-year-old women that occur outside of marriage has more than doubled in the United States since the early 1970s, rising from 18% in 1970-1974 to 41% in 1990-1994. Additionally, women who become pregnant before marriage are less likely to marry today than they were in the early 1970s (23% vs. 49%). A Census Bureau analyst examining women's marriage and childbearing patterns considers the increasing tendency of women to delay marriage in favor of education and career, as well as the growing prevalence of cohabiting relationships, to be contributing to these changes.

The analysis is based on data from fertility and marital history supplements to the June 1980 and 1995 Current Population Surveys. Women were classified as having had a premarital birth if their first child was born before their first marriage. Those whose first birth occurred within seven months after their first marriage were said to have had a premarital conception. Women whose first child was born eight months or more after their first marriage were classified as having had a postmarital conception. The analyst looked at first births because their status is often predictive of women's future reproductive choices.

In the early 1970s, among women aged 15-29 who became first-time mothers, about one in three infants were born or conceived premaritally. This proportion rose to one in two in the early 1990s, but the pattern of change was very different for premarital births and conceptions. The proportion of first children who were born before their mother married increased from 18% to 41%, while the proportion conceived premaritially decreased from 17% to 12%.

The proportion of premaritally pregnant women who married before the birth of their first child also decreased from the early 1970s (49%) to the early 1990s (23%). According to the analyst, this decrease may be attributed, in part, to social changes that occurred from the early 1960s to the early 1980s. She notes that although fertility control was reaching new heights in these decades because of the pill and easing of abortion laws, women were postponing marriage longer to pursue education or a career and were becoming sexually active at younger ages. She also speculates that women became less likely to marry the father of their child simply because they were pregnant.

Patterns of marriage and childbearing differed considerably according to a woman's race. Among black women, 86% of first children were premaritally born or conceived in the early 1990s; the proportion had been 74% in the early 1970s. In both periods, premarital births far outnumbered premarital conceptions. One in 10 black women in the early 1990s married before their premaritally conceived child was born, half the proportion who had done so in the early 1970s." (…)

Reference by:

Bachu A, Trends in premarital childbearing: 1930 to 1994, *Current Population Reports,* 1999, Series P-23, No. 197.

http://www.guttmacger.org/pubs/journals/3209900.html   3/8/06

Problems at home and the desire to leave home
Teen marriages
I Want to Move Away From My (…) Parents (...)

"Are you thinking about getting married because you are having trouble with your parents and want to move out? Realize that being married is definitely not about freedom. You have a lot of responsibility (housework, money, jobs, bills, etc...) and a major commitment and obligation to another person.

If you argue, you can't just stomp off to your room and close the door. You can't just walk away and go home, because you are home. You won't be free to just come and go as you please or do whatever you want, because you'll have another person and involve him or her in all your decisions.

Instead of just talking about how much fun it will be to live together, talk about the aspects of your daily life that won't be so much fun, and how you will deal with that.

Money and Responsibility

How will you budget your money for bills? How will you spend that left over, free-time money? Do you agree on how this will be spent? How much will you put into savings, and for unexpected emergencies? What if there is no left over money? How will you relax and spend your free time then?

Do you agree on all of these issues? Money is a huge issue with couples, whether married or living together, and one of the chief reasons given in marriage surveys for marital problems. It may seem unimportant now, or like a minor detail, but these are major things that need to be worked out.

What if there's a special treat that you give yourself every week or month, such as dinner out, a new c.d. or video game, whatever? Will you be willing to sacrifice this without grudges when money is short? What about the stuff that your parents buy you that you take for granted: Soda in the fridge, school supplies when you run out, doctor's bills, new clothes? Transportation money?

And what about the extra responsibilities: Grocery shopping? House work? Meal fixing?
How will you divide up the chores?"
http://www.wholefamily.com/aboutteensnow/relationship_peers/crushes_and_dating/teenhtml3/8/06

THE RISE IN PREGNANT WEDDINGS   Pages 1 – 2 [7]
by Kent E. Heaton Sr.

"The bride glides down the aisle into the waiting arms of the one who will take her hand and in love join in matrimony their lives together. Families weep as young ladies become wives and young men become husbands. It is a time of great joy and excitement as a new home is begun. All too often it is a home begun with a child in the womb.

Young people face many challenges in their lives and the greatest of these is to remain pure. Bombarded by television that exploits the sexual temptation between a man and a woman, young men and young women struggle to maintain a balance of knowing what is right and what is wrong. Through the movies and the music blaring from the sexually dominated themes, young lives are drawn to experience and enjoy relationships that are sacred to the marriage bed. More and more of the weddings performed today include a child.

While it is obvious to know the reason for the pregnancy, it is just as easy to deny the cause and result of the act. Pregnancy happens as a result of sexual intercourse between a man and a woman. The relationship of the sexual act is holy to the marriage bed and not to the relationship of dating couples. Young people find themselves drawn to one another in the beginning by common ties and interest. They begin to spend time together and grow in their love for one another. As this process continues, they begin to be attracted to one another in a physical way. This is how God has planned the union of two people together.

These feelings of yearning for one another – while natural – is to be kept in check with the understanding of how God has made the physical body. Paul described this emotion in 1 Corinthians 7:9 – 'But if they cannot exercise self-control, let them marry. For it is better to marry than to burn with passion.' Burning with passion is a blessing God has given in the marriage bed as wholesome and satisfying. To fulfill this passion outside of marriage is fornication – it is sin!

'Now concerning the things of which you wrote to me: It is good for a man not to touch a woman. Nevertheless, because of sexual immorality, let each man have his own wife, and let each woman have her own husband.' (1 Corinthians 7:1, 2) The passion shared by young people is a wonderful thing to enjoy in the marriage bed but only in the marriage bed. The act of sexual enjoyment before marriage is why brides come to the wedding pregnant with the father becoming the husband. God has some very strong words about this matter: 'Marriage is honorable among all, and the bed undefiled; but fornicators and adulterers God will judge.' (Hebrews 13:4)

A wedding where the bride is pregnant is a marriage that is begun with defilement and we need to understand that and teach that to our young people. Even the child born will be able to understand that when they grow up and realize they are older than mom and dad have been married – consequences of sin continue years after the act.

The greatest blessing God has given mankind is the avenue of repentance and forgiveness. We rejoice in this knowledge and love and appreciate those young people who correct their lives and grow to be great men and women of the Lord's body. But we must work even harder to keep young men from believing the lie of the devil to enjoy the fruits of sex and to encourage our young women to fight for the purity of their bodies.

Pregnancy is the product of sex and sex is the product of fondling and petting. Heed the words of the Lord through Paul in 2 Timothy 2:22, 'Flee also youthful lusts; but pursue righteousness, faith, love, peace with those who call on the Lord out of a pure heart.' Keep the heart pure and the hands clean. Fornication is a sin! Let the wedding be pure!"

'We must learn from the mistakes of others for we do not have time to make all of them ourselves'.-Mark-Twain"

drtucker@alltel.net
Web page: www.newportweb.com/churchofchrist/
http://www.newportweb.com/churchofchrist/I104.html3/8/06

Another Real Problem is Idealism.

The idealisms that come into play in relationships, and that can create a great deal of stress in a relationship, a person is (human). There is another factor and a driving force in the relationship some people are highly motivated being successful and others care less about success in relation to a job and the idealism of how much success is successful? Women are more likely to think in turns of the marriage and having a nice home.

A person needs can also drive and motivate them, but a person cannot let it dominate their life and relationship, there is a need for successes, another thing when a person thinks of themselves as failures, and people do make mistakes.

There are failures to live with along the way and that can seem like a paradox. Success does not guarantee happiness. Then on the other hand we have the people that are failures because they don't try, as for as society's standards, people learn to live with failures in their life, it does not mean they cannot have some successes in their failures. You say that sounds like you're either successful or you're not. May I say this in defiance of these statements; I think it to be true idealism has a lot to do with the concepts of success or failure, but when they are unrealistic they have become a problem.

"We cannot always judge a book by its cover" or "until we have walked a mile in (his or her) footsteps". The scripture says "judge not least ye be judged". We cannot always tell what is going on in the mind of a person. We want a person to take a good look at what (he or she) is going through and the outside influences. Most people think they have dealt with their problems, but in reality they usually have not. They have just covered them up or they are not dealing with them at all. We hope to prove and expand on this point as we go on; again, I know I felt bad about my failures. I can only assume others feel the same way, because I see so many troubled marriages today.

The Love Formula – Find Mr. or Ms. Right – Relationship
Pages 1 – 5 [8]
by Dinah S. Temple
Relationship Coach and Author of *Picking Up The Pieces:*
A Guide to Recovery from Betrayal and a Broken Heart © 2004

"Have you ever sworn to yourself that you are going to be more selective in who you choose for a relationship partner? Many have and will even hold fast to the resolution. The problem is that the line of thinking usually stops there without further reflection. It's foolish to think that just because you plan to be more selective that you will be more successful in the dating arena. You have to be selective the right way and for the right reasons.

There is no magic love potion that can change your image in the eye of the beholder. This is however a logical method of selection that will increase the likelihood of relationship success. This is if you follow it, all of the time.

The Love Formula highlights your past unsuccessful relationship patterns so you can change them. And it illustrates important 'deal breaker' requirements that must be present in your future-relationships.

Give The Love Formula a try and see if it doesn't revolutionize the way you select future partners with increased results. Your next date could be Mr. or Ms. Right

The Love Formula
$F + P + CS = R + N = $ Mr. or Ms. Right
$F = $ The Fizzle Factor
$P = $ Pass
$CS = $ Changes you would make in yourself if you could go back and

choose over

R = Requirements (Those non-negotiable things that absolutely must be met in your next relationship 100% of the time).

N = Needs (Those things you wish to have in a relationship that will not cause the relationship to fail if they are not met all of the time).

Using the Love Formula

The Fizzle Factor = (Why past relationships didn't work)

Pass = (The reasons why you would not choose this partner again)

CS = Changes in Self (Changes you would make in yourself if you could go back and choose over)

R = Requirements (Requirements are required relationship elements that must be met in your relationship. Requirements must be set in stone. Ask yourself if you could still be happy in this relationship if X requirement was not being met 100% of the time. If the answer is No, then this is a requirement and if even one requirement is not met, the relationship will fail. If you answer yes, then this is a need that does not have to be met 100% of the time for you to be happy.)

Questionnaire II *Creating the Love Formula Analysis Form*
Make 4 vertical columns on a piece of paper.
Label the first column F with the heading ("The relationship failed because it was....")
Label the next 3 columns with the name of your last 3 significant long-term relationships.

Name   **Name**   **Name**
F= failed.   Last relationship   Second to last relationship   Third to last relationship

Now make 4 horizontal columns on the same piece of paper.
The first column is already labeled F.
Label the next column P with the heading ("I would pass on this partner because the following requirements were not met 100% of the time") (below F).

F = Fizzle   P = Pass   CS = Changes   R = requirements

Label the next column CS with the heading ("If I had been, done, had (fill in the blank), I would not have chosen this partner"). (below P).
CS = changes

Label the last column R with the heading ("Requirements that must be met 100% of the time for me to be happy in a relationship") copy this from column P.
R = Requirements

---

*Create your own Love Formula Form by using the form below as a guide. It will aid you in determining what elements must be present in your next relationship for you to be happy and date successfully.
The Love Formula: F + P + CS = R + N = Mr. or Ms. Right
Partner 1
F
The relationship failed because it was...._____
(describe the relationship)

P
I would now pass on this previous partner because the following requirements were not met 100% of the time.
List the requirements._____

CS
If I had (been, done, had)
I would not have chosen this partner

R
List requirements that must be met 100% of the time for me to be happy in a relationship
(copied from column P)

The Love Formula: F + P + CS = R + N = Mr. or Ms. Right
Partner 1 – 4

F
The relationship failed because it was....
(describe the relationship)

P
I would now pass on this previous partner because the following requirements were not met 100% of the time.
List the requirements.

CS
If I had (been, done, had)

I would not have chosen
this partner

R
List requirements that must be met 100% of the time for me to be happy in a relationship
(copied from column P)

Review Your Past Relationship Patterns and Vow to Change them

Underline the common repeating words or phrases from column P and insert them by completing this sentence: I will no longer stay in a relationship that lacks…..(insert the underlined words.) These represent your past relationship patterns.

Your Needs

List all functional and emotional needs you would like to be met by your partner most of the time. These will be used in the next step.

Formulate Your New Definition of Your Mr./Ms. Right

Write a descriptive page of your new relationship with Mr. or Ms. Right. Begin your sentence with "My perfect mate will bring the following things to our relationship 100% of the time". (Use your list of relationship requirements)

(fill in the blanks from your list of needs above)

And there you have it! Now you can say that you know what you want in a perfect mate! You are now locked and loaded to date consciously!"

If you're interested in learning more about conscious dating, request information on <u>Love Quest Training for Singles.</u>
http://www.bellaonline.com/erticles/art30656.asp.hmtl3/23/06

Identifying Adultery

Finding love on the side is nothing to be looked at lightly and is often well justified grounds for **divorce**. To add a little historic cultural perspective, throughout the ages adultery has been a subject and even today, adultery has been grounds for **divorce** under most fault-based divorce laws. I just wanted to emphasize not to be shrugged off lightly and it will not be by a court for sure.

How is it possible for one to ever go back to having a normal sexual relationship with the spouse after such an upset and disappointment? If one chooses to continue the relationship, how does one get past this, the thought that the spouse was in someone else's arms? Does one not wonder if the adulterer goes through a thought process, a comparison between the spouse and the adulterous partner? If it was only a physical attraction and how can it not be an emotional relationship, does one not wonder if their spouse misses or desires what the other provided? How does one surpass this emotional or validate their actions? If they say it was not an emotional experience that is an excuse? Is it more than an attraction, the best way is to call it adulterous act? How does one give of oneself sexually again without some feelings during the act? The women is more likely to experience remorse. The man is more likely to feel it as and an ego to his pride.

Next, let's consider two people having sex that are not married, what are their thoughts and emotions each person will feel different because of their emotional involvement. Even if the act is without a loving partner there is a sexual connection, one might not think of it that way, they might be thinking it might matter, they might be just thinking it is a physical experience, but the real-truth-it-involves-both-people.

I might be wrong here, but I think for men it's a lot about the physical sensations and less about the emotional involvement. I do think that men love the emotional connection they have with the women derived from just being with a woman that wants him. Maybe in a sense it is a statement-of-self.

I also think that the sex in a marriage has to be considered as another reason for an affair in this case I am assuming that they are not loved and that caused the involvement. There is a physical need within the body and there is a physical experience, it much better when people love each other, how do couples cope with that? Let's assume that a person is consumed with those thoughts of lusts after the affair let's assume they have destroyed the relationship, the friendship, and the marriage has nothing to build on! They did cross the line by breaking (his or her) vow, I think that needs to be addressed separately.

MARRIAGE – FAMILY & ADDICTIONS

The previous relationships are very important in helping the family a just because this could be where the relationship is gotten off on the right or wrong foot. Each relationship can be very fulfilling or bad, and yet difficult to define in the difference between a good relationships or bad one because of the different personalities and some cases it could be cultural differences or social differences. There are so many different variables to deal with such as abuse in previous or current relationship, such as ego, emotional feelings of love, the fears associated, hope and anticipation of fulfillment. The stress levels in each aspect of the situation, the element of communicating those feelings in a marriage relationship/and other relationships before and after marriage.

There are all kinds of relationships as I have tried to point out and each one can be equally rewarding. First, it is important to focus on the dating and premarital problems and how those relationships failed in this first session, don't minimize each relationship that relates to the premarital relationships and the marital family relationships. The next six sessions on the marriage relationship, because each relationship outside is just as important to a person's well-being and state of mind in the relationship of the marriage. These two sections 2 sections we have discuss two main issues and how they can be self-defeating form within and how it affects the individual and the outside influences of relationships. Personal counseling maybe needed in dealing with the specific issues in a person's life and relationships, the problems may involve the circumstances of the relationship or personal problems that need to be dealt with, one, maybe depending on the severity of the personal conflict between the couple or they may need individual counseling before going into marriage counseling.

I want to emphases there are problems maybe in the line with unresolved past relationships, bad family relationships that need to be dealt with, or cultural or interracial relationships takes more time because of the many different backgrounds that have to be dealt with in time and I want to be sure that addictions are not involved.

We as counselors want to reassure them if they have too many unresolved problems, it is not a good time to start a marriage counseling and the more they know about themselves and how to solve their problems. Studies have proven those who have resolved issues in their life end up in divorce within a few years, and that is not what they want to happen to their marriage. I hope not, or the real question is do they want a successful marriage, or do they just want to get married, or being lonely, or leaving home because they think this is the solution to their problems.

At this point we have two types of couples, one who want to have a successful marriage which brings us to our counseling program for marriage, or the different kinds of counseling services available for the individual or a couple who needs help, or those who want to go a step farther into relationships in marriage.

You don't seem to know if you can trust them again, was it just a sexual relationship or an emotional one find out WHICH? Counselors can help both in understanding WHY, and it will help BOTH of you to work at resolving those issues in the affair it can be done.

1) Is there a lack of intimacy?
2) Does it even matter at this point?
3) It should, because a lot can be riding on your decision to divorce

These are not the only questions you will need answers if you are unwilling to abide by the matrimonial covenant you should agree to the essence you have agreed on when you married.

You are responsible for assessing the degree of depression or other symptoms so that you can decide whether to do marriage counseling. Individual counseling for psychological problems usually damages *the troubled marriage* because the counselor becomes the advocate for the individual client and disturbs whatever tenuous balance of power existed prior to counseling. However, if the client is seriously depressed, marriage counseling may not be what is needed at that time to protect the client. I thus recommend that the client pursue individual counseling (usually with a different therapist so that the depressed client and I will not form a special bond that impedes future marital counseling) until the depression is under control. Then the couple should return for marriage counseling with me.

If the depression is not severe, I usually treat the couple for marital difficulties and include individual counseling within the marriage counseling.

NEW BEGINNINGS I, MARRIGE & FAMILY

Chapter 2

PREPARE YOUR HEART AND MIND FOR MARRIAGE AND FAMILY

Why are you interested in making your marriage and relationships better? Do you know at this point what problems are affecting your marriage or future marriage, how are both of you going to face them, and to what degree are you going to do something about your marriage relationship.

There are two definite aspects to look at, one how are you dealing with your relationship. Separate the second aspects of how each of you are hurting each other and how to make the marriage better.

If *you* are not happy why, *could it bayou* have had bad relationships with others!

Example of a man: A married couple and the husband says, "when we were first married, "I came home from the office and my wife would bring me my slippers, and our dog would run around barking. Now my dog brings me my slippers, and my wife is barking".

Example of women: when a wife feels stuck in a marriage, she never dreamed the marriage would get in such mess. Through all her tears she says, "I love him, but I'm not in love with him." Another case where the love has grown cold the wife is usually the first to say the marriage has gone bad, and the first say we need help. The man is more likely to say nothing is wrong, "it is just a bad time in our marriage, and it is not that bad."

- Most will agree a marriage is not easy.
- Most will agree that there is no perfect marriage.

MARRIAGE – FAMILY & ADDICTIONS

Recipe for a Happy Marriage: Fact or Fiction
Recipe for a Happy Marriage:
FACT or FICTION?   **Pages 1-5 [9]**

"If you go on the internet and search for the term a recipe for a happy marriage, you'll find all sorts of cutesy wedding sites listing actual "recipes" for a happy marriage. You'll find 'ingredients' like "1 cup courtesy", a dash of humor, a sprinkle of in-laws and so on.
In an idealistic world, you could pass a recipe for a happy marriage on to friends who would put it together and 'create' a happy marriage. But of course this world is not ideal. What most people are probably searching for is actually more of an "action plan"…than a *recipe*.

Action plans are different than recipes. They are personalized…like a blueprint. If you're really looking for an action plan, then great - I'll lay it on the table for you. (But I'm sorry to say, I don't do *recipes – Actually, I can't even cook!* ;-)

Consider this your Marriage Action Plan

This recipe for a happy marriage (a.k.a. Marriage Action Plan) is based on the program I developed that helps individuals and couples stop a divorce - even AFTER the papers have been filed.

STEP 1: Find out where you are on *the Secret Path to Divorce*

After working with couples for over 12 years, I noticed a pattern that ALL couples travel when they are headed toward divorce. I call this 'pattern' *The Secret Path to Divorce*. It starts with a couple entering a marriage with Ultimate Expectations of each other and ends with a frustrated man or woman crossing the "Point of No Return".

1. Determine whether or not you can save your marriage….and…
2. Find out exactly WHERE you are on this dangerous path.

If you've crossed the "Point of No Return", **it may be too late to save your marriage.** *This free report will help you decide.*

STEP 2: Identify Which "Country" You're from

I know, I know, you're probably thinking, *"Huh? What does my country have to do with my marriage?"* Well let me tell you…. it's <u>NOT</u> the kind of country you're thinking of.

You see, over the years, I've discovered that there are 4 different kinds of people in the world. I've created a file for you to download so you can get a better understanding of each of the 4 countries.

I drew each of the characters myself based on 27 years of researching these people. Once you know what to look for, you'll be identifying the countries of your family, friends and coworkers. It's a quick and easier way to understand people.

I'll go into a brief description of each of the 4 countries, but if you want the WHOLE story, you can read about it in my book **Softhearted Woman Hard World**.

I have every couple read this book that I take through the Environment Changer Program because of the positive results this book has shown in helping caring, compassionate and sensitive women get along with their strong-willed, direct and impatient husbands.

(It also works in the opposite scenario too. A strong-willed wife and a laid back, sensitive husband.)

Okay, back to the 4 countries…

Let's start with FUN Country

People from FUN country smile often, are VERY sociable and need to go out and do something with people instead of staying home alone. **What causes conflict in their marriages-** One issue that causes conflict in FUN people's marriages is when they marry someone who is NOT social. If you ARE married to someone from FUN country, realize that they NEED to be around people.

Don't be offended that they would rather go out with friends than stay at home and watch a movie with you. THIS IS THEIR NATURE…it's what makes them happy.

Another area of conflict is that FUN people seem to be irresponsible. This creates resentment in their spouse because they feel the "burden of responsibilities" is entirely on them.

Next is CONTROL country

These people are very direct and to the point when they talk. It's difficult for them to listen if they feel someone isn't getting to the point. They are results driven and put great value in accomplishment. They are often great leaders…when others choose to follow them.

What causes conflict in their marriages?

Because CONTROL people tend to be impatient; they can become angry when their spouse doesn't do things as quickly as they'd like….or the way they would like.

If you're married to someone from CONTROL country, GIVE THEM APPRECIATION for all they do. One Important Note: ASK them to do things. Don't TELL them. (Believe me, my wife is from CONTROL country and she HATES when people tell her to do things, she'd much rather be ASKED.)

The People from PEACE country

These people avoid conflict at all costs and want very much to get along with everyone. You can identify these people easily because the expression on their face rarely changes. PEACE people are happier with a quiet evening than a night on the town.

What causes conflict in their marriages-

PEACE people plan what they're going to do before jumping into an activity. If you're married to one of these people and you like to be spontaneous rather than planning your every move, you'll end up upsetting your spouse.

Their reaction won't be yelling though. Instead, they will either walk away or simply ignore you. In fact, that's a common problem PEACE people face in their marriages - their spouse wants to deal with issues on the spot and head on, while PEACE people would rather avoid conflict altogether.

Finally…PERFECT country

No, they are not "perfect." Everyone from PERFECT country is still "human" but these people are in the endless pursuit of perfection. Perfect country residents NEED sensitivity to their feelings.

What causes conflict in their marriages- PERFECT people have strong ideals and the desire for things to be RIGHT. If things go wrong, they can get quite upset. Since PERFECT people are easily hurt by the most innocent comments, they tend to remember negative events for extended periods of time.

So when they marry someone from CONTROL country who might be very direct in their language, they often struggle with issues over the PERFECT person's sensitivity level vs. the CONTROL person's insensitivity to his/her spouses' feelings.

Here's the point:

If conflict is an everyday occurrence in your marriage, step back and think about WHY these arguments are happening in the first place. Remember, the 4 countries are very different. The quickest way to resolve these conflicts is to ask yourself these questions:

1. What country is my spouse is from?
2. What are the REAL issues in our marriage?
3. Could this conflict be happening because the two of us don't understand each other's countries, values and ways?

STEP 3: Discover Your INVISIBLE LIFESTYLE

Read the FREE Special Report, "*Your Invisible Lifestyle…Is it Helping or Hurting Your Marriage?*" This report is the other half of the 2-part solution you can use to find the REAL source of the conflicts in your marriage.

The first step is to understand your spouse and have them understand you, and the second is discussing your values and beliefs.

Get this free report to find the source of the conflict in your marriage.

If you follow this 3-step recipe for a happy marriage or as I call it, your marriage building action plan, you'll notice a positive difference in your marriage.

Remember, these three steps are not a definite "recipe for a happy marriage" because there is still a chance they may not work for everyone.

Those couples, who are so far along on *the Secret Path to Divorce*, can't even bring themselves to take the first step in improving their marriage. So even a clearly defined "recipe for a happy marriage" or a 3-step action plan like the one I just laid out for you won't work with those couples who are too far along on the Secret Path to Divorce.

If this is true of your situation, the Environment Changer program can help you transform your marriage, even when your spouse is completely unwilling to participate in any way.

No long counseling sessions, no 'stress relieving drugs', just the same, simple tools and techniques that I used to save my own marriage."
http://www.marriage-success-secrets.com/recipe-for-a-happy-marriage.html   1/18/2012

Why would *you* want this study on marriage, "if at the end of this study you are getting the same results we have failed?" I want you to understand relationship changes over the years for the better or if it gets worse that is why you will want know how to build a better marriage. I want *you* to focus on facilitating growth in the marriage, rekindling the romance from time to time, helping couples obtain the knowledge and skills that will build and sustain a healthy relationship in the marriage.

Marriage counseling is like going to the "ER" (emergency room) we are here to help you get *your* marriage working, and provide healing. I want *you* to think in the vernacular of making the marriage better. A great analogy is when your relationship is in trouble; *you may think you need* to go to the "Mayo Clinic" or *you* need a specialist that is not necessarily the case and that why we want *you* to find ways to fix the problems before they start.

I want *you* to provide a safe supportive environment while dealing with the conflicts, and averting the other obstacles in *your marriage*. The one problem each couple will want is to feel safe emotionally with one another. When someone does not feel emotionally safe it affects the love channel between two people. On the other hand when a person feels safe emotionally they open their heart, and the love flows, and the connection takes place. Open communication is the secret that brings about trust and support for each other.

I want to let *you* know *your* marriage matters. Couples are more likely to follow through with their marriage when they invest in following, is *your* marriage worth the time it takes to make it right, if *you* do this chapter will help *your marriage*. I can only go as far as *you* are willing to go in building *your marriage*.

People get too passive and don't care for each other or they become (selfish)

Not enough emotion, passion, and love (self-involvement)

Taking each other for granted and being (self-centered)

Dominating, controlling, and abusiveness (self-destructive)

Are there any doubts about the relationship (self-commitment?)

The "Big Question" is how much do *you* love each other, and how far are you willing to go to prove your love for each other? Here is where the contradictions of who loves each other the most and this can be because one feels they are not loved enough. If they go back to the way they loved each other before they got married both of you were willing to move mountains and swim the widest sea to prove their love for each other. The thing is knowing how much you loved each other and was it easy to forgive because your love was strong, what happened; selfish motives become more a parent after *you* get married. The need is even more important after marriage; there is still the need to prove *your* love after *you* get married. Right or Wrong, and what is good or bad in the relationship ultimately is up to the couple to decide if the marriage is working?

Mark 3:25 (KJV) "And if a house be divided against itself, that house cannot stand."

The need to love and the need to be loved is an innate part of life!
I think everyone has the need to be loved and wants to be loved, not everyone has the nature to love and love in return. Another question is being able to give love for some and others it comes easy, while others have a hard time showing their love, but the need is still there. A person's love is probably influenced most in hoe they love their (children) or in some cases how they were love in their home and how bad their relationship was with their parents).

Maybe it's just a little too easy for some to love because they care and put up with the worst circumstances imaginable, (why) while others wear their feelings on their sleeves and can't give love in return.

Some people love and see the romance as an adventure, (some go from one romance right into another), but the hardest part of making a relationship work is loving each other when things go wrong.

Believe it or not the hardest thing maybe the gage of how a person likes what the other person does and says, but a person can still love them in spite of how they act or what they do.

Another is a physical attraction between the man and a woman that is important, but usually that is not enough to hold a marriage together. The passion that goes into lovemaking is accelerating, and yet that may not be enough to make the relationship work, and yet the passions may not be the same in each other and the same is true their love-making.

Now we come to the fact of love is a part of the relationship, and again it's a two way street the (give and take.)

I think there has to be a little more to it than love just because a person says they love someone love is more than emotion, there is more to it, respect, *you* have to work on love for it to grow. (It is like growing old together) it should get sweeter, not bitter over the years. I have learned that there are many kinds of love and degrees as to how much a person can love someone.

What is the acid test in a relationship and marriage, it is "LOVE"

Assessment of your LOVE"

Did *your* love last through the courting stage? Yes ___ No ___
Has *your* love survived the storms arguments? Yes ___ No ___
Has *your* love endured hard-ships? Yes ___ No ___
Has *your* love gotten better? Yes ___ No ___
Can *your* relationship stand the test of time? Yes ___ No ___
Unconditional love that supersedes all else
Quotes & Poems {1}

Let's look at some quotes and poems, see if we can come up with a clearer understanding of love.
   a) Love Quotes
"To the world you may be one person
      But to one person you may be the world"
      -Bill Wilson-
      "Love is more than a feeling
      it's a state of mind"
      -Lisa Grude-
      "Love is when you look into one's eyes
      and see their heart"
      -Jill Petty-

   (b) Love poems
    "I love you not only what you are
   But for what I am when I am with you"
    -Elizabeth Barrett Browning-
    "Grow old along with me
    the best is yet to come"
    -Robert Browning-
  "Love is not blind – It sees more and not less
  but because it sees more it is willing to see less"
      -Will Moss-

(c) Love from the Bible assignments:
(1) God' is Love

Luke 6:35 (KJV) "But love ye your enemies, and do good, and lend, hoping for nothing again; and your reward shall be great, and ye shall be the children of the Highest: for he is kind unto the unthankful and *to* the evil."

Luke 6:28 (KJV) "Bless them that curse you, and pray for them which despitefully use you."

Luke Verse 38 Give, and it shall be given unto you; good measure, pressed down, and shaken together, and running over, shall men give into your bosom. For with the same measure that ye met withal it shall be measured to you again."

Read Matt. 5:44-48
Read Luke 6:27-38

(d) Commitment to love and marriage is the glue that keeps a marriage together
(1) Poem

The Meaning of
The magic of Love
Love is like magic
And it always will be.
For love still remains
Life's sweet mystery!!
Love works in ways
That are wondrous and strange
And there's nothing in life
That love cannot change!!
Love can transform
The most commonplace
Into beauty and splendor
And sweetness and grace.
Love is unselfish,
Understanding and kind,

> For it sees with it's heart
> And not with it's mind!!
> Love is the answer
> That everyone seeks....
> Love is the language,
> That every heart seeks.
> Love can't be bought,
> It is priceless and free,
> Love, like pure magic,
> Is life's sweet mystery!!
> -Helen Steiner Rice-

Luke 6:48 (KJV) "He is like a man which built an house, and digged deep, and laid the foundation on a rock: and when the flood arose, the stream beat vehemently upon that house, and could not shake it: for it was founded upon a rock.

(E) Loving someone is God's way;

(1) Poem

I asked God

> "I asked God for a flower, he gave me a bouquet
> I asked God for a minute, he gave me a day
> I asked God for true love, he gave me that too
> I asked for an angle and he gave me you."

God's greatest gift to us is love and marriage, which was given in **Gen 2:24 (KJV)** "Therefore shall a man leave his father and his mother, and shall cleave unto his wife; and they shall be one flesh."

Some believe that "relationships are made in Heaven", but we have to live with them on earth, the humanity of a (man or women) is what we have been dealing. I'm not too sure that relationships or marriages are made in Heaven, but I certainly believe God can lead us in the right decisions and choices. I do believe in seeking God's guidance in all matters of life and in *my* relationships. My hope is that *your* relationships/marriage is a good one and blessed of God. I hope (he or she) is an angle sent from God.

Questionnaire III

How do you feel about your job/school, spouse, friends, relatives, and especially your abilities?
    1) Do you feel socially-accepted?   Yes ___ or No ___
    2) Do you feel comfortable around others? (or just shy)
        Yes ___ or No ___
    3) Do you copy trends, behaviors, and dress accordingly?
       (are you a wall-flower?)   Yes ___ or No ___
    4) Are you influenced by society's standards? (or dance
       to your own tune)   Yes ___ or No ___
    5) Are you rebellious according to social standards,
       morals, and values?   Yes ___ or No ___

How does self-acceptance affect the other person's in your relationships?
    1) Now are you ready to compare your goals with the
       other person?   Yes ___ or No ___
    2) Are you able to forgive others for what they have done
       Yes ___ or No ---
    3) That does not mean you have to have something new to make
       you happy?   Yes ___ or No ___
    4) It does mean being able to cope with others goals and
       future plans.   Yes ___ or No ___
    5) It means dealing with their behaviors. Yes ___ or No ___

How do you feel accepted in your relationships?
    1) Are others comfortable with you and your actions?
       Yes ___ or No ___
    2) Does it make you feel comfortable spending time with
       Yes ___ or No ___
    3) Do you put yourself down to make others feel good?
       Yes ___ or No ___
    4) Are you pushy or controlling?   Yes ___ or No ___
    5) Are you judgmental or overbearing? Yes ___ or No ___

6) In general do you feel others put you down?
   Yes ___ or No ___
7) Are you able to make others feel better? Yes ___ or No ___

How to improve one's self-worth in relationships.
1) Are you confident but not egotistical?   Yes ___ or No ___
2) Are you caring and considerate of others?
   Yes ___ or No ___
3) Are you patient with others down falls and short comings?
   Yes ___ or No ___
4) Are you willing to help others with a kind word?
   Yes ___ or No ___
5) Are you being harsh or sarcastic with others?
   Yes ___ or No ___
6) Are you jealous of others and what they do and have?
   Yes ___ or No ___

How do you accept individual differences?
1) Do you love people for who they are?   Yes ___ or No ___
2) Do you accept people with different personalities and cultures?
   Yes ___ or No ___
3) Some are on the surface and others are not visible.
   a) Surface = age, gender, looks, and height?
      Yes ___ or No ___
   b) Personality = feelings, behaviors, and temperament?
      Yes ___ or No ___
   c) Prejudices = race, color, creed, and religious?
      Yes ___ or No ___
   d) Discrimination = treatment, unfair, and dislike?
      Yes ___ or No ___
4) Are you honest in your goodwill toward others?
   Yes ___ or No ___
5) Learn the value of others in your life? Yes ___ or No ___
6) Do people enrich and enhance your life?
   Yes ___ or No ___
7) Do you feel better for knowing them? Yes ___ or No ___

MARRIAGE – FAMILY & ADDICTIONS

Are you helpful and supportive in *your* relationship?

1) Are you willing to help another?   Yes ___ or No ___
2) Are you there or do you wait until its convent for you?
   Yes ___ or No ___
3) Do you offer advice or do you criticize? Yes ___ or No ___
4) Do you know when to say no or when to say yes?
   Yes ___ or No ___
5) It is better to offer to do something however small the task?
   Yes ___ or No ___
6) Is failure a sign of weakness?   Yes ___ or No ___
7) By helping others you usually strengthen the relationship?
   Yes ___ or No ___
8) People need to learn how to communicate and interact?
   Yes ___ or No ___
9) Emotional healthy people can balance their needs and wishes, while respecting others needs of others?
   Yes ___ or No ___
10) Learn to get along if they have problems and don't agree?
    Yes ___ or No ___
11) Are you able to work through difficult situations?
    Yes ___ or No ___
12) Are you able to respond to others needs and wishes?
    Yes ___ or No ___
13) The most important aspect in a relationship is forming a bond and kinship with each other? Yes ___ or No ___
14) Be kind one to another, even if *you* are not getting along. (do you show respect and kindness)? Yes ___ or No ___
15) Don't take advantage of spouse/family, friends, and relatives.

Remarks:_____

Summary for dating and engaged couples

At this point the couple should have a pretty good idea whether their relationship is going to work or not, they should be more excited than ever and that problems are just stepping stones for happiness in their marriage and they want to continue with the plans they have made for marriage, everything is workable if two people are willing to work on their problems, their actions, and emotions fitting for their ideas and goals for their marriage. If this is the case you are ready to proceed with the marriage and preparing for the marriage ceremony, others maybe trying to reconcile their relationship before the marriage.

I would like to say don't make something out of dating or premarital relationships that really didn't happen. That does not mean a person is not to be kind to the people who have come into their life, try hard to fit as many people into a person's life as possible, because every relationship is important, and the experiences may help a person grow, but that does not mean they have caused the bad marriage, because they may not be good for you ("oil and water don't mix") and if they have cause personal damage or abuse to one's self image and character, they may destroy the person's ability to love another person later. Be very careful and patient if you are contemplating a divorce there should be one marriage and of course these other relationships should lead you to be a better person, and there are other outside relationships that have an impact a person's life, the family relationships and friends.

When a person marries a person for the wrong reason they are not only messing up one person's life, it could mean messing up both person's life in the process! And both person's affect the family members and other relationships usually suffer too.

A personal relationship takes effort on each individual's part believe it or not, and a good relationship does not just happen! These past relationships are factors as we have discussed in the past session. That tells me as a counselor a lot about the present relationship you are in, because people have a tendency to make the same mistakes in a marriage relationship. I will look at a person's attitude toward relationships and marriage; this will be the final signature that seals the kind of relationship it is going to become.

If not the answers may lie in the individual who is unhappy because of what they have found out about themselves or the other person in the premarital study and now they are ready for marriage. One or both may need help in some areas of their life before going into the marriage, or it could be that one or both are not ready for marriage for many reasons at this point and don't want to continue into the marriage until they get the problems solved.

They may need to deal with the specific issues in their life and the problems may involve the circumstances of the relationship or personal problems that need to be dealt with from a past relationship, one, maybe depending on the severity of the personal conflict between the couple, or they may need individual counseling before going into the marriage.

I want to emphases there are problems with unresolved past relationships, bad family relationships are just as bad if someone is causing problems that need to be dealt with, or cultural or interracial relationships take more time because of the many different backgrounds that have to be dealt with and I want you to be sure that addictions are not involved. At this point we have two types of couples, one who want to have a successful marriage which brings us to our study on marriage,

Couples usually go through at least one Surge-Euphoria-Relapse cycle, sometimes two. Actually they may go through even more, but if they have stuck through counseling, they have learned to expect and cope with them. So additional cycles are not as damaging as they experience cycles without warning. When they begin to progress, I want to warn the couple about their need to continue in counseling. I might say, "You are doing very well. You seem to be enjoying each other more than you did a few weeks ago, and you are recapturing some of the romance you had earlier in your marriage. Without dampening your enthusiasm, let me encourage you to keep working. Even though things are going well right now, I have found that we need to keep working on counseling through at least two or three weeks more to make sure these changes are lasting. After all, we want to have these changes last and just not fade away once your enthusiasm decreases."

I do not imply that their changes will not last. I encourage them to make sure the changes do last. This positive expectation helps the couples then act confidently in expressing their new behaviors as indications of real love for each other.

NEW BEGINNGS I, ON RELATIONSHIPS

Chapter 3

DEFINING THE RELATIONSHIP, MARRIAGE AND HAVING CHILDREN

This is important when children come into play this is another factor that we need to explore and that is how stress figures into having children. Stress is relevant in any situation or relationship, but especially when raising children are you a child of divorce, a break-up, or separation, if so at what age did it happen? The result of these influences when children are raised by a single parent or when children are involved in blended families they will have some influences from these situations. This is something to be considered in the relationship and having more children. Your back grounds in these areas will influence the way you feel about having children, you may want to weigh all these things before having children.

One, how do *you* deal with the different aspects of the situation, circumstance, or crisis? Two how do *you* as a person feel about the demands in *your* relationship in general, do *you* feel stress in *your* relationships and future marriage?

Now, I want you to define *your* personal relationship, how do both families feel about the relationship, and how they relate to *your* relationship. I think all of us will agree we have families; this is especially true when it comes to a marriage relationship. Let me emphases at this point people take their situation personal. When a marriage has gone wrong, and on the other hand the sweetest thing is when the marriage is going right, can we agree on either or both statements.

When *you* look at this part of the study let's see if both of *you are* wanting out this relationship? Who wants it more is a good question to ask of the other person involved? I want each of you to know how to deal with these guide lines.

There is one thing for sure, what *you* put into *your* life and marriage is what *you* are going to get out of *your* life and marriage. Another thing that is just as certain is *your* conduct, temperament, and character will influence *your* marriage. May I ask another question does either one of *you* feel controlled going into and after *you* are in the marriage? Who would *you* say is in control of *your* relationship now, if *you're* not, *who is*? Let's look at this question more closely.

First, let's look at the Stages in the marriage relationship. {2}

Marriage has many entities, it has several parts and functions, which are enter related!
   1. Couple = Husband-Wife, 2. Children = Mother-Father, 3. Family = In-laws-Out-laws

Demonstration Chart I, Axiom:

Second, the Life Line Age + Stage (illustration) with an evaluation scale +5 best to -5 worst score.

+5 perfection +4 very best ♥ +3 best♀♂   ♀♂ +2 better +1 good
-1 poor -2 bad -3 controlling -5 abuse   - 1 to -
5 is below average, -2. poor -3. bad, -4. very bad,-5. abusive
1. growth. 2. rebellious stage 3.family life   4. health& prosperity 5. retirement

Birth - 14   Teens 15 - 25   Young Adults 26 - 45
establishment 46 - 65   Golden Years 66 - up

(Three, is defining: "The Life Cycle" in relationships and marriage)

(Age + Stage) enters the picture as *you* look at the marriage, and then having a family!

The **first birth** brings a couple into a wonderful experience now the couple becomes family. The parents take care of a child and then guidance leads to what *you* do as parents you will largely determine the child's growth and happiness. What you teach the child will determine to some degree their possible.

Be careful as parents this is when things can trip *you* up, and do most of the damage in a child's life. The primary time for guidance is done from 1-6 years of age; if *you* as parents fail during this time a child will reinforce the good or bad teaching and training during years 7-13. The teen years 13-18 years of age will only add to the good, this is when they pick-up bad habits.

My dad said "if you don't have control of a child by the time they are 5 or 6 you will never be able to control them when they become teenagers". I have to say and a lot studies say the same thing there is a lot of truth in that statement. There is another problem if a parent has abuses a child they will be a troubled teen and young adult. I think most psychologists and therapists would agree with that statement as well it is based on my studies on child behavior.

Saying all of that their childhood should be a wonderful time. They start to declare more independence as they grow up; I call this the **Exploratory Stage**. Which creates some conflicts, how you deal with the conflicts and teach them discipline as a child will either make or break their will, on the other-hand it can create some major crises if dealt with in the wrong way.

There is one thing about being young they are optimist and feel there are no boundaries while others who feel abused will deal with depression and anxiety. If *you* have had a bad relationship with *your* family, *you* need to be careful not to fall into the same trap of being like *your* parents. As a parent and as they grow up and become teens it is important to set the right kind of example.

As parents of young adults you should be there for them, but even more important don't say one thing for them and do the opposite they will pick the double standard and they will hold you accountable one day they are looking to find out *who they are and where they are going and even who they will marry?*

Refining: "a parent in relation to their children"

- As the parent – *your* responsibility is to do *your* best.

- God – help us to be good parents, "I can do all things through Christ which strengthened me."
- Parent – how you relate to children
- *WHO are you as parent?*
- *WHAT kind of parent are you?* What are dealing with as a parent?
- *WHERE are your children going to become?* What is their destiny and how does that fit into how you have raised them?
- *WHY are they acting this way*, how am I doing as a parent?

(What are some of the real problems in your children)?
What are the-problem areas?
   1) Is when everything is going good!
   2) I know that it sounds odd, but it's true when children go bad!
   3) Do you feel invincible and feel nothing could go wrong!
   4) A person can use bad judgment in raising there children!

What are your motives & motivation as a parent?
   1) Money - Wealth - Prestige - Position – Family!
   2) Personal Ethics – Principles - Standards – Values!
   3) Success - the ultimate challenge is raising good productive children!
   4) Happiness - the excitement of having good children!

The **marriage** of a husband and wife and the family unit children add to the home and life, the many duties, and responsibilities of a family, job, etc. All of this can contribute to being tired, over-worked, and in some cases burnout. In most cases the day-to-day humdrum sets the pace in the marriage, but it can drag into days and even years of frustration if the children are raised in bad environment. The marriage and family and even the daily decisions /choices become arguments and they influence the family. Then, when it comes to the big or major decisions/choices how *you* make those decisions, if there is hurt and anger in the children, why?

Marriage ABCs Product Reviews Articles Forums Help
Pages 1-2 [10]

"Marriage how does your marriage measure up?

- A = Abandon or Selfishness
- B = Bestow Praise on One Another
- C = Call Home if Running Late
- D = Dream a Lot of Dreams Together
- E = Enjoy Learning New Discoveries About One Another
- F = Flowers Say A lot
- G = Grins are Life Giving
- H = Hands are for Holding
- I = Invest Your Time, Talent, and Treasure on Your Marriage
- J = Journey Together
- K = Know How to Have Fun Together
- L = Love is a Decision
- M = Make Time for Being Alone Together
- N = Negativity is Death Dealing in Any Relationship
- O = Obliterate Jumping to Conclusions
- P = Plan for Passion
- Q = Quit Quarrelling - If it's Over 48 Hours old, Let it Got
- R = Remember Those Special Days, e.g. Anniversaries
- S = Share Feelings on a Daily Basis
- T= Take Lots of Pictures and Create Great Memories
- U = Unity Creates Joy
- V = Vacations are Not Luxuries - Take Time to Re-Create
- W = Write Love Letters to One Another
- X = Xmas is a Time for Building Traditions, Not for Creating Tension
- Y = Yearn for a Great Marriage, Not Just a Good One
- Z = Zestfulness Breeds Excitement

Do you have any to add?"

http://marriage.about.com/library/weekly/aa070697.htm 7/20/04

Personality, temperament, behavior, & patterns = Character!

There are many aspects to a person's) **personality**. A person will have to deal with the personal side and the human side of (his or her) personality. Each (gender and sex) has their own peculiarities, and characteristics within themselves. Each person has their own personality and different sets of principles, values and standards, because of their parents and their social upbringing. Whatever influences have come into *their* lives help create their personality, that shows up as the *couple* deals with this study and how it affects the way the other person sees themselves sometimes this becomes a mountain in the relationship.

There is an interaction within the relationship and family, but on the other hand a person may feel alone. If *you* see *yourself* as a bad person and you blame others for *your* problems may be dwelling too much on what *you* don't like about *yourself*. Rather than seeing yourself as the problem, but see yourself as a problem solver. (Not the judge and jury).

I believe God honestly loves everyone, and deals with every person in *their* own situation. Every person has (his or her) own personality, Christian values, and a church preference. I believe that God is a Holy and Righteous, Loving God, (not a tyrant), as some would believe.

I find this to be the most reveling in a person their **temperament** these beliefs are very reveling, but usually not readily accepted by the personal acts and to what degree *they* understand themselves. It is important to deal with such characteristics because they do affect the family.

To sum up what I am talking about, or to understand what I am saying Examine YOUR MOTIVES; look at YOUR ATTITUDE because they are major influences. This is a reflection of what is or has happened in *your* life. In most cases it will determine what *you* do and say. It will show up in how *you* are dealing with *your* relationships and children, and how *your* relationship is affecting *you*.

There are **behaviors** which usually lead to strong emotional behavioral patterns, such as being out of control, uncontrolled temper, violent actions, and abuse. In extreme situations a person may want to hurt a person in this kind of emotional environment. Have these arguments become hostile in *your* relationship; if so a person has major problems, you need to deal with them if the marriage is-going-to-succeed.

Illustration

I have used this illustration before, but bears repeating at this point. I know a sweet Christian young lady who says, "all my husband wanted to do was sit and watch TV with the remote in his hand (TV – games, computer or suffering the web)", while I do all the work around the house. She works a full time job and helps support and raise the child. If I get the picture, now the annoyances became a big problem. I'm sure there were other situations that contributed the breakdown that lead to the divorce after a few years.

Blame game, and shame

1) Blame everyone else for what happens or goes wrong, but not themselves
   a) blames God, the Devil,
   b) They blame their spouse because they never do anything right.
2) Game player is one who plays with another's life.
a) For their pleasure they play with everyone's life and their always right.
   3) Shame is one who feels and takes the blame for everything
       a) they are usually an unselfish person, or they are dealing with low-self-esteem and with an inferiority complex.

(Illustration) that might help in understanding each other better:

I have used this illustration before. Let's think of a tire on a car and *you* can usually see if it is flat. It is much harder to see how much air is in a tire. *You* can usually tell if it is low, but *you* usually can't tell if the pressure is too high by looking at the tire.

If it is properly inflated the car will run better and smoother. "Right"!

Now let's look at a marriage and see if the **pressure** is too high or too low, if tire is too low it will be wobbly going from side to side, one the evidences *you* don't feel the love *you* use to have, the enthusiasm for the marriage is gone. This is typical of burnout and if there is too much pressure in the marriage it will be bumpy and bouncing up and down, and if it is too high there will be arguments and fighting. Then if the tire is flat! Guess what? The marriage is in real trouble, they are going nowhere, until it fixed!

How do you know if the (pressure is right) the marriage it will be smooth; it is only going to experience an occasional bump in the road.

- Now I am going to ask if any part of this illustration fits *your* marriage?
- How have *you* been dealing with the bumpy problems?
- Have *you* been surveying from side to side dodging the problems, sooner or later the bumps will be too much and they are going to catch up with the person, marriage, or relationship.

Love and marriage "go together like a horse and carriage" I have spent some time on the individuals before and after they go into the marriage.

There should always be peace of mind in any situation and as *you* go into and deal with the marriage. If not I want *you* to know how our studies reflect how to deal with any situation. Keep *your* chin up, be positive, even in the worst of circumstances having peace of mind "is worth its weight in gold", and enjoy getting to know the person *you* are going to marry or married to.

I think at this point a person should have an idea **who they are**, and be headed in the right direction and they should have *their* priorities straight.

What are *both of you* are wanting to accomplish in *your* marriage, what are your goals for the marriage and children, and what do *you* want out of *your* life in relation to *your* marriage, and then what is the purpose for *your life* and *marriage*?

Love and Marriage in Relation to Your Identity

Another situation is when *you* get lost in a marriage and loss your identity in a marriage, especially when *you* have children. This is something every marriage has to deal with on an everyday bases. We put all these in a group category for the purpose of personal identity and being able to identify with social disorders. There is a direct correlation between Co-dependency/Addictions/Abuse in a marriage and that is why I have put them together now and we will with addictions later in this study. They are social problems and in some cases the result is a bad marriage.

You have to find your identity and interdependence from the problems in the marriage. Then this study can be of help. There are many ways to deal with social problems, but the first step is to identify if any of these are affecting *your* marriage.

When the other person is uses drugs, both may not know how to deal with it! You can lose your identity as a person, low self-esteem, and depression sets in. A person may feel inadequate, helpless, and unsure within themselves. Also a person may become a co-dependent to drugs or alcohol and when either one becomes abuse within the marriage.

First, there are some miss conceptions out there "love can cover multitude of sins". (True) But, love can only go as-far-as the other person will let them love them, but when there is rejection and no love in return, and when it comes the point of abuse. If the love has been violated then what?

Now let's take a look at some real situations of abuses and how it hurts the person involved. When someone **abuses** there trust. In some cases the (reaction) is hate, vengeance - wrath, anger - revenge (getting even). That

MARRIAGE – FAMILY & ADDICTIONS

is (human nature) at work, if a person has an affair the other person may have an affair to get even.

There are some very basic needs in every person's life, and when someone <u>takes advantages of that love,</u> it hurts and abuses *there* love, it is WRONG, but it happens. <u>Even worse is when abuse and infidelity is involved</u> in this need for love, and the other person falls in love with another person. This relationship is in real trouble, and <u>something needs to be done</u>. That person may need some HELP when they feel betrayed because of what happened, their love will suffer, can the love be restored?

Co-dependency can become abusive in nature. I get calls all of the time where a person gets assaulted, abused, and can't break off the relationship because they feel responsible, or feel they deserve the abuse. But, what about those who have been raped, this falls under a violent crime, and authorities should be involved.

Abusiveness is relevant to personal convictions and there are two interruptions, one the laws of man and two God law, each person is different in nature and personality, moral character and belief, and (Biblical) beliefs.

Those natural safety devices within a person's life is based on convictions which has been violated in some way, and in that way their life has been altered and there are reasons why a person wants to hurt a person in return. Because they were hurt, whether they wanted to or not, sometimes they hurt a person subconsciously or wants to retaliate.

To intentionally abuse or hurt someone is a completely different story. That must be dealt with too. God will in my personal belief judge the heart within one's self. That is why we have no room to judge another. "Judge not, that ye be not judged. (verse 1) of Matt. 7:1-5; and (verses 2-5) gives a spiritual application to judging.

Look at yourself and what you do unto others, it could fall back the person who judges. "Whatever you sow ye shall also reap". Look at Rom. 2:7-16 (verse 11) "For God there is no respect of persons with God" "Dearly beloved, avenge not yourselves, but *rather* give place unto

wrath: for it is written Vengeance is mine; I will repay, saith the Lord."
We all need to work on these principles (daily).

The root of the problem lies in the basic needs and desires of a person. Is your heart and motives right, you are more likely to make the right decisions, and be able to forgive others.

Dealing with *your* emotions

A state of physical or emotional pressure and how *your* body reacts.
- There is a reaction to anything that places demands, normal demand usually people adapt quickly.
- Understanding how emotions affects *your* body is important.

Emotional Responses = are usually automatic reactions to a situation.
- Emotional responses are normal, even if they are "good" or bad".
- Emotions reaction to the response when there is something wrong?
- Automatic responses – nervousness/anxiety/worried,
- An emotional response – blushing, gasping in surprise, and/or weeping/crying.
- Strong emotional response - reactions headaches, stomach pain, and/or sleeping problems.
- Emotional responses – exhaustion and fatigue.

How emotions relate to the thought process, first a subconscious feeling and then a conscious reaction to an emotional situation. These responses can cause physical changes to the body, or a change in the mind-set. Regardless of the emotional reaction people are going to experience emotional feelings to the stress signals.

I call them one of the warning signs. "The cries for help"

- How do *you* react to **a situation** in a relationship and marriage?
- When *you* face **stress** *you* should want to know if it the relationship is **"good or bad"**

- *You* should look for the **"right** and be aware of the **wrong"** in any situation.

Illustration: If spouse says, "I want to talk with *you* about something, what is *your* reaction or feedback, are *you* able to communicate and understand their feelings.

- *You* may think it is bad news if you've been in an argument, or think something wrong.
- *You* might ask *yourself,* what might be wrong now and how serious is it?

Examples:

- *Your* heart may beat faster, perspire, and shortness of breath.

Emotional Stress Relief –

- Note - regular exercise can reduce stress, and make coping with any situations easier.
- Note - take time to eat properly, and get the proper amount of rest and sleep.
- Note – reading, good movies, and activities.

How to avoid emotional stress?

- Everyone reacts, but do they understand their thought process, conscious and subconscious feelings.
- After the reaction to emotional stress, then relax.
- Control and resist the emotional stress.

The fighting emotional impulses –

- Fighting, when something threatens or angers *you, you* may feel an impulse to fight back.
- Fighting, may simply be a way of fighting back because *you*
are angry, or standing up for *your* rights.
- Fighting is a part of living to stay alive.
- If you flee it may mean *you* don't want to fight for many reasons.
- It could be that *you* will comeback some other day to fight.
- The worst kind of fleeing is because *your* are afraid, or don't want to fight because it hurts too much.

If a person is in a dark room and *you* hear a noise then what? You can react by covering *your* head or turning on the lights. *You* try to find out what those noises are. It could be a cat playing, it would be a normal situation if *you* have cat, and if it was not the cat was it *your* imagination at the time, or was it something else.

It probably caused some emotional stress reaction in some way, if the obvious answer came up little or no emotional stress, if one of the other answers came up, it is more likely raise the level of emotional stress. The question is did *you* do something about the situation in a positive manner.

How do you get rid of the emotional stress, or avoid the emotional stress, did *you* feel much better when *you* relieved emotional stress? (RIGHT) Managing Emotional Stress

    1) How are emotions linked to stress?

    2) How does a person handle emotional stress?

Emotional Stress-relief, coping / makes a person feel better mentally & physically**.**

NEW BEGINNINGS I, CONFICTS IN MARRIAGE

Chapter 4

The QUITE BEFORE and AFTER THE STORM.

Describing the different power struggles and how each affects a relationship and marriage.
Formula for marriage and family problems.
Describing the different power struggles and how each affects a relationship and marriage. Newlyweds' 5 Biggest Pitfalls
Pages 1 – 2 [11]

Experts say unrealistic expectations, avoiding conflict after marriage can lead to disaster.

By Leanna Skarnulis, WebMD Feature
Reviewed By Michael Smith, MD

"Love and marriage may 'go together like a horse and carriage,' but most newlyweds set off without a shared road map. Each partner comes to the journey with their own set of directions including – assumptions about roles, expectations about how to spend time and money, and deeply held beliefs about children. Then there's also – baggage. Experts say it takes desire, honest communication, and hard work to move a relationship from the romantic stage through the power struggles to a loving marriage based on shared meaning. Get off to a good start by avoiding these five major pitfalls:

1. My family does it this way.
2. Marriage will make me happy.
3. My partner will change once we're married.
4. Talking about issues like his rowdy friends, her credit card debt, when to have kids, and who should clean the toilet, will take the bloom off romance.
5. We should avoid conflict at all costs.

My Family Does It This Way

His family sits down together around the dining room table for dinner every night. Her family scatters and grabs dinner on the run.

Couples often underestimate the influence of their families. 'People go into marriage with expectations that are engrained almost subconsciously,' says Addie Leibin, MS, LMHC, a private mental health counselor in Winter Park, Fla. 'They think, I'll get married, and I'll do it like my family did it. But you can't build a house with two sets of blueprints. The whole object is to come up with your own set of plans. It's not your mom and dad's house."

Mark Freeman, PhD, agrees with Leibin that families operate on both conscious and subconscious levels. He counsels couples and teaches a class called 'Marriage and the Family' in his roles as director of personal counseling and instructor at Rollins College, also in Winter Park. On a conscious level, he says, when there's interference from one of the spouse's family members or a person doesn't have total allegiance to his or her spouse that creates problems within a person's marriage.

On a subconscious level, families provide the frame-of-reference that individuals bring to the marriage regarding money, gender roles, and other important issues. 'Know each other well enough to find out what the stated expectations are, and recognize sometimes there are unconscious expectations. For example, you could say 'I'm open and like to deal with things,' but in your own family when conflict arose, you shut down. So it's the stated vs. the unconscious. Sometimes we have the best intentions to be one way, but then a coping strategy from our own family comes up and violates the thing we are. We're human, not perfect.'

Marriage Will Make Me Happy

He's lonely and has no friends. She feels inferior to her prettier, smarter, and wealthier sister. Both believe marriage will make them happy.

'In the early stages of a relationship, everything is beautiful,' says Leibin. 'Couples have to understand that love is never enough, and marriage doesn't make you happy. Happiness is a do-it-yourself job.'

According to a 15-year survey reported in the *Journal of Personality and Social Psychology,* an individual's level of happiness before marriage is the best predictor of happiness after marriage.

My Partner Will Change

She assumes he'll stop having lunch with his ex-fiancée. He assumes she'll give up expensive spa weekends with her friends.

Marriage inevitably means compromise, but couples need to compromise without giving away too much of what they value. Freeman advises articulating a marital contract that addresses the expectations each has for the other. 'The expectations can be high, but make sure they're realistic,' he says.

One task he addresses with couples in pre-marital counseling involves helping them overcome romantic illusions and unrealistic expectations. 'When the romance diminishes, the relationship moves to a power struggle, and for a while, each person tries to change the other. Even though people mouth the words that they don't want to change the partner, they still try. It's a developmental stage, and if couples resolve it in a healthy way, they move into stability and long-term commitment. Marriages that blow up early have a romantic view, and once that's dissipated they think the marriage is broken and can't be fixed.'

Leibin tells WebMD that rather than compromise and share, some couples continue to lead separate lives after marriage. 'They end up pulling apart. Couples should be friends and learn to work together. I believe in a Saturday night date, and maybe she makes the plans for one week and he does the next week. It's a time to share their lives and try to understand each other's worlds.'

She says love starts a relationship, and communication makes it grow into a good working relationship in which partners respect one another's differences. She sees many couples who don't make an effort to learn about each other. 'One newly married couple divorced over crumbs in the sink. He'd go off on her if there were crumbs, and she couldn't stand it.'

Talking about Hard Issues Will Take the Bloom off Romance

She doesn't tell him that once they have children she wants him to quit working. He doesn't tell her his company might relocate him to Singapore.
Leibin tells WebMD that in recent years she's seen an increase in the number of couples in trouble as early as the eighth month of marriage. 'Often they'll say, 'I wish I'd known such-and-such.' People present their best selves before marriage, and they overlook serious issues, like alcohol abuse, that can destroy a marriage.'

Far from ruining romance, talking openly and honestly fosters acceptance and deeper understanding which is essential if partners are to feel safe with one another. 'When you feel safe with someone you love, you won't find anybody prettier, richer, or more desirable,' she says.

We Should Avoid Conflict at All Costs

He leaves and goes for a drive when she confronts him about viewing computer porn. She learns to stifle her feelings about computer porn and keep quiet.

Couples who claim 'we never fight' are missing an opportunity to build their relationship. 'It's how couples handle the conflict that matters,' says Freeman. 'Do you de-escalate situations? Can you repair the relationship? Do you validate your partner after a big fight? When people give up on each other, it's usually because they've stopped trying to resolve conflicts.'

The research of John Gottman, PhD, has had a profound impact on the field of marriage counseling. Freeman says Gottman can tell with 95% accuracy which couples will stay together. 'He puts them in a room and videotapes them discussing their relationships. Then he observes their verbal and nonverbal behaviors, and counts positive behaviors, such as nodding or placing a hand on a shoulder, and negative behaviors, such as whining or stern criticism. With successful couples, the ratio is five positive behaviors to one negative. What makes them successful is the ability to reduce the negative feelings.'

'Even good marriages will have criticism and defensiveness, but there's danger when people stonewall or feel contempt. If you hold someone in contempt, you don't think the problem can be resolved. Contempt replaces hope.'

Freeman says some important lessons emerging from the research are different for men and women. 'Wives who stand toe-to-toe with their husbands and don't give in do well. But when wives raise their tolerance levels, the marriage is doomed, because the husband makes a power play. Husbands who can calm themselves down and lower their anger are more likely to have happy marriages.'"

Originally published May 24, 2004.

Medically updated May 10, 2005."

SOURCES: *Journal of Personality and Social Psychology,* March 2003. *Why Marriages Succeed or Fail,* John Gottman. WebMD Medical Reference with the Gottman Institute: 'Relationship 101.' Mark Freeman, PhD, director, personal counseling and instructor, Rollins College, Winter Park, Fla. Addie Leibin, MS, LMHC, mental health counselor in private practice, Winter Park, Fla.

Http://www.foxnews.webmd.com/content/article/87/99551.hmtl?printing=true　　　　　　　　　　　　　　　　　3/15/06

Questionnaire IV Marriage Profile

Let me emphasize at this point, a **marriage** is the hardest thing to deal with because people take the situations personally, a friend could say the same thing and it's not so personal. When a **marriage** has gone wrong it creates problems in each situation, and the sweetest thing is when the **marriage** is going right.

I am saying to each of *you* do *you* agree with statement?
                                                            Yes___ No___,

Both statements are correct.

What do both of *you* want out of this **marriage**?

Comments:

Husband: _____

Wife: _____

Now that I have heard from both of you, let me give *you* some guide lines.

(Input & output forum):

There is one thing for sure, what *you* put into *your* life and **marriage** is what is going to come out of *your* life and **marriage**. Do you both agree?   Yes___ No___

Another thing about *your* life that is just as certain, *your* conduct, temperament, and character will influence *your* **marriage**. May I ask another question? And I repeat:

- *Who are you* in the **marriage**?

  _____

- Second, does either one of *you* feel controlled in the **marriage**? Her, Yes___ No___
  Him,   Yes___ No___

- Let's look at this question more closely do *you* feel *you* have an equal say.
                           Her, Yes___ No___ Him Yes___ No___

  - Do either of *you* feel there needs to be any changes in the decision making?
                 Her answer, Yes___ No___ & His answer, Yes___ No___

Demonstration Chart II: {3}

Evaluation of the marriage relationship, the <u>Life line</u> Age + Stage

Evaluation scale +5 best to -5 worst. Now let's look at the chart below:

<u>+5 to +1 = +5 perfection, +4 very best, +3 best, +2 excellent, + 1 good</u>

<u>*The Life Line*</u>

<u>- 1 to – 5 = -1 below average, -2 poor, -3 bad, -4 neglected, -5 abused</u>

Breakdown

There is a need to understand the scale and how to evaluate the marriage, I have drawn a line which I call the "**Life Line**" and how it works. Anytime a situation in negative it is an indication of something bad, the line going above the "**Life Line**" in chart II means a positive action or reaction is taking place. If an action or reaction is taking place below the "**Life Line**" negative actions and reactions are taking place. All negative actions and reaction are not bad because life is not always made of highs or good things happening. That is the reason I ask *you* to evaluate all the actions and reactions taking place in the **marriage** relationship.

Use numbers in Scale:

Example: +3 is (best) under the situation.

Now fill out questionnaire in your home.

Questionnaire V
SOS study guide principles in marriage"! (+5 to -5)

(1) How do *you* feel about the marriage?   Scale____
(2) How do *you* feel about *your* marriage partner?   Scale____
(3) Do *you* feel the marriage will last?   Scale____
    (4) Evaluate their character.   Scale____
(5) How do *you* feel about *your* life?   Scale____
(6) Do *you* feel the problems are solvable?   Scale____
(7) Do *you* feel *you* may have used bad judgment?   Scale____
(8) Do *you* feel safe in marriage?   Scale____
(9) Do *you* feel nothing is wrong?   Scale____
Example, add the pluses and subtract mimes   Score____
  (1) Do *you* feel everything is going bad?   Scale____
  (2) When things go bad, do *you* feel vulnerable?   Scale____
  (3) Do *you* feel *your* marriage is wrong?   Scale____
(4) Do *you*   (4)   feel everything is against the marriage?   Scale____
(5) Do *you* feel what is the use, why try?   Scale____
(6) Do *you* feel unhappy with *your* life?   Scale____
(7) At this point do *you* feel the need for changes?   Scale____
(8) Use the same Scale when it comes to score: Score____
(9) How important is *your* family?   Scale____
(10) Money - Wealth - Prestige – Position?   Scale____
(11) Personal Ethics – Principles - Standards – Values! Scale____
(12) Do *you* feel the ultimate challenge is to succeed! Scale____
(13) *Your* happiness?   Scale____
(14) Do *you* feel any excitement about new challenges! Scale____
Total the pluses   Score____
Total the mines   Score____
Subtract the mimes from the pluses   Score ____
    YOU SHOULD HAVE MORE PLUSES THAN MINIUES

If you have all pluses great, if your score has too many minus you have problem.
Now you know what to work on, see if you can change the score later? (like 6 months later)

Take your time when it comes to making changes!

What are the problems, or do you know at this point how to solve your problems look at the differences in a person, marriage and relationships and to what degree are they affecting you personally, and your marriage relationship.

The next thing I want *you* to know about *you* as a person think about how you are going to make these changes, how they have been affecting *your* **marriage** relationship. Let me say these changes are enviable if *you* are going to have a better **relationship**, and what happens after the changes. Let me explain how it will affect the (men), and how the (woman) will respond to the changes in both are there any changes. If *you* want changes they usually happen in very subtle ways, it is only natural for a person not to think about the psychical and emotional changes over time, because they have become a way of life, but it is important to make changes and adjustments when needed. It is usually the one who thinks it is the other person who needs to change, but in reality it may be *one* or *both* who have to change their ideas.

There are going to be major changes when *you* have children, and that affects both of *you*, but in different ways, be aware of the impending problems. Most **marriages** have unresolved problems, and it usually involves some selfishness in each person, and what they think of themselves.

Formula for marriage and family problems

Let's look at **Ages & Stages** of the **marriage** relationship.

*I want you to know how "The **Life Line**" fits into "Demonstration Charts I, II: as we look at and go into your own lifeline, how do both of you deal with the different aspects of the situation, circumstance, or crisis, and even demands/stress; and to what degree does each set of circumstances influence the marriage relationship. Then, the different Ages & Stages, a person has to deal and how to deal with the different issues in their marriage relationship, which we will go into next. All of us deal with life and co-exist in the marriage.*

Input & Output, Forum: *(God or self) let's make no mistake about one thing you are responsible for your conduct and actions. You may want God to help, but you're accountable for your actions, every word, and the deeds done in this mortal body. How does a person deal with the pursuit of life, happiness, and God?*

*This is **his lighted** to show you how a person goes through changes in their life and changes in their marriage. Marriage has many entitlements, it has several parts and functions, which are enter related.*

*They will need to read, or take notes as you go through this study. It will go much quicker and easier as we discuss the different problems relating to your **marriage**, and how you have dealt them, and set them in order. Improving the **marriage** relationship is the ultimate goal for each of you. Each person well determine their own speed and progress.*

Defining: "the persons in relation to their marriage"

- The person – *your* responsibility is to do *your* best
- God – please help us help ourselves
- Person – if *you* can't relate to your partner

Before we finish I want both of you to know it is import to *review* questionnaire I at this point, you can use the evaluation questionnaire later on and compare *your* progress later.

Age + **Stage** + **Circumstances** are another way of looking at the influences that affects the **marriage life cycle** of a (husband and wife).

Marriage ABCs Product Reviews Articles Forums Help.
                             Pages 1-2   [12]

Marriage, Marriage ABCs
   "How does your marriage measure up?
   A = Abandon Selfishness
   B = Bestow Praise on One Another
   C = Call Home if Running Late
   D = Dream a Lot of Dreams Together
   E = Enjoy Learning New Discoveries About One Another
   F = Flowers Say A lot
   G = Grins are Life Giving
   H = Hands are for Holding
   I = Invest Your Time, Talent and Treasure on Your Marriage
   J = Journey Together
   K = Know How to Have Fun Together
   L = Love is a Decision
   M = Make Time for Being Alone Together
   N = Negativity is Death Dealing in Any Relationship
   O = Obliterate Jumping to Conclusions
   P = Plan for Passion
   Q = Quit Quarrelling - If it's Over 48 Hours old, Let it Got
   R = Remember Those Special Days, e.g. Anniversaries
   S = Share Feelings on a Daily Basis
   T= Take Lots of Pictures and Create Great Memories
   U = Unity Creates Joy
   V = Vacations are Not Luxuries - Take Time to Re-Create
   W = Write Love Letters to One Another
   X = Xmas is a Time for Building Traditions, Not for Creating Tension
   Y = Yearn for a Great Marriage, Not Just a Good One

Z = Zestfulness Breeds Excitement
http://marriage.about.com/library/weekly/aa070697.htm 7/20/04

Certainly bad health, a catastrophe illness can add to the problems in a **marriage,** if there is a crisis it will add to the everyday circumstances a couple has to deal with, this will test your faith in yourself and God.

Age + Stage X Factors =

There are good and bad factors that come from your personality. Each (gender and sex) has their own peculiarities, and characteristics within themselves. Each person has their own personality and other influences that have come into *their* lives help create a personality *they* will have to deal with, but more importantly is how these relate within the **marriage.** There are many aspects from within one's self, and in this study we want to expand on how little things can affect the other person in the **marriage.** *You* need to recognize and reflect on how they affecting you. Sometimes these personal characteristics can become a mountain in a person's life and **marriage.**

There is an interaction within the relationship, but is it good for you to take a personal look if you feel anything is bothering your **marriage** relationship.

These factors are going to tell a lot about the person if that is not perplexing enough, people lose *their* individual identity, and *they* get tangled up in *who they are.*

If this is the case *you* may not seem so bad and the reason that happens people blame the other person for how they are reacting may be *you* are dwelling too much on their personality traits or you may not like something about them. Rather than seeing the person for who (he or she) is, and what they may be contributing to the marriage.

I believe temperament characteristics are the most revealing about who a person is. Those traits are very revealing to others, but usually not readily accepted by the person personal actions. To what degree do *they* understand themselves it is light of understand the other person and how you are dealing with other characteristics in your mate.

To sum-up what I always to have a person examine their MOTIVES and their ATTITUDE toward *their* mate, because they are a major influence in how you see them. This may be a reflection in how they see in *you*. If they feel *you are mad*, they are going to react defensively, and they are going to react to the bad attitude or mood. In most cases a person's reactions are governed by what is said and none by the other person.

It will show up in a person's **marriage**, and these influences can take on different characteristics and destroy the **marriage**.

There are strong emotional behavioral patterns, such as being out-of-control. I know jealousy is big one and I will deal with it later, but right now let's look at the anger and what it causes, it can affect the **marriage**. Let's characterize some of these other behaviors as we go on.

(A short temper or impatience that causes aggressive or passive behaviors, and/or dominating, controlling behavior patterns when a person reacts violently, gets angry or mad over the least little thing).

The person's life style and the way they were brought up, that is how someone sees themselves, (personal preference, prejudices, and basis set forth in a person's life). All of these can become a way of life for the person. The hurt, anger, and bitterness may have become a part of their personal make up. (Personality Temperament, Behavior, and Patterns makeup shows up in the character of a person).

When viewed from the **normal** or **abnormal reactions,** the **emotional** make-up will interact with their **temperament,** but when a person let's it get out-of-control, or out-of-balance a person may have personal **emotional** problems to deal with before they can go on with the **marriage**. There are set influences by which a person has to deal with, and there are other providential influences.

After being **married** there are many minor annoyances, or they could be a particular flaw in a person's personality and they are magnified when a couple gets **married**.

They may love that person, but can't overlook those little things. What if they are big annoyances and human traits that they don't like, they have a problem, don't they?

- **How does a psychologist's evaluate behavioral symptoms and characteristics?**
- **The normal and abnormal behavior defines how bad the problem is.**

I am giving four suggestions about how to handle these different areas and influences:

- Be honest with yourself and your spouse.
- I'm not talking about divorcing someone, or starting all over again.
- I'm not talking about erasing *your* past that is a part of you.
- People tend to make the same mistakes over and over again, they usually follow a pattern, show up as self-defeating habits, and behaviors!

I look at the particular behaviors as well, and how they relate to principles that work and help, but I do look at the scriptural applications in (**human nature**) and **personality, temperament, behavior, and patterns**. Ultimately the decisions/choices will rest in your hands as to what you are going to do.

Here are three **personality axioms**: **temperament, behavior, and patterns**, the question is how does **temperament, behavior, and patterns** affect the **marriage**. It may be a personality trait that is affecting the **marriage** in some way. Remember earlier in this chapter, how I used the **Chart breakdowns** relate to a **Breakdown**. The problem we are dealing with is the personal aspects in the **marriage,** and they can be just as damaging as the **stress/demands** put on the **marriage**.

Some questions or problems will never be completely answered to either one's satisfaction as long as there are (women and men) that can't forgive and forget. But, people can come to a better understanding of each other. Picture this, if each person tries to understand each other better there should be less conflict, tension, and stress.

The mathematical equation will not help in finding out the degree of the problem, on the other hand temperament, behaviors and patterns are predicable. Now they have become personal **actions** and **reactions** that are predictable because a couple follows patterns and that is not difficult to understand, and in some cases it is harder to change those bad patterns.

Our hope is to help you find helpful ways to deal with a couple's outlook for changing bad patterns and we want to show them how to change those patterns and behaviors.

The other aspect of this study is to help a couple evaluate the of amount stress in their life and relationship that will differently help them in solving some of their **marriage** problems. To be able to **evaluate** the **actions** and **reactions** in relation to the emotional up each person is dealing with, and when and why they **overreact**, that is where our **evaluations** are definitely helpful.

The reason people have problems identifying their problems their safety devices are over loaded or shut off; stress over loads limits how to understand these factors in life and in the **marriage**. When a couple doesn't pay attention to the warning signs and they don't understand why *their **marriage** relationship* is not working, or why they keep having the same **marriage** problems, and why they are dealing with the issues regarding their **marriage**. Look no farther than bad habits and patterns in the **marriage**.

The **marriage** relationship should be equally important to each other, and it should be equally rewarding, don't minimize each other's role, because the success or failure of the **marriage** is equally important to each person's happiness, well-being, and *who they are*.

When putting all of those elements together in *your* **marriage**, *you* must try to deal with the hurt, anger, and bitterness first; *you* need to stop the fighting and arguing.

Then evaluate the daily stress the family is dealing with and if both have jobs how that is contributing to the stress. Yes, a person can go to church and be a Christian with all of these elements, and there can be abuse in *their* life too.

This means everyone has to deal with their own stress and their emotional level at the same time. The time and effort should be short in nature when there is a problem, and should not make it harder to get back to a **normal pattern** in life.

But, when *you* have **abnormal stress** a person may be experiencing depression, anxieties, and worry from time to time. Especially when a person gets down on themselves for no reason, the other person should be helping the other person get up, and then both of them are pulling together. That will help, but if there are problems pushing both of them down, the sooner they can get things back to normal in the **marriage,** each person's life will run smoother and things will get back to normal, but if they don't, what happens in those cases.

In that case a **breakdown** has not been dealt with, there has been some damage, but can *you* as a couple get over it and go on. This breakdown also has to do with a stress point, (*you* could be stressed-out) over a crisis, but it has exceeded the normal demands on the **marriage**, or (*you* could have over reacted to a demand) and caused an emotional breakdown (for instance if *you* are yelling at the kids or the spouse too much).

This could result from being over worked on the job, stressed out, or dealing with a bad relationship at work. (When the fire and romance has gone out of a **marriage.** It could be because the relationship has too much stress over a period of time). Another thing a person should watch out for is not enough time and energy and feeling stressed out. There are other reasons such as financial obligations, discouragement, worry and anxiety, being impatient with *your* expectations of *yourself* and *your* spouse.

The big thing about dealing with problems in a **marriage** they get on each other's nerves and they can't agree on anything, even worse is getting victory over those feelings, and a couple usually doesn't spend enough time finding the right answer. When the stress in the situation gets to be too much, a person may want to back off for a while, and then talk and evaluate the situation before it gets any worse. Then tackle them, but what if it doesn't get better? The idea of things will get better over time usually doesn't work unless something is done to solve the problem.

I think these same principles will apply in building a better marriage and we will present them for everyone.

11 Principles for a better marriage

1. **Be explicit.** Talk through the differences each other brings to the marriage and negotiate a compromise for solving the situation. Listen to the other person and empathize with them in a loving and caring ways. Take turns talking and listening to the solutions even if they don't workout, be understanding, and be open to each other's ideas. Remember each of you is the expert on your own kids, and for kids-related decisions, the biological parent's preference in how to meet those needs should take priority in most cases. Try to find a win-win solution in any situation.

2. **Take time together.** Regular couple time, focusing on your relationship and having fun, is vital for success. This may require pulling back on time with friends and family, church, and other responsibilities. Kids take a lot of time; couple's must take time and protect the family. Set aside time for weekends get a ways with the children, for yourselves, and try to take a weekend getaway every few months.

3. **Talk through expectations.** Both of you should bring good and wholesome ideas to be considered to have a good relationship, but base them on the needs in your relationship. Take about what you want in a wife or husband, and get to know what you want your spouse likes best about you and build the good qualities of each other. It is not your spouse's job to make up for your mistakes. It is both of you working together to identify and communicate your expectations to each other and negotiate any differences.

4. **Empathize with the kids and the ex-spouse.** Like many aspects of remarriage, a great deal of maturity is required to do this well, perhaps more it is than you can muster on some days, so you have to work on the relationship every day.

5. **Be flexible.** This includes everything from discipline in the way both of you spend money. Vacations and time alone together have to

work around the kids' needs as well as the adults'. For example, if Mother's Day happens to fall on a weekend outing, the adults should be flexible so the kids don't have to miss it, plan another time.

    6. **Be open and honest with each other.** Communication and compromises are necessary to solve the problems.

    7. **Resolve your problems without upsetting the children.** Take time to resolve marriage problems through therapy if needed, and prayer. In some cases pastoral counseling is a good idea and each person must be considered to determine the type of pastoral counseling care necessary for healing.

    8. **Tell the truth about money.**

    9. **Be yourself.**

    10. **Be patient with the process of building a family.**

    11. **Kiss each other goodnight every night.**

When couples have problems one of the considerations may be divorce, because the marriage failed for some reason and again the personal-well-being of the person is at stack. I didn't understand what my heart and mind was saying and why the divorces had happened to me. This section will be particularly interesting to those who have had problems. I am going to show you how this helped me and how it saved my life at the same time, and then how it saved me from a fate worse than death. Then I will give you the steps I took to restore my mental-well-being at the same time.

You may think that would enough to destroy my life, and my health problems almost destroyed my life, let's look at the positive aspects, first all of the bad things have helped make me to be who I am today and how I have to live with these past relationships.

I have to get along with myself and believe in my convictions, values, and (character) I had to learn to believe in myself before I could move on. I had to for-give myself and each person involved, the hurt was a big issue for me, and how I dealt with the emotional influences in my life at the same time, or at least be willing to see their side of the story. That does not mean I have to agree with them or what they did or why.

I found from time to time my feeling did change in some ways for the better. I stopped blaming them and criticizing myself and I hope they have settled things in their heart and mind or maybe they have had similar feelings, if not, then I wish them the best.

That brings us to the issues of today there is a lot more information and counseling along these lines and self-help books. We believe in support information and groups help build relationships. I am of the opinion that is a start in the right direction or at least it was in my life. That is one of the reasons for writing my life story and study guides. I believe in the openness of today's society and I have put my heart into this particular study, I have my personal feelings, and these studies have helped me to understand my life in a better way. I think I have a better understanding of myself and the inter self. I am satisfied that this is the best way to go about helping families, children and other's going through marriage problems.

NEW BEGINNINGS I, WARNING SIGN

STOP
LOOK
LISTEN

Chapter 5

THE WARNING SIGINS IN RELATIONS & MARRIAGE

Fine tuning the relationship, and marriage

That means a person needs to PAY ATTENTION TO WARNING SIGINS in their relationships and marriage! A person can get so busy living their life they don't realize the impending dangers during courtship and then marriage. Usually they have not paid attention to the **Busy Signals**, the rush of life, busy schedules, and your job, and we hope the excitement of getting married or being married is there.

I want *you* to look for the **Busy Signals,** the danger and the perils to the marriage. I believe **busy signals** can be **cries for help**. However, are times when a person just doesn't see the **warning signs** because they are hidden, if the safety devices have been altered or damaged, and in some cases they become (doormat) because a person's feelings become numb? There is a danger when a person doesn't see them as a problem there are ways to detect them, if there are improper balances from within or from the outside influences.

A person may say "I didn't know there were any problems in the relationship or marriage," at this point there is usually the need for, "HELP"! Not like a <u>HELP Wanted Sign,</u> but there has been **Warning Signs** all along the way, some are in <u>**Big Capital Letters**</u> a person can see, but at times they are in very <u>**small print**</u> and a person doesn't see or fails to see them.

In the meantime the **Warning Signs** were there, they may have been ignored (this maybe characterized by withdrawing from the problem) a person may say "leave me alone, or nothing is wrong let me suffer through it, it will get better." What if it doesn't get better, what then? They maybe feeling sorry for themselves, "RIGHT". Other **Warning Signs** are DEPRESSION or UNUSUAL EMOTIONAL STRESS over things in the relationship or marriage. That brings about anger and hurt feeling if these symptoms persist and cause conflicts, and the emotional stress increases.

Another way to know if there are contradictions in their feelings toward someone or is it one's self; if a person is hiding *their* true feelings, those are not good signs at all that means something is wrong. When a person is not able to live with those feelings of hurt, anger and bitterness and yes disappointments in the relationship and marriage. That is "OK" if a person feels they can do something, but when a person can't hide those feelings. They feel they do not have to involve the other person directly, but it will affect the relationship or marriage, it is good to solve the problems when they happen.

Usually those hidden feeling can come out when a person least expect it, can a person or couple should find ways in those kinds situations. The question, if nothing is done it will become an even (bigger problem)?

Another **Warning sign** is built into how a person spends their money or thinking shopping makes them happy in most cases it is an avenue where buy the things we need. There are those who are very tight with their money, those who spend wisely, and others who spend because they enjoy buying things. The worst case scenario is when a person is unhappy, and they are only happiness comes from buying something to sooth their feelings, if you see this before the marriage work out those differences, but when they are married a person may able to adjust their differences in spending.

I was in a barber shop some years ago, in small town in the state of Missouri. The barber was talking to the man in the chair. "Did you hear about the rich men in town", his name I can't remember to this day. He said to the man in the barber chair, "if I had his money I'd take a trip around the world to see things". The rich man reply was, "if you have half as much fun spending your money as I do saving my money, you are a happy person". He put the man in his place in a polite way, as the barber told the story everyone laughed to hear of the man who saved his money.

The moral to the story is everyone has their own way of being happy, and that is what I want for *you*, but if *you* are unhappy there is reason, and I will spend some time trying to help *you* find some happiness. Buying things and spending money is a temporary fix to the real problems in *a person's life*. If there is need to buy things other than to survive, food, clothing, a home and a car, and so on, but if it is to buy something to buy something, think about why?

Those were some of the personal **Warning Signs**; now let's look at the **Danger Signs** in relationship or marriage! Every, life is intertwined with the person's in the relationship, family, vocation, etc.

Are you able to evaluate the danger signs?

- Sometimes it hits a person from the blind side, usually when they are not expecting it, or not prepared to handle the situation, then what?
- There is also ("the law of sowing and repeating") and how does a person deal with it.
- Also, there is another aspect in a person's life, when a person changes, and they are going in different directions, and have different goals?
- Another is when a relationship or marriage goes bad just remember, **"People will have a bad day"**.

Put all of this in perspective, when a person has problems in their relationship or marriage, it is important how they deal with the circumstances and their personal conflicts. Be aware of the differences in points view, harboring bad feelings for instance. In other words when a person dwells on trying to hurt someone it usually because they have been hurt. This only damages *their* own self-wroth; *they* become a victim of their own feelings, and thoughts.

A person should have the heart and mind-set to find the point of agreement if possible, people do not always do that, but usually it's best to wait for the right time and place to confront the other person.

Take on the personal responsibility for *your* actions, and trust the other person's judgment too, before *you* come up with the final decision. Remember *you* may not be able to change the other person's way of thinking, but *you* should be able to find some common ground, but if you can't, then what?

I think the next step will be just as helpful, don't make a decision until both of you can come to an agreement or point of view that will meet both of *your* needs.

Be aware of disagreements and even arguments that have to be dealt with! Both of you need to see the bad (negative), then look at the bad, and look at the ultimate consequences? Now *you* need to try and find some good if possibly, then identify with the good (the positive aspects if possible). "RIGHT". *You* need to separate the two as you discuss both points of view.

It wasn't just one day when something went wrong, then **BAM**, *you* have had the problem all along, usually it has been coming on over a period of time, and there is usually something that triggered the reaction. One or both of you may not realize the impact until the crisis has hit. Now someone is paying attention because they have ignored it too long, **"The Warning Signs"** were there! What happens, somewhere along the way someone or both of you got off track, people really don't know just when, where, and how? Now they have dealt with the problem?

Another, of the most common occurrences is the changes in the relationship when a woman or man is more likely to experience mood changes, and unhappiness. They may become unhappy and may not accept the status quo as before.

I hope I haven't been too tough on you; we're just trying to get you to realize there are potential troubles some are within the person and they don't see themselves as a problem. Notice when there are **Busy Signals, Warning Signs, & Danger Signs** there needs to be something done before it gets out of control, and it becomes a serious problem, a series of problems or it becomes insurmountable problem to deal with. It is much easier to deal with each problem as they come along, don't let them build over time, and then something happens.

It well help a couple to deal with larger and bigger problems down the road if they have not taken care of the small problems in their relationship and marriage. Human nature is to wait or procrastinate; another reason most couples can't deal with larger problems they haven't learned to deal with the hurt feelings, arguments, and disappointments of the past.

Now we are ready to deal with the assessment of the relationship

The assessment is a vital part of any thing we do, but it is not at all conclusive in the validation process of the relationship. The success depends on the insight into each other and being able to solve problems, and seeing how they relate to *you* as a couple. God is able to forgive, but are *you* able to forgive is big factor, remember healing comes from God's love, but the couple must be willing to forgive each other, be able to for get to some degree, and be able to put things in the past. To what degree they are able to do this will determine the success in the relationship or marriage.

Some of the biggest arguments come in regards to how the money should be spent, raising children, others are over political views, religion, and personal prejudices you must agree to disagree if you are going to have a good relationship or marriage.

1. The definition of "assessment" says a lot about the process:

First, the act or instance of assessing the problem: APPAISAL
Second, the amount assessed;
Webster's Ninth New Collegiate Dictionary MERRIAM-WEBSTER INC., *Publishers* Springfield, Massachusetts, U.S.A. (1988)".

This introduces what the assessment means to the relationship or marriage and how comfortable they are with each other, because there are going to be questions and problems to deal with. They need to be able to communicate; I want to give you some idea of how these assessments are going to help you have a better marriage and family.

Believe it or not being able to talk to each other is good, but are they able to make an assessment of themselves and the importance of communicating with each other about the marriage. One way a couple can do this by talking things over, not making demands of each other, I want insure *you* the assessment will help you if you realize there are two sides to every argument.

Ask each other what they think will help make the marriage and family better? It will be helpful in analyzing the situation and take time to discuss a troubled area in your relationship or marriage ask each other:

- How stressful is the situation to each person,
- Are you able to talk about a provocative subject or problem without arguing?

Second, these emotional hurts are not healthy; these problems will bring out the emotional stress in a situation within the relationship.

Third, when this leads to some form of dependences, abuse, such as mental, physical, and sexual abuses.

Fourth, do these behavior patterns lead to strong violent actions such as out-of-control, uncontrolled temper, and abuse.

Fifth, in extreme situations do you want to hurt a person because they have hurt you?

Sixth, when the arguments are hostile in nature, *you* need to learn how to control your anger.

Questionnaire VI Questions to (ask each other):
1) Can you as a couple distinguish between the major and minor issues at this point in the discussion?
Yes ___ No ___
2) Can *you* control the problems and be specific in the way you are going to deal with the problem or problems and are you able to find a solution?
Yes ___ No ___
a) How does it make *you* feel as a person and about the other person?
b) How do *you* feel about the other person that *you* are involved with?
c) How do *you* feel about the relationship at this point?
d) How bad is it?
3) Do you see any hope at this point?   Yes ___ No ___

That is a good start, have *you* considered all these problems and were you able to solve them, do *you* characterize them as minor in nature, if not you may not have made a true assessment. If all the problems are major in nature are *you* over evaluating the severity of your problems or are they real problems.

Then the next step is to see if *you* can evaluate, state the problem, if yes that is a very good sign.

- Another thing at this point can *you* talk about the problem without arguing, it would be helpful if *you* can define the problem or problems and what is causing the problem, in that case *you* may be able to deal with one part of the problem and still not be able to find the major cause. As a counselor I want *you* to look at the real issues either way?
- If *you* can't tell them what is wrong, can *you* tell them how bad *you* feel or how they have hurt *you* can (*you*) describe the pain at this point.
- If both of *you* are feeling the pain who is more likely to give-in or who is not likely are both of you willing to deal with the problems at this point. If they are unable to deal with the problems there is not

much hope until they are able to talk about the problems, or if you can't solve any issues at this point this could bring about: **Confusion, angry, frustrated, and/or out of controlled feelings.**

• If you can't describe the pain and hurt, there is a need to describe how bad it feels, some of this can helped by talking about those feelings, if a person is not able to talk about things, they are in serious trouble, and so is the marriage. They are going need lots of help before they can go on with the marriage.

At this point they need to be referred to a personal counselor that deals with personal issues or a marriage counselor. At least at this point they should know of a good counselor, that is a starting point for each person.

Appraisal

Each person at some point needs to make an appraisal of themselves and what they want out of the marriage. Their appraisal of the other person is not relevant because they need help before they can go on with marriage, and also if they can't look at each other as a valued partner or (an equal partner), (each person) needs to evaluate their self-worth to themselves, and to the marriage.

Some people value themselves better than the other person because they are per-say a better person or Christian. There is a bigger question when a person thinks they are better than the other person, and takes advantage of their feeling superior. This can become a weapon of superiority over the other person making them feel bad instead and if their problem stems from an arrogant personality. I'm afraid if this is the case they have two problems, they do not understand their self-worth, and their own temperament.

How much emotional stress and pressure can a person take is directly tied to their ability to make an assessment of the success or failure in their marriage? Some people can take more and give more, while others are just the opposite in nature and temperament; they take and give very little in return.

I want *you* to still have *your* dreams, but face them realistically in relation to the relationship or marriage. My life would not be the same without my dreams, but as a child and young person I looked at my life and dreams differently. Let's take another step in dealing with the reality of the relationship, marriage and family.

- Show your love by listening and communicating, and being affectionate is always appropriate, a hug is always appropriate and a kiss that fits the occasion.

My hope is that you of will give more of yourself and have a better understanding of each other in the relationship or marriage. These axioms helped me understand my relationships in a better way.

NEXT, I want to reestablish your ties to your character, standards, values, and personalities do inner into a relationship too, and how you communicate them?

Awareness is a key in understanding happiness in a relationship.
    1) The key to understanding one's self and their personality.
    2) Is accepting yourself for who you are and as a valued person...
    3) Is the key to understanding ones feelings, wants, and desires?
    4) Is the key to understanding ones goals and destiny?
    5) Is the key making good choices in your life?

The key is what you know about one's self
    1) Are you physically and mentally comfortable with how you relate with each other?
    2) Are there unanswered questions about one's self?
    3) Are you being realistic with one's self, and fair with others?
    4) Are you comfortable with your looks and appearance?

Communication makes for good relationships and marriage.

1) Communication is the bases for a good marriage and relationship.

2) Communication can mean talking, writing, and knowing when to be quite (take heed to that one)

3) Communication is also touching, and by listening to each other's problems.

4) Communication has a *sender* and *receiver*.

5) Communication is successful when messages are received in the same spirit as the *sender* and *receiver* receives the same intent.

6) Communication is successful when *you* communicate and make purposeless.

7) Communication should communicate good-well and intent.

8) Communication is being involved in a good a marriage relationship.

Bad communication from the *sender* can make for an unsuccessful marriage relationship.

1) A selfish intent or purpose.

2) A mixed message or deception.

3) A poor choice of words (have either of *you* said something *you* could take back later)

4) Poor body language (*you* can tell a lot by what is not being said)

5) Controlling the conversation (do *you* feel left out of the conversation?)

6) Wrong intent or boring. (are *you* able communicate in the conversations)

Bad communications from the *receiver* can make for an unsuccessful marriage relationship.

1) Bad listeners interrupt while the other person is talking. (Waite and listen to what they are saying)

2) Pretend to be interested. (be honest and sincere while listening)

3) There could be distractions, noises, and interruptions. (if so what should you do?)

4) They lose their train of thought. (be patient and give them a chance to gather their thoughts and they should do the same for you)

5) When they lose focus and their attention in the conversation. (stop and say what is wrong, or why don't you understand what I am trying to tell you)

Example:

Your friend may say *you* have a new haircut or style. *You* may think it is too short you might say something about a new haircut or style. What do *you* say to them, say something nice without hurting their feelings? *You* may say, "do *you* like their new haircut or style?" (The term may depend on whether you are a (male or female.)

You have not have hurt their feelings in *your* reply, but they know *you* have seen the new look.

The dialog may proceed from there. *You* have opened the door for more conversation or maybe that is as far as the comments should go at the time.

How are *you doing* now, communicating, and getting along?

Is it better? Can *each of you* do a better job of communicating and getting things done?

(This not a test, but a good time to ask questions)

Questionnaire VII

How to maintain a good relationship is being able to communicate with each other?
Know your communications' Skills Quiz:
- We've all had times with our spouse or even with very good friends where the conversation dragged on and nothing was accomplished. Both of you went away feeling drained or frustrated.
- Fortunately, we have also had times with our relationship or spouse when the conversation was very satisfying. The time flew by as you talked.
- We have met people that we could not converse at all, while meeting others in the conversation. They were easy to talk to:
- Why? _____

- Was it a bad time of day for them? For you? Was one of you talking too quickly before the other could not speak?
  Yes ___ No ___ Why?
  _____

- Have you ever wondered why a person was so hard to get to know and get along with. Why?
  _____

- Have you ever wondered if people think you are hard to get to know and get along with?
  _____

- Did this quiz answer some of your questions?
  Yes ___ No ___
- Do these questions give you insight into your own patterns of conversation and communication skills? Yes ___ No ___ & How?
  _____

- Do they provide a clue about your communication preferences and skills? Yes ___ No ___
  - Now describe your communication skills?
  _____

Read these statements and rate each one with the number that best describes *you*. There are no right or wrong answers.

Ratings:

0 Never
1) Seldom
2) Sometimes
3) Often   I absorb information quickly. _____
4) I am talkative early in the morning. _____
5) I am talkative late at night. _____
6) I pay attention to visual details. _____
7) I give short, concise answers to most questions. _____
8) I keep most of my thoughts to myself. _____
9) Much of the time I am absorbed in my own ideas. _____
10) It is easy for me to identify my feelings. _____
11) I believe most of my thoughts are of interest to others. ____
12) I believe most of my thoughts are not of interest to others. ___
13) I believe most of my thoughts are none of anyone else's concern. _____
14) I have difficulty expressing my thoughts. _____
15) I have difficulty expressing my feelings. _____
16) I base my decisions more on logic than emotions. _____
17) I like to talk about intimate and/or emotional matters. _____
18) I have a hard time knowing what I'm feeling. _____
19) I feel overwhelmed or confused when people jump from one idea to another. _____
20) I am a fast talker. _____
21) I quickly tire of a subject. _____
22) Speak slowly, often pausing to think. _____
23) I feel bored or anxious if my partner talks too slowly. ____
24 I feel bored or anxious if my partner talks too quickly. ____
25) I like to be the center of attention. _____
26) I vigorously defend my thoughts and opinions. _____
27 I like to talk about what I am feeling. _____

MARRIAGE – FAMILY & ADDICTIONS

28) I like to have good conversations when I eat. _____
29) I don't like to talk when I eat. _____
30) I like to talk to someone when I drive. _____
31) I don't like to talk when I drive. _____
32) I do not like to talk about money or financial matters. ____

- Now answer the following questions in a few words or a few paragraphs, whatever your "style."

1) As a general rule, the times of day and general situations when I feel most available to talk. _____

2) I listen most attentively when people (examples: talk slowly, talk quickly, don't dwell on one subject too long, speak with enthusiasm, speak in a calm voice, share their emotions, etc.)

_____

3) It is difficult for me to pay attention when others (talk at length, about home, work, jump from topic to topic, talk only about problems, etc)

_____

4) It is difficult for me to talk when (people ask too many questions, when I am tired, I first wake up, etc.)

_____

- Do you recognize any patterns in your answers? Yes ___ No ___ Don't Know ___
- What pattern may express your individual style of conversation and communication?

Conversation ___ Argumentative ___ Factual ___ Fun ___ Don't care ___

- This personal insight help *you* with conversation with *your* partner and others. Yes___ No ___

5) Acknowledgement While Talking & Communicating

- You are talking to a friend. He or she tells you a long story containing things you don't agree with. What do you do?

_____

- Often when your child, lover/partner, or friend tells you a story or voices a complaint, are they just asking for acknowledgment.
  Yes ___ No ___ or want a reply explain
  _____

- This does not mean that he/she wants an agreement or compliance; or does it merely indicate a desire to be heard and understood is he or she really talking to be understood.
Explain: _____

- Many conflicts in your personal relationships can be avoided if you will take the time to acknowledge the other's feelings and points of view. In fact, understanding communication is not all about you.
Explain _____

Describe your communication Skills:

Try these three steps in acknowledgment:
Acknowledge by repeating back to your child, friend, lover/partner, what has said in similar words to show them you have heard and understood. Examples: "You were upset today because I was late." "You feel like I have treated your sister or brother better than you, I understand that you are upset by what happened."

> 1) Don't Invalidate: It is not necessary to agree with the person you are acknowledging. You do not even need to feel that what he/she said is the truth. However, do not invalidate him or her in some way.
> 2) Don't Try to Change the subject

Examples of bad invalidation include:
"You're too sensitive."
"You're certainly wrong. I don't treat your sister or brother better than you."
"There is no reason for you to feel like that." "That's a crazy way to feel."

Be satisfied just to acknowledge don't try to change (him or her).

3) **Attention when in conversion and attention when conversing.**

Conversations and attention when in conversing: Attention when conversing means focusing, looking, and paying attention. These three components of a conversation are easy to understand and produce more satisfying conversations.

- Paying attention to someone in a conversation will get and keep their attention. It means that your ears, eyes, your body, and your feelings are all focused on that person at one time. Attention is a very important part of all conversations and any relationship, it includes:

Physical Presence

- Relationships are a building process. Your friend, child, lover (and you) gradually share interests, feelings, and goals. Usually this sharing is done in part through conversations.
- That often requires being together physically or by phone, internet. Also, your physical presence shows the other person that you care about them. It affirms that (he/she) is important to you.

Focusing

- Focusing means all of your physical and psychological attention is directed toward the other person and what they are saying during the entire conversation. Your body language is very important be open and relaxed. You should look at them squarely and face them and slightly inclined toward the person. Your facial-expressions convey interest and comprehension.
- Keep the focus on the other person. Relating similar personal experiences or offering solutions to problems takes the focus away from them and places it on you. Even though you may feel you are offering empathy or sympathy in this manner, in this way you can turn any conversation around to what you have to say, make sure it relevant to the subject.

Looking

- Remember to look with your eyes.
- A classic example of looking with "your eyes" a child coloring or drawing while the mother cleans the kitchen. The child finishes a picture quickly and repeatedly says, "Look at this one, Mommy."

The mother mumbles, "Good, Meagan" or "That's great," while continuing to rinse dishes.

Finally the child, "Look now, Mommy. Look with your eyes."
- Looking at another person shows that you are there for (him or her) during conversations. It usually requires eye contact.

Listening is a Communication Skill:
Listening is a Communication Skill: Listen during conversations. Learn listening skills & listening habits. A good conversationalist listens more than they talk. Beneficial listening; listen attentively, you're listening skills produce meaningful communications.

Are You REALLY Listening?
- Most of us do not realize the importance of listening as a communicative tool. Studies have shown that we actually spend 50% more time listening than we do talking. We often take listening for granted, never realizing that it is a skill that can be learned.
- Watch someone who listens attentively. (He/she) makes eye contact and focuses on the other person while (he/she) listens. (He/she) listens with their eyes as well as their ears. While listening, he nods or makes attentive noises from time-to-time. This is a skilled listener and an attentive listener.
- When a person is listening they feel a sense of communication. Everyone wins with beneficial listening.
- After *your* next conversation, test your ability to benefit from listening to that conversation. Analyze and ask yourself:
  1) What did I learn from the other person(s)?
  2) What did I learn about the other person(s)?
  3) Who did more talking?
  4) Who did more listening?
  5) Where there any interruptions while you were talking?
  6) What questions should I have asked?
  7) What questions should I have answered more

thoroughly?
8) Was I absolutely certain I understood everything?
9) Did I ask for clarification?
10) Did I practice acknowledgment?
11) Did he or she practice acknowledgment to me?
12) Were both parties showing attention?
13) Was the conversation balanced?
14) Did anyone keep changing the subject?
15) Did anyone get angry?
16) Did anyone appear sad?
17) Was everyone paying attention?
18) What will I do different in my next conversation?

- The ability to listen is a skill that can be improved with use. This skill can and will improve your overall relationships spouse, children, and co-workers and boss.

Fifteen Ways to Say, "I'm Sorry." {4}

Do you need to apologize? Here are 15 ways to say "I'm sorry" to someone you love.

1) I'm feeling defensive. When I feel defensive, sometimes say things I don't mean.

2) I'm not talking to you like you are someone I love. Let me start over because I do love you.

3) I know I'm sounding angry, but I'm feeling extremely threatened. Let me take a deep breath and try again.

4) I know I'm feeling harassed please bear with me; I will make up for it later.

5) I'm afraid if I say I'm sorry, you'll make everything my fault.

6) I'm sorry. I think I was using a tone of voice I did not mean.

7) I think I'm overreacting.

8) I guess I haven't been listening very well. Please give me another chance.

9) Please forgive me?

10) I know I've hurt you what can I do that would help us to be happy again?

11) I've said some mean things. Can I take them back?

12) I'm making it sound like it was all your fault I know that is not the case.

13) I know I sound mad now. I'm sorry and I haven't stopped loving you.

14) I love you, I hate fighting, and I'm sorry for my part of this one!

15) I feel lousy about what just happened. Can we just make up?

Don't forget the best two words of all, "I'm sorry."

Don't forget the best three words of all, "I love you."

Don't forget the best four words of all, "Please forgive me

Are you comfortable with this information?

                 Yes _____ No _____

How do you feel after reading this information?

    Reply to: _____

Breaking down old patterns and building new relationships

We have looked at some practical ways to say I'm sorry **breaking down old patterns, and building new relationships**, and how this relates to the marriage relationship. Using principles that work and help in such cases as a couple looks at the application of (**behavioral patterns**), and how they relate to **the cry for help in a person's life and marriage relationship**. Ultimately the decisions/choices will rest with *you* as a person and couple.

Demonstration Chart II, 1– 6 Reactions Axioms

Next we're going to break down the different types of **reactions** as we look at **Demonstration Chart II Graff Layouts** that deals with the normal, abnormal emotional reactions and breakdown.

Emotional Reactions (Axioms),
- [(1)] Normal Reactions
- [(2)] Normal Highs & Lows
- [(3)] Normal Breakdown

Abnormal Reactions (axioms)
- [(4)] Short-term Breakdown
- [(5)] Long-term Breakdown
- [(6)] Struggle & Overcoming

Questionnaire VIII. Normal and abnormal is defined by good and poor emotional control:

A. Abnormal self-defeating, habits, patterns, and behaviors name those that apply:
   _____

B. Normal habits, patterns, and behaviors name good ones
   _____

C. Abnormal level of competency in *your spouse* if any name some?
   _____

D. Abnormal indictors in the relationship.
   _____

E. Abnormal rejection, insecurities, inferiority, and introvertedness.
   _____

Learn from past mistakes

1) Be willing to learn from past mistakes and how. Explain
   _____

2) Name some mistakes that have happened over and over again.
   _____) _____
   _____

3) Name some patterns or a downhill spiral.
   _____

4) How do you feel about breaking the barriers in your life?
   _____

A philosopher once remarked it is up to you what you choose to make of yourself. In our book B on self-image and self-awareness we use "Thinking Strategies", William Altier shows how creative thinking begins with recognizing opportunities as they present themselves in everyday life. Once these 'triggers' for creativity have been spotted, the person then needs to assess the possibilities, often overcoming barriers to new solutions. Creativity is achieved through breaking down existing relationships and analyzing the elements of the problem. Then moving these into new patterns until a solutions are found. Creativity requires a desire to experiment, an ability to understand problems and ask questions, and a refusal to be afraid of failure. Developing these traits is not easy, but it can be done.

The world and even Christians have a broader view of marriage today, living together, to premarital sex, teenage pregnancy, abortions, and same sex marriages are all issues of the day, as a counselor we need to be able to turn these people away from making a bad decision or do they could try and look for God's guidance in their life.

Personal responsibility in the marriage relationship

When a person looks at *themselves* and says everything is alright, the question is it? I like to look at our studies from different points of view, and let's have some fun doing it. A person should try their best to prevent something from happening, and then how does a person deal with it after it happens.

In our **SOS Life Enhancement** book we use a familiar story line about one's self. "Who is that person in your mirror" when I looked at myself I saw a lot of problems.

If *you* were to see *yourself* as others see *you*, would *you* recognize *yourself*, or would *you* even like that very same person if *you* saw them walking down the street. If *you* do, *you* may even have a big problem in recognizing *your* own personal faults, but don't kid *yourself* into thinking it is okay because it is just *me*! Don't think that way.

We have looked a person's actions and how to say please forgive me, while not criticizing the other person for their actions and conduct. A person may think how could they do that in good conscience? It's when a person's thinks they are better than the other person, but in reality that is what a person is doing when they say I can't forgive or think it was their fault?

A person can get caught up in this kind of thinking, and it becomes their way of life. If a person sins, they should not condemn the other person, Christ speaking in

Matt. 5:41-42 V 41 "And whosoever shall compel thee to go a mile, go with him twain." V 42 "Give to him that asked thee, and from him that would borrow of thee turn not thou away." And in **Luke 6:27-29** Christ teachings on love V 27 "But I say unto you which hear, Love your enemies, do good to them which hate you," V 28 "Bless them that curse you, and pray for them which despitefully use you." V 29 "And unto him that smith thee on one cheek offer also the other; and him that taketh away they clock forbid not *to take thy* coat also."

These Biblical principles should stand out because they will influence a person's life and relationship. It is only human to make mistakes, and some of them turn out bad. (You may just happen to think that *you* would not have made those same choices.)

Look at **John 8:7-11**; look at verse V 7b "Christ speaking "He that is without sin among you, let him cast a stone at her." and V 11b "Christ says even more, Neither do I condemn three; go, and sin no more." Read all of the verse to get the whole story.

And some people are so hard on themselves and feel like they have sinned in either case these are misconceptions in a person's life.

These principles are good, and there are other study-guides just as good. However, our methods in dealing with the situations in relationships, and the problems associated within a person and their marriage are you able to get a mental picture of what I'm talking about at this time.

As a Clinical Psychologist & a Cognitive Behavior Counselor I relate to the mental & as well as the physical aspects of life.

I love people, how about *you* I want to pass this on as we have looked at how *you* have looked at *your* feelings, look for the real joy and possibilities in *your life*, even in the worst set-of-circumstances look up and count *your* blessings. I hope each *person* and couple will make a commitment to carry on the good work that you started in *your relationship*.

The key to success is a "proper knowledge and understanding of the situation". I know I've said that before, I think this is one of the greatest things that has changed my life, I find it is important to share each other's burdens, that is one of the joys in having a good relationship. If *you* are not doing this I want to help *you* learn how to do this in a better way. I want to help *each of you* to work on making *your* relationship and marriage better.

I think as *you* look at *your* life, my hope is *you* are living for today and tomorrow, and you have a successful marriage.

NEW BEGINNINGS I, SEX IN THE MARRIAGE Wedding Rings & Wedding Voles

Chapter 6

PREPARING FOR SEX IN THE MARRIAGE

This happens all too often in homes and even ministers of the Gospel do not live up to Biblical principles and application in the marriage valves. I say this in love and kindness as a warning and as a professional clinical counselor. There was a change in society around the 1960's about sex and that does not mean I don't understand today's acceptance of sex outside the marriage. I believe this is the best way to present the problems in sex not everybody will see the Biblical view as I do, but I want young people to look at it. If you are having problems how does sex fit into the problem and I will say this is the best way to deal with sex within the marriage and it is in good test. Everyone looks at it in their own way?

It that has to do with the sex in the marriage; every couple should read this charge from the Bible on marriage and sexual conduct by Paul. **I Cor. 7:1-40** a couple should read this every year or so, I hope giving these scriptures will help and clear up some miss giving about sex in marriage.

1 Corinthians 7: *(KJV)*

"**V 1 Now** concerning the things whereof ye wrote unto me: It is good for a man not to touch a woman.

V 2 Nevertheless, to avoid fornication, let every man have his own wife, and let every woman have her own husband.

V 3 Let the husband render unto the wife due benevolence: and likewise also the wife unto the husband.

V 4 The wife hath not power of her own body, but the husband. and likewise also the husband hath not power of his own body, but the wife.

V 5 Defraud ye not one the other, except it be with consent for a time, that ye may give yourselves to fasting and prayer; and come together again, that Satan tempt you not for your incontinency.

MARRIAGE – FAMILY & ADDICTIONS

V 6 But I speak this by permission, and not of commandment.

V 7 For I would that all men were even as I myself. But every man hath his proper gift of God, one after this manner, and another after that.

V 8 I say therefore to the unmarried and widows, it is good for them if they abide even as I.

V 9 But if they cannot contain, let them marry: for it is better to marry than to burn.

V 10 And unto the married I command, yet not I, but the Lord, Let not the wife depart from her husband:

V 11 But and if she depart, let her remain unmarried or be reconciled to her husband: and let not the husband put away his wife.

V 12 But to the rest speak I, not the Lord: If any brother hath a wife that believeth not, and she be pleased to dwell with him, let him not put her away.

V 13 And the woman which hath an husband that believeth not, and if he be pleased to dwell with her, let her not leave him.

V 14 For the unbelieving husband is sanctified by the wife, and the unbelieving wife is sanctified by the husband: else were your children unclean; but now are they holy.

V 15 But if the unbelieving depart, let him depart. A brother or a sister is not under bondage in such cases: but God hath called us to peace.

V 16 For what knowest thou, 0 wife, whether thou shalt save thy husband? or how knowest thou, 0 man, whether thou shalt save thy wife?

V 17 But as God hath distributed to every man, as the Lord hath called every one, so let him walk. And so ordain I in all churches.

V 18 Is any man called being circumcised? let him not become uncircumcised. Is any called in uncircumcision? let him not be circumcised.

V 19 Circumcision is nothing, and uncircumcision is nothing, but the keeping of the commandments of God.

V 20 Let every man abide in the same calling wherein he was called.

V 21 Art thou called being a servant? care not for it: but if thou mayest be made free, use it rather.

V 22 For he that is called in the Lord, being a servant, is the Lord's freeman: likewise also he that is called, being free, is Christ's servant.
V 23 Ye are bought with a price; be not ye the servants of men.
V 24 Brethren, let every man, wherein he is called, therein abide with God.
V 25 Now concerning virgins I have no commandment of the Lord: yet I give my judgment, as one that hath obtained mercy of the Lord to be faithful.
V 26 I suppose therefore that this is good for the present distress, I say, that it is good for a man so to be.
V 27 Art thou bound unto a wife? seek not to be loosed. Art thou loosed from a wife? seek not a wife.
V 28 But and if thou marry, thou hast not sinned; and if a virgin marry, she hath not sinned. Nevertheless such shall have trouble In the flesh: but I spare you.
V 29 But this I say, brethren, the time is short: it remaineth, that both they that have wives be as though they had none;
V 30 And they that weep, as though they wept not; and they that rejoice, as though they rejoiced not; and they that buy, as though they possessed not;
V 31 And they that use this world, as not abusing it: for the fashion of this world passeth away.
V 32 But I would have you without carefulness. He that is unmarried careth for the things that belong to the Lord, how he may please the Lord:
V 33 But he that is married careth for the things that are of the world, how he may please his wife.
V 34 There is difference also between a wife and a virgin. The unmarried woman careth for the things of the Lord, that she may be holy both in body and in spirit: but she that is married careth for the things of the world, how she may please her husband.
V 35 And this I speak for your own profit; not that I may cast a snare upon you, but for that which is comely, and that ye may attend upon the Lord without distraction.

V 36 But if any man think that he behaveth himself uncomely toward his virgin, if she pass the flower of her age, and need so require, let him do what he will, he sinneth not: let them marry.

V 37 Nevertheless he that standethstedfast in his heart, having no necessity, but hath power over his own will, and hath so decreed in his heart that he will keep his virgin, doeth well.

V 38 So then he that giveth her in marriage doeth well; but he that giveth her not in marriage doeth better.

V 39 The wife is bound by the law as long as her husband liveth; but if her husband be dead, she is at liberty to be married to whom she will; only in the Lord.

V 40 But she is happier if she so abide, after my judgment: and I think also that I have the Spirit of God."

Sex in the marriage

Sex in the marriage **Proverbs 5:15-19; I Corinthians *7:2-5***

Here are two scriptures that teach us about sex in marriage and the purpose for sex in a marriage is to enhance the relationship – bearing children are some of the other uses of this gift, it teaches man was given a spouse I would like to explain, why.

For a solid marriage it is important to understand what the Bible teaches regarding sex; and not only regarding sex it prohibits sex outside the marriage, but the Bible teaches us a lot about sex within marriage it has a good purpose. The Bible gives instruction about this part of a husband's and wife's behavior which is clear in I Cor. Chapter 7.

Both the Old and the New Testaments has something to say about sex in marriage. In Proverbs, King Solomon instructs his son about sex all through the book of Solomon. In the first letter to the Corinthians, Paul answers questions put to him by a young man about the problems in marriage - questions about fornication, about marriage and divorce, about fathers giving away their daughters in marriage and, yes, questions about sex in marriage.

The Apostle Paul gives instruction in I Corinthians 7 about sex in marriage, and points out that it is necessary, blessed, and God-Glorifying.

Sex in marriage is NECESSARY "to avoid fornication". This is a very realistic approach to sex in the marriage. Realism is when we acknowledge there is a strong desire created in the man and woman, a lesson some people don't adhere to.

The apostle Paul says, "To avoid fornication, let every man have his own wife, and let every woman have her own husband" (verse 2). All by itself, this overthrows the teaching that sex in marriage is only for producing children. Second, Paul says, "it is better to marry than to burn" (verse 9). Although if one gives in to his or her sexual urges outside marriage without repenting, he or she needs to make it right with the spouse. Paul means that it is better to marry than to burn in one's *lusts*. Marriage is the remedy for that.

Sex in marriage is also necessary because it is a "debt" one spouse owes to the other. I Corinthians 7:3 says, "Let the husband render unto the wife due benevolence: and likewise also the wife unto the husband." "Due benevolence" is God's careful way of referring to the sexual obligation of one spouse to the other. They are there for their spouse and to give themselves to each other physically.

In the next verse, Paul explains how this can be called a debt. "The wife has not power (really 'authority') over her own body, but the husband: and likewise also the husband does have not power ('authority') over his own body, but the wife." Husbands and wives have "authority" over their spouse's body. This does not mean that the husband may say, "You have a debt to be paid." The Christian viewpoint is different each spouse must ask themselves, "What do I *owe* my spouse?"

If Christian couples do not live in this way, Satan will tempt them. This is the teaching in I Corinthians 7 verse 5. When a husband does not give himself to his wife, or the wife to her husband, the devil grabs that opportunity to tempt the other person, and that could lead them into unfaithfulness. Then the fault belongs as much to the one who withheld (himself or herself) as to the one who was unfaithful. This is confirmed when Jesus said, in Matthew 5, "that the one who puts away his wife for unbiblical grounds, *causes* her to commit adultery."

Sex in marriage is not only necessary; it is BLESSED. We do not stop with saying that it is necessary; as though that's the only reason couples give themselves to each other.

Hebrews 13:4 says, "Marriage is honorable in all, and the bed undefiled." All by itself, sex in marriage is a blessed, sanctified gift of God.

Geneses 2:24 shows that sex is not the result of sin, but was blessed by God before the fall. "God blessed them and God said unto them, be fruitful and multiply, and replenish the earth." They had no shame, as 2:25 shows: "And they were both naked, the man and his wife, and they were not ashamed." They clothed themselves because God could not look at them in a sinful state. Let me say this in good conclusion Adam and Eve did not feel nicked until they had to face God; this had been natural for them to see each other that way. Now they felt the need to be clothed for those who were around them.

For us, the grace of Jesus Christ restores us to the right attitude and the right use of this gift of God. The Song of Solomon is unashamed in its description of this gift (chapter 1:3). Or, read how a wise father describes the blessedness of married life also in Proverbs 5:15-19.

However, sex is blessed only when we keep in mind the *Christian* view of it, the world may see it differently. In the thinking of non-Christians, the marriage partner is only a tool for his or her self-gratification. The Christian perspective is different, because it is one of the definitions of one's love for each other. The Christian does not ask, "How can my wife please me?" He asks, "How can I please my wife?" Not: "What does my husband owe me?"

What do I owe my husband?' This is perspective of love that *gives* instead of *takes*.

If this is the Christian perspective, then Christian couples ought to be ready and willing to say yes, even jealousy teaches this in principle, as parents teach their children and warn them about sin the misuse of this gift of sex. The message is to teach them the good and how blessed it is in the marriage? What is wrong in the world's view will result in a warped thinking and undue distress in the children's marriage.

How and where should they be taught? Not in school this subject is too sacred, in the privacy of the home and should not be taught in the public school where the boys snicker behind their hands out of embarrassment. The school teaches them how to prevent and control six. This is the parent's duty and privilege. If parents, lets the television and the movies educate their children about this gift, it can ruin their view why it is wrong to have sex before marriage. It is in obedience to God's calling for us to be holy and to "flee fornication" - I Corinthians 7 V6.) In addition to the warnings, parents have a responsibility to teach them the need for having a good family life. Good parents want to do this and are not ashamed to talk to them about other things concerning marriage. Here is some very good information for and your children on marriage.

Increasing Intimacy in Marriage   Pages 1 – 1 [13]
What Is Marital Intimacy?

"Intimacy is the closeness of your relationship with your spouse – emotionally, spiritually, intellectually, sexually, and in many other ways. Intimacy is not an end goal but rather a journey that lasts throughout your marriage. Marriage and family researchers Schaefer and Olson (1981) describe attaining intimacy as 'a process that occurs over time and is never completed or fully accomplished' (p. 50).

As you both grow and develop, each of you changes. If you neglect intimacy in your marriage, you will grow apart. The time to work on intimacy is now.

Benefits of Intimacy in Marriage

Studies show that marriage offers many benefits. According to Olson and Olson (2000), 'Married people tend to be healthier, live longer, have more wealth and economic assets, and have more satisfying sexual relationships than single or cohabiting individuals. In addition, children generally do better emotionally and academically when they are raised in two-parent families' (p. 3).

The physical benefits of marriage are widely supported by research. Several recent studies, for example, found heart benefits that are particularly dramatic for men. At Case Western Reserve University in Cleveland, researchers assessing the marital intimacy of 10,000 married couples asked the husbands: 'Does your wife show you her love?' The husbands who answered yes reported having significantly less chest pain within the next five years than the men who answered no (Ornish, 1998). In another study of 119 men and 40 women, Yale scientists found that husbands who reported feeling loved and supported by their wives had less artery-blockage than those who did not (Ornish).

Mental health is also better for couples with healthy intimacy. Researchers Firestone and Catlett (1999) say, "In our opinion, love is the one force that is capable of easing [depression]" (p. 13).

(For a detailed discussion of marital benefits, see *Making the Case for Marriage* on this website.)

Forms of Intimacy

Intimacy can take many forms, including the following:

- **Emotional intimacy** is the closeness created through sharing feelings. Because girls are encouraged to recognize and express their emotions from an early age, women generally understand emotions better than men. Unfortunately, society tends to discourage men from feeling or showing emotion. Men who didn't learn how to be emotionally intimate while growing up can learn as adults. If they do, their marriages will be stronger and healthier.

The first step to emotional awareness is to pay attention to your feelings, identify them, and think of possible reasons for them. Work on noticing the differences between strong emotions such as terror and fury and the differences between more subtle emotions such as anxiety, insecurity, and irritation.

Emotional intimacy can occur once people know what they are feeling, convey those feelings to each other, and express concern and understanding of their feelings to each other.

- **Mental or intellectual intimacy** involves a mutual understanding about all the important issues in your marriage. Setting goals together is one way to further intellectual intimacy. For example, you might set goals to improve your intimacy, to save a certain amount of money, or to go for daily walks together.

- **Spiritual intimacy** involves sharing religious beliefs and observing religious practices together, such as praying and attending church. As you share spiritual experiences, you will become united in your attitudes and goals. Dr. Ed Wheat (1980) suggests that couples become active in a church where they can learn, grow, and serve God along with others. (If you and your spouse struggle with differing religious beliefs, see the article on this website, *Strengthening Interfaith Marriage*.)

- **Recreational intimacy** is enjoying activities together, like running, golfing, or reading. Things as simple as popping popcorn and watching a movie or preparing a meal together can be good ways to build recreational intimacy.

- **Financial or monetary intimacy** comes with discussing and sharing your finances. If you have separate accounts and separate incomes, you probably lack financial intimacy in your relationship. (Schaefer & Olson, 1981; Stanley, Trathen, McCain, & Bryan, 1998; Wheat, 1980)

- **Sexual intimacy** is one of the most important dimensions of healthy marital intimacy. Healthy sexual intimacy includes sexual frequency that both partners are satisfied with, sexual activities both partners enjoy, and an open dialogue about sex. Olson and Olson (2000) say, "A major strength for happily married couples is the quality of the sexual relationship" (p. 126). They found in their research that the most common sexual concern is differing levels of interest in sex. Happier couples tend to agree in their definition of sexual satisfaction and have fewer worries about their sex lives than less happy couples.

More than half of all married couples, they note, have trouble discussing sexual issues.

Characteristics of Intimacy

Relationships with healthy intimacy have several factors in common, including the following:

- **Mutual trust** builds a sense of security for both spouses. You can show it be having no desire to injure your spouse in any way. Though you might unintentionally cause hurt, you won't hurt one another on purpose.
- **Tenderness** includes gentle expressions of caring. Through touch you can express your love to your partner. This affectionate contact 'is absolutely essential in building the emotion of love' (Wheat, 1980, p. 184).
- **Acceptance** is unconditional approval in a relationship. No one is perfect, but acceptance means not holding weaknesses against one other. If you find yourself frequently pointing out your spouse's faults, work on focusing instead on the qualities you fell in love with.
- **Open communication** is the ability to discuss anything with your spouse. It includes sincere expression of thoughts and feelings as well as careful listening. Signs of poor communication include feeling reluctant to tell your spouse about the events of your day or being unwilling to listen when your spouse is explaining how he or she feels.
- **Caring** is genuine concern for your spouse's well-being. If you do things you know hurt your spouse, you cannot have healthy intimacy. You can develop a more caring heart and mind by learning to think of your spouse's feelings before your own. Always ask yourself before acting or speaking, 'If I do this or say this, will I hurt my spouse?'
- **Apologies** are the remedy for mistakes that spouses inevitably make. Recognizing mistakes, taking responsibility for them, expressing remorse for any hurt caused, and making a commitment to change the hurtful behavior are all essential to mending the relationship after a mistake. For spouses who have created a chasm of hurts that separate them, offering a sincere and humble apology is the first step in building

a bridge over that chasm. Even if you believe your partner made the mistake, you can begin the healing by finding something you did that calls for an apology.

- **Forgiveness** is the process of letting go of anger, desire for revenge, and obsessive thinking about times your spouse has hurt you. It includes giving your spouse permission to have weaknesses, make mistakes, and change. Seeing the goodness and strengths of your spouse along with the weaknesses can open up emotional space for good will to build toward your spouse. Forgiveness does not automatically create trust or reconciliation, nor does it mean you approve of bad behavior. But it is an important early step toward rebuilding a fractured relationship.
- **Appropriate boundaries** are the limits you place on a relationship. The limits can be created individually or as a couple. These limits include saying 'no' when your spouse asks you to do something that goes against your values or is more than you can handle. By setting firm, clear boundaries for yourself and respecting the boundaries of your partner, you create feelings of safety and trust. If your relationship is in trouble, one or both of you might decide to write a "Bill of Rights" that clearly defines the conditions necessary for staying in the relationship. For example, one woman told her husband that she would stay in the marriage only if there was (1) mutual respect, (2) no drinking/drugs, (3) no hitting or emotional abuse, (4) no name-calling, and (5) no cheating/affairs.

Can There Be Too Much Togetherness?

When we think of intimacy, we might think we can't get too much of a good thing. But sometimes spouses forget the need for separate time and try to spend too much time together. If a spouse feels guilty about spending any free time alone or with friends, he or she might begin to feel constrained in the relationship. Usually this feeling doesn't mean love has diminished, only that a healthy sense of self is getting lost.

Most intimacy needs can be met through a spouse or significant other, but no one person can meet all our needs. A husband, for example, might find his wife a wonderful confidante for his insecurities and dreams but not a good companion for sports events. For a night at the hockey rink, he'll need to go with a brother or friends. A wife may need a regular night out with friends so she can do things that don't interest her husband, like shopping or scrapbooking.

Healthy intimacy includes pursuing some of your own interests independent of your spouse and encouraging your spouse to do the same. These pursuits should not get in the way of building intimacy or involve inappropriate relationships with members of the opposite sex, but spending reasonable time on personal interests helps each partner be happier and a more interesting and well-rounded companion.

Interdependence

Imagine for a moment that you and your spouse are standing with the palms of your hands together and leaning against each other with all of your weight. Together, you look like an upside-down "V." If one of you becomes tired and stops leaning, the other topples over. Similarly, a spouse who depends completely on the other person runs the risk of exhausting the partner and causing him or her to back away. Without the other spouse's support, the dependent spouse would crumble to the ground. Now imagine that you and your spouse are standing up straight and holding hands. You lean in a little, but only enough that you support a portion of one another's weight. If one or the other or you moves, you won't fall. You're responsible for most of your own weight, but you're still connected to your spouse and lean in for extra support from time to time.

As this analogy shows, over-dependence in marriage can lead spouses to become tired and resentful of carrying the burden for the other's happiness. Over-dependence creates feelings of powerlessness and weakness because your happiness is in someone else's hands. Complete independence is also unhealthy because it causes spouses to feel unneeded and lonely. *Interdependence* is a balance between overdependence and independence. In an *inter*dependent marriage, spouses feel needed without being overburdened. They feel a sense of freedom and power, understanding that their happiness is in their control and not in the hands of another person.

Suggestions for Developing Intimacy

Developing intimacy is much like gaining muscle. Just as a body builder regularly goes to the gym and works on specific muscles, you must regularly work on the different types of intimacy in your relationship. Olson and Olson (2000) say, 'You must take care of your marriage as you would any living thing if you want it to thrive' (p. 33). The first step to increasing intimacy is to evaluate where you are. After you and your spouse read this article, talk about how close you are in the different forms of intimacy and how well you communicate. If you find yourselves lacking in some areas, discuss ideas for improvement as guided by the information below.

Understand the Different Love Languages

Chapman (1995) suggests there are five different love languages: (1) words of affirmation such as compliments and appreciation, (2) quality time, (3) receiving gifts, (4) acts of service, and (5) physical touch. He says that what is considered an act of love differs for each person, so 'we must be willing to learn our spouse's primary love language if we are to be effective communicators of love' (p. 14).

When you give love in a different language than your spouse understands, he or she may not recognize the message as an act of love. For example, a husband might compliment his wife on how beautiful he thinks she is, and she might respond, 'If you really loved me, you'd help more with the kids and housework.' She's telling him that in her 'love language,' she feels loved more if he eases her household burden than if he compliments her. To communicate his love effectively, he needs to speak "her language," which means helping more with the kids and housework.

If you're not willing to learn your spouse's love language, chances are you'll create distance in your marriage. The husband in the above story, for example, could open a rift if he responded to her remark with, 'I don't know if you love or need me anymore. Ever since we had children, you give all your attention to them. If you really cared, you'd give more attention to me.' Both husband and wife then start wondering why their spouse doesn't see how much they give to the relationship. Eventually, feeling discouraged and unappreciated, each might unwittingly create distance in the relationship.

The good news is that you can learn to 'speak' and understand different love languages. You don't have to read your spouse's mind to determine his or her primary love language. You can learn what it is by asking what expressions of love mean the most to him/her. For instance, would she prefer flowers, a back rub, or you doing the dishes? Would he rather go on a hike together, be given a hug and kiss, or be complimented on how hard he works at his job?

Do the Things that Build Intimacy

Below is a list of actions that create intimacy, adapted from a list by the Relationship Institute (n.d.). Discuss these ideas with your spouse and try to learn more about his or her love language. Talk about obstacles that might be getting in the way of your relationship. Come up with ideas for how you can work together to improve your marital intimacy.

- **Regularly express caring and tenderness as defined by your partner.** Surprise him with spontaneous acts of kindness. Buy her a present for no particular reason. Create regular time alone together, such as a weekend vacation without the kids, a weekly date night, or frequent walks together. Make sure you give consistent attention to one another and the relationship. Make time for passion, excitement, and fun together.

- **Be affectionate.** Give frequent small gestures of affection, such as a touch on the shoulder, a squeeze of the hand, or a peck on the cheek. Take the time to cuddle, hug, and kiss without always moving on to sexual intimacy.

- **Genuinely respect one another and the relationship.** Accept your partner's personality and characteristics. When you're annoyed by something, don't let the annoying behavior become a negative label of his entire character. Instead, focus on his good qualities. For example, switch from thinking 'He always leaves his shoes in the living-room – he's so lazy!' to 'He may forget to clean up sometimes, but he really is a loving, caring husband.'
- **Communicate.** Express your feelings regularly, resolve anger or resentment rather than let it fester, and communicate realistic expectations. Take the time to listen to what your spouse thinks and feels. Avoid mind reading – making assumptions – by checking your understanding with your spouse. Ask for what you want, be positive, and find solutions to problems rather than let them build.
- **Live in the present while envisioning a positive future together.** Avoid focusing on past mistakes that are no longer relevant. Focus on what you want your relationship to be like, and work together toward that vision. Some couples enjoy displaying art work or photos in their home that represent the vision they have for their marriage.
- **Promote your spouse's growth as an individual.** Be supportive of your spouse's wishes and dreams and help him or her achieve them. Encourage your spouse's growth through education, learning, and life experiences.
- **Say and do what is truthful and honest for you.** Be honest and straightforward with your spouse.
- **Promote physical and emotional safety.** When your spouse feels physically and emotionally secure, he or she will feel safe being close to you and expressing honest thoughts and feelings with you. Physical aggression and verbal abuse destroy this feeling of safety and are never acceptable. Abuse includes name-calling, put-downs, contempt, forcing your spouse to do something, intimidating, and hitting.
- **Take responsibility for your relationship and your life problems.** Rather than blame your spouse for your relationship problems, focus on what *you* can do to improve your marriage. Each person has enormous, untapped power within, and something almost magical

happens when you think about what you can do, what you have, and what you feel instead of what you can't do, don't have, or don't feel.

Increase Communication Skills

Healthy communication is vital to developing and maintaining intimacy. According to Olson and Olson (2000), 'Communication is the one crucial ingredient that defines a relationship. . . [and] remains the key skill for maintaining intimacy' (pp. 23-25)

Healthy communication is clear, open, honest, direct, and appropriate. When marital communication is healthy, good feelings between spouses increase and problems resolve more easily. Communication makes it possible for your spouse to know you. It's the tool for expressing love and support and for working through problems.

Basic communication patterns are established during the first few years of courtship and marriage and often remain fairly stable throughout a marriage. You might find that after being married a few years you can generally predict how your spouse will respond to your comments. You know what will please her and what will make her angry, frustrated, or annoyed.

Marriage researchers Gottman and Levenson (1999) have found that the positive or negative feelings spouses experience when they talk together have a far greater effect on marital stability than what is actually said. They discovered that couples who had five times more pleasant (feel-good) experiences with their spouses than unpleasant (feel-bad) experiences had significantly more stable marriages. Gottman and Levenson (1999) call this the 'ratio of positivity to negativity.' This ratio teaches us that (1) it is important to pay attention to our spouse's feelings when we're talking, and (2) we should regularly express much more love and acceptance than criticism to our spouses – at least five times more.

Ask yourself the following question: 'Do I ever speak with my spouse in such a way that he or she feels put down, blamed, or rejected?' If your answer is 'yes,' follow up with this question: 'How can I speak in ways that will help my spouse feel more understood, loved, and respected, even when I have a complaint?'

This article touches only briefly on the subject of communication in marriage. For more information, consult John Gottman and Nan Silvers's book *Seven Principles for Making Marriage Work* (1999). Another resource is a workshop called *Couple Communication.* Its purpose is to improve day-to-day communication, learn how to resolve issues in the marriage, and increase marital satisfaction. For further information on where the workshop is available and costs call 1-800-328-5099 or go to www.couplecommunication.com.

Give Compliments and Express Appreciation

Offering compliments and appreciation are powerful ways to increase good feelings in your marriage. Olson and Olson (2000) say, "Giving your spouse at least one complement each day may sound simplistic, but it can have a remarkable effect on your relationship" (p. 36). Complimenting your spouse helps him feel loved and admired.

Be Self-Disclosing

Self-disclosure is 'making yourself known to [your spouse] by verbally revealing personal information' (Pager, 1995, p. 45). Discussing deep personal information with one another is a bonding experience. It can also be threatening because it opens you up to judgment and criticism. But in a healthy marriage, you can trust completely that your spouse will never use any information you disclose to injure you. As you reveal who you are, sharing your innermost thoughts and feelings, you will come to truly know one another.

Because you and your spouse are always experiencing new things, you're both constantly changing and so is your relationship. When you don't share current feelings with your spouse, he or she can't share your life. If you want to be understood, you must help your spouse understand you. It's not always easy to talk about deep experiences and feelings or even to know what to share. The Family Centre (n.d.) suggests self-disclosure conversation starters listed below. Allow these starting points to increase the self-disclosure in your marriage.

- The kind of relationship we have is. . .
- One way in which we are alike, is. . .

- One way in which we are different, is...
- If our relationship were a movie it would be called...
- The needs you satisfy in me are...
- I feel most tender towards you when...
- What I like best in our relationship is...
- In the future, I would like our relationship to become more...
- In five years, I see us...
- Some of my needs that are not being completely satisfied are.
- Something you have helped me learn about myself is...
- One of the feelings with which I have most trouble is...
- I have most fun with you when.... (p. 1)

Try the "Magic 50 Minutes a Week"

Olson and Olson (2000) suggest that couples set aside five minutes a day and fifteen minutes on the weekend to discuss three questions:

- What did you enjoy most about your relationship today?
- What was dissatisfying about your relationship today?
- How could things be made better for each of you? (p. 35)

Handle Unresolved Anger

One of the greatest contributors to marital distance is ongoing unresolved anger. Lashing out with name-calling, negative labels (lazy, stupid, selfish, etc.), and words intended to hurt, such as 'I never loved you,' can cause great pain in marriages. Lashing out, as harmful as it is, can look like its working because it gives us a sense of power, disguises feelings of helplessness, and temporarily numbs our hurt feelings. But in the long run lashing out creates further conflict and distance. In fact, Gottman and Levenson (1999) found that frequent angry expressions are a strong predictor of divorce, even expressions that might seem milder, such as disgust, contempt, and stonewalling (the silent treatment) (p. 146).

Complete suppression of anger isn't healthy either. Disagreements may be hidden temporarily, but over time suppressed anger often turns into resentment, indirect expressions of anger like guilt-tripping and ignoring, or explosions of rage. "When we suppress, deny, and disguise anger, we do not rid ourselves of it. Rather the anger lingers as growing hostility" (Cox, 2002, p. 40).

The answer is to neither lash out nor suppress, but rather to 'bridle' your anger – which means to express angry feelings in a calm and non-confrontational way. Communicating dissatisfaction in a straightforward and constructive way is not a bad thing in marriage. In fact, if done appropriately, it can lead to increased understanding, new solutions, and closer intimacy.

If you're angry enough, though, you might not be able to discuss the problem constructively. Gottman's (1999) research indicates that when people become very angry or distressed in an argument, their pulse rate increases and their body enters a stage of *fight or flight*. You'd have the same fight or flight reaction if you were about to get shot or eaten by a bear. Your body gets ready to duke it out or run for dear life. When you're in this state you're not in a good frame of mind for talking about sensitive issues. Instead of talking, take a moment to cool off. Use the old adage 'take a deep breath and count to ten.'

When anger is especially intense, you'll need more than 10 seconds to simmer down. For these situations, follow the suggestions below, adapted from Gottman (1999):

• Tell your spouse you need time to cool off. If you think your spouse is the one who needs to cool off, don't call the time out for him or her. Say you feel uncomfortable talking right now and need some time to think.

• Set a time to talk about the subject again.

• Separate yourself physically from your spouse by going into another room or sitting on the other side of the room.

• While you're separated, soothe yourself by thinking calming thoughts or doing relaxing activities. Don't rehash in your mind all the reasons you're mad at your spouse.

• Come back at the appointed time to discuss the issue. If you're still too angry to talk, set a new time to come back and start the process over again.

After you calm down, you'll be ready to discuss the issue. Always begin with an (I) statement, which helps you express your own feelings rather than place blame on your spouse. For example, if your spouse said something that upset you, say, "I felt hurt by. . . ." Once you're conversing, listen carefully, repeat back what you think you heard to make sure you've understood, and double-check your understanding by asking questions like 'Is this what you mean?' When expressing complaints, it's especially important to validate your spouse's worth.

For further information on communication skills see the articles, *Handling Conflict in Marriage* and *Solving Your "Solvable Problems"* on this website.

Not all problems can be worked out. Even with perfect communication, some problems will remain unsolvable (see the Forever Families article, *Moving from Gridlock to Dialogue*). The important thing is that you're able to maintain positive feelings toward one another even if you can't agree.

For more information on bridling anger and resolving anger issues, see the article *Bridling Anger* on this website.

Offer Apologies and Be Forgiving (Revisited)

Apologies and forgiveness are two of the most powerful ways you can heal pain in your marriage. They allow both husbands and wives to learn from their mistakes and start anew. Often people are reluctant to apologize because they think doing so will mark them as a flawed person. Feeling flawed leads to feelings of shame, which people always try to avoid. Understanding the difference between guilt and shame can help, say researchers Harper and Hoopes (1990). We feel guilt when we recognize a flawed *behavior* and we feel shame when we see a flawed *self* (p. 3). Guilt helps us feel sorry for making a mistake but does not decrease our feelings of self-worth. Shame generalizes a mistake to our entire self, making us feel like we're unworthy, unlovable, and a failure. Many people who feel a lot of shame are afraid to apologize for fear that if they admit their weaknesses, their spouse will respect them less. What they don't realize is that expressing remorse for past mistakes usually connects people rather than distances them. Since we all have weaknesses, we are comforted when we see others have them, too.

If you've hurt your spouse and want to repair the damage, consider writing an apology letter. You might include things like:

(1) how you believe you have hurt your spouse,
(2) the sorrow you feel over having caused the hurt (leave out excuses for your behavior),
(3) what you would do differently if given another chance,
(4) a *re quest* for forgiveness when the person is ready but *not a demand* or expectation of forgiveness, and
(5) a commitment to how you will behave differently in the future. If you follow through with your commitment to change, trust will rebuild over time.

Forgiveness does not require an apology, and an apology doesn't require forgiveness. But if the relationship has been harmed and you want intimacy restored, both apologies and forgiveness need to happen. Think of each as half of the relationship bridge. Some days you will need to say 'I'm sorry' to rebuild the bridge and other days you will need to say 'I forgive you.' Bishop and Grunte (1993) state:

Forgiveness remains a challenge to everyone–except maybe hermits. Despite periods of good will toward all, nobody gets to stay an expert forgiver. No sooner do we pat ourselves on the back for the high degree of enlightenment that we've attained than we find ourselves stuck in some hugely petty attitude that persists in thumbing its nose at us for hours or months. (p. 107)

Bishop and Grunte (1993) add that deep emotional wounds tend to take much more time to heal than everyday squabbles. Letting go of anger and resentment from such wounds happens in slow stages and sometimes only with the help of a higher power. When there are significant relationship injuries, such as infidelity, marital therapy and help from spiritual leaders may be needed. To learn more about forgiveness, read *How to Forgive When You Don't Know How*, by Jacqui Bishop and Mary Grunte (1993). When infidelity is the issue, read *After the Affair*, by Janis Abrahms Spring (1996).

Improve the Sexual Health of Your Marriage

Research consistently shows a link between sexual satisfaction and the quality of a marital relationship. When overall happiness in the marital relationship is higher, so is sexual satisfaction, especially for women (Brecher, 1984; Blumstein & Schwartz, 1983; Edwards & Booth, 1994). Hawton (1994) found the marital relationship to be the most important contributor to women's enjoyment of sex. Men often discover that when their wives feel loved outside the bedroom, they will respond more inside the bedroom. Similarly, Weiner-Davis (2003) find that when wives are sexually responsive to their husbands, their husbands are more open to helping in areas outside the bedroom, such as with the housework.

None of these findings means that you should behave in ways inside or outside the bedroom that manipulate your spouse into doing something you want. Rather, use these principles to increase the intimacy in your marriage.

For both men and women, meaningful and satisfying sexual experiences require a safe and nurturing emotional environment. In relationships with mutual trust, tenderness, acceptance, open communication, caring, and forgiveness, spouses feel free to try new things, be vulnerable, learn from mistakes, and express and receive gestures of love. Sexual problems are higher in relationships that have power struggles, resentments, conflict, fear of making mistakes, and feelings of being rejected, used, or not good enough (Wincze& Carey, 2001).

Not all sexual problems result from a poor relationship, but many if not most do. Simply put, improve your relationship and you'll improve your sex life. Masters, Johnson, and Kolodny (1988) offer these practical suggestions for improving sexual intimacy:

- Good sex begins while your clothes are still on. You can't have good sex without a good relationship. If you improve intimacy in other areas, you can dramatically improve your sexual intimacy.
- Take responsibility for your own sexual pleasure.
- Talk with your spouse about sex.

- Make time for regular sex.
- Don't let sex become routine. Allow plenty of time to make sex fun for you and your spouse.
- Use fantasy, such as role-playing. This can be a powerful aphrodisiac.
- Don't carry anger into your bedroom.
- Realize that good sex isn't just technique.
- Nurture the romance in your life.
- Don't make sex too serious.
- Don't always wait to be "in the mood" before agreeing to have sex. Foreplay can help create the mood.
- Realize that you and your spouse don't have to agree about everything involving sex.
- Don't be afraid to ask your spouse for help.
- Try to keep your sexual expectations realistic. (pp. 452-461)

Common Sexual Problems

Sexual problems are not always related to relationship quality. Other factors can lead to problems in sexual functioning, such as stress, lack of education or experience, time-constraints, exhaustion, aging, previous unpleasant sexual experiences, and biological problems. Almost half of all couples experience some kind of sexual problems in their lifetime.

In a sample of 1,768 men and women in the United Kingdom aged 18 to 75, Dunn, Croft, and Hackett (2000) separated sexual problems into categories. For men, the most common sexual complaints were erectile problems (48%), sex not being pleasurable (45%), and premature ejaculation (43%). For women, the complaints were arousal problems (54%), sex not being pleasurable (47%), orgasmic dysfunction (40%), painful intercourse (24%), and vaginal problems (22%). Laumann and colleagues (1999) state:

Sexual problems are most common among young women and older men. Several factors may explain these differential rates. . . . [Young women's relationship] instability, coupled with inexperience, generates stressful sexual encounters, providing the basis for sexual pain and anxiety. Young men are not similarly affected. Older men are more likely to have trouble maintaining an erection and to lack an interest in sex. Low sexual interest and erection problems are age-dependent disorders, possibly resulting from physiological changes associated with the aging process. (p. 542)

Some sexual problems seem to affect sexual satisfaction more than others. Results from the U.S. National Health and Social Life Survey (Laumann, Paik, & Rosen, 1999) indicate that sexual problems most related to sexual dissatisfaction are low desire, men's erectile problems, and women's inability to become aroused. It is important to note, however, that having sexual problems does not always drastically decrease sexual satisfaction. In a study published by the *New England Journal of Medicine*, 80% of couples studied said they were happy with their sexual relationship (Frank, Anderson & Rubenstein, 1978) even though 63% of the women reported arousal or orgasmic problems and 40% of the men said they had erectile or ejaculatory difficulties.

Dealing with Sexual Problems

Many resources are available to help couples struggling with sexual problems. The least expensive and least intrusive resources are self-help books and websites. These resources can provide basic education and give suggestions for common problems (see suggested self-help readings at the end of this article). When self-help isn't enough, marital and sex therapy can be helpful.

Sex therapy helps couples work through conflicts, distorted beliefs, sexual myths, boredom, frequency debates, performance anxiety, aging issues, and other stresses that may be interfering in their sexual relationship. In 1984, Brecher found marital happiness was related with couples' ability to talk about sexual issues. Couples who have trouble talking about sex can learn in therapy to talk more openly. Sarwer and Durlak (1997) reported a 65% success rate for couples seeking weekly sessions of sex therapy, which included education, communication skills training, and sensate focus exercises.

Initially developed by Masters and Johnson (1970), sensate focus exercises are assigned to couples to do at home. The exercises teach couples to approach physical intimacy in a slow, non-threatening way. In the early stages of sensate focus, couples engage in non-sexual touch (like backrubs or holding hands). This step helps those who are anxious about sexual performance to relax. It also teaches couples that there are more ways to be physically intimate than having sex. As couples become more comfortable with non-sexual touch, they are then assigned to engage in more erotic kinds of touch (mutually agreed upon by the couple) and eventually sexual intercourse. Sensate focus exercises can be particularly useful when one of the spouses has experienced past sexual abuse or trauma.

Sometimes, sexual problems require medical attention. Before beginning any kind of sex therapy, it's wise to get a checkup from your physician. When medical complications are the problem, minor surgery, medication, or medical sex therapy provided at specialized clinics can usually resolve the difficulty.

Choosing a Sex Therapist

Sex is a sensitive subject. If you're considering sex therapy, be cautious as you choose a therapist. Your relationship with him or her is one of the biggest predictors of success in therapy, so it is important that you make a good choice. Therapists have different specializations, approaches, and personalities. Not all therapists are specialists in working with marital and sexual problems. Ask potential therapists about their credentials and experience in marital and sex therapy. Many people try out several therapists for one or two sessions before deciding whom they feel most comfortable with. Once you choose a therapist, if you haven't seen progress within five to six sessions, discuss your concerns with the therapist.

Some sex therapists prescribe masturbation and erotic media to treat problems like painful intercourse, sexual trauma, and arousal difficulties. If you believe these practices are immoral, look for a therapist who respects your beliefs and your limits. Find one who will encourage you and your spouse to participate in activities you agree on and you both feel comfortable with.

Since sexual health is so connected to the quality of the marital relationship, sex therapy is generally not appropriate until major marital conflicts have been resolved. Don't be surprised if your therapist recommends marital therapy as a first step before sex therapy.

Sexual Intimacy Self-help Resources

Below is a list of recommended books on sexual intimacy. They cover topics such as sexual anatomy, sexual response cycle, relational aspects of sex, suggested exercises, and tips on preparation for intercourse. *Becoming One, The Act of Marriage*, and *A Celebration of Sex for Newlyweds* are geared toward conservative Christian audiences and focus on basic how-to information. *The Sex-Starved Marriage* spends less time on the how-to's and concentrates more on resolving conflicts about differences in levels of desire for sex.

- *Becoming One,* by Robert F. Stahmann, Wayne R. Young, & Julie G. Grover (2004).
- *The Sex-Starved Marriage,* by Michelle Weiner-Davis (2003).
- *A Celebration of Sex for Newlyweds,* by Douglas E. Rosenau (2002).
- *The Act of Marriage,* by Tim LaHaye & Beverly LaHaye (1998).

Marriage Enhancement Resources

Descriptions of marital enhancement programs and contact information are available in the *Strengthening Marriage Through Marriage Enrichment Programs* article on this website. Another good resource for information on marriage enhancement is www.smartmarriages.com . This website contains the most current information available. It is frequently being updated with articles written by some of the most well-known researchers in the field of marriage. You can search the articles for specific information.

Conclusion

Creating and maintaining intimacy is challenging, and it is well worth the effort. The poet Rainer Maria Rilke said:

It is also good to love, because love is difficult. For one human being to love another human being; that is perhaps the most difficult task that has been entrusted to us, the ultimate task, the final test and proof, the work for which all other work is merely preparation. (quoted in Firestone & Catlett, 1999, p. 68)

After you have read this article as a couple, have a conversation about the level of intimacy in your relationship. Once you've determined where you need to improve, go to a library, bookstore, or website to find information that will help you tackle your issues. Read the information *as a couple* and brainstorm ways to customize the ideas to your marriage.

Marital enrichment programs, books, and counseling may not have all the answers, but they can provide new ideas and direction as you seek strengthen your relationship. As you do, be sure you commit with absolute determination to build a stronger relationship. This determination will help you gain the humility to learn from past mistakes, repair relational wounds, work through problems, express tender feelings, and make the sacrifices necessary for creating a meaningful, satisfying, and intimate relationship."

Written by Derek Willis Hagey, Research Assistant, and Amber L. Brewer, Graduate Research Assistant, edited by Rachel V. Jamieson, Graduate Research Assistant, Robert F. Stahmann and Stephen F. Duncan, professors in the School of Family Life, Brigham Young University."

References

Bishop, J., &Grunte, M. (1993). *How to forgive when you don't know how.* New York: Station Hill Press.

Brecher, E. L. (1984). *Sex and aging: A consumers' union report.* Boston: Little, Brown.

Blumstein, P., & Schwartz, P. (1983). *American couples.* New York: Morrow.

Chapman, G. D. (1995). *The Five Love Languages: How to express heartfelt commitment to your mate.* Chicago: Northfield Publishing.

Cox, F. D. (2002). *Human intimacy: Marriage, the family, and its meaning.* Belmont, CA: Wadworth/Thomson Learning.

Dunn, K. M., Croft, P. R., Hackett, G. I. (2000). Satisfaction in the sex life of a general population sample. *Journal of Sex & Marital Therapy, 26,* 141-151.

Edwards, J. N., & Booth, A. (1994). Sexuality, marriage, and well-being: The middle years. In A. S. Rossi (Ed.), *Sexuality across the life course* (pp. 233-259). Chicago: University of Chicago Press.

Frank, E., Anderson, C., & Rubenstein, D. (1978). Frequency of sexual dysfunction in "normal" couples. *New England Journal of Medicine, 299,* 111-115.

The Family Centre. *Intimacy in relationships.* Retrieved October 20, 2003.

Firestone, R. W., & Catlett, J. (1999). *Fear of intimacy.* Washington, DC: American Psychological Association.

Gottman, J. M. (1999). *The Marriage Clinic: A scientifically-based marital therapy.* New York: W. W. Norton & Co.

Gottman, J. M., & Silver, N. (1999). *Seven principles for making marriage work: A practical guide from the country's foremost relationship expert.* New York: Crown Publishers.

Gottman, J. M., &Levenson, R. W. (1999). What predicts change in marital interaction over time? A study of alternative models. *Family Process, 38 (2),* 143-158.

Harper, J. M., &Hoopes, M. H. (1990). *Uncovering shame: An approach integrating individuals and their family systems.* New York: W. W. Norton & Co.

Hawton, K., Gath, D., & Day, A. (1994). Sexual function in a community sample of middle-aged women with partners: Effects of age, marital, socioeconomic, psychiatric, gynecological, and menopausal factors. *Archives of Sexual Behavior, 232,* 375-395.

LaHaye, T., &LaHaye, B. (1998). *The act of marriage: The beauty of sexual love.* Colorado Springs, CO: Alive Communications, Inc.

Lauer, R. H., & Lauer, J. C. (1994). *The quest for intimacy*. Dubuque, IA: Brown and Benchmark.

Laumann, E., Paik, A., & Rosen, R. C. (1999). Sexual dysfunction in the United States: Prevalence and predictors. *Journal of the American Medical Association, 281,* 537-544.

Masters, W. H. & Johnson, V. (1970). *Human sexual inadequacy*. Boston: Little, Brown.

Masters, W. H., Johnson, V., &Kolodny, R. C. (1988). *Masters & Johnson on sex and human loving*. Boston: Little Brown.

Olson, D. H., & Olson, A. K. (2000). *Empowering couples: Building on your strengths*. Minneapolis: Life Innovations Inc.

Ornish, D. (1998). *Love and survival: The scientific basis for the healing power of intimacy* . New York: HarperCollins.

Prager, K. J. (1995). *The Psychology of intimacy*. New York: The Guilford Press.

The Relationship Institute. *Creating intimacy, creating distance*. Retrieved October 20, 2003.

Rosenau, D. E. (2002). *A celebration of sex for newlyweds*. Nashville: Thomas Nelson, Inc.

Sarwer, D. B. &Durlack, J. A. (1997). A field trial of the effectiveness of behavioral treatment of sexual dysfunctions. *Journal of Sex and Marital Therapy, 23,* 87-97.

Schaefer, M. T., & Olson, D. H. (1981). Assessing intimacy: The PAIR inventory. *Journal of Marital and Family Therapy, 7,* 47-60.

Spring, J. A. (1996). *After the affair: Healing the pain and rebuilding the trust when a partner has been unfaithful.* New York: Harper-Collins Publishers.

Stahmann, R. F., Young, W. R., & Grover, J. G. (2004). *Becoming one: Intimacy in marriage.* American Fork, UT: Covenant Communications.

Stanley, S., Trathen, D., McCain, S., & Bryan, M. (1998). *A lasting promise: A Christian guide to fighting for your marriage*. San Francisco: Jossey-Bass Publishers.

Sternberg, R. (1987). Liking versus loving: a comparative evaluation of theories. *Psychological Bulletin,102,* 331-45.

Walster, E. & Walster, W. (1978). *A new look at love*. Reading, MA: Addison-Wesley.

Wheat, E. (1980). *Love life: For every married couple*. Grand Rapids, MI: Pyranee Books.

Wincze, J. P. & Carey, M. P. (2001). *Sexual dysfunction: A guide for assessment and treatment*. New York: Guilford Press.

Weiner-Davis, M. (2003). *The sex-starved marriage: A couple's guide to boosting their marriage libido*. New York: Simon and Schuster.

This article can be found online at
http://www.foreverfamilies.net/xml/articles/marital_intimacy.aspx?
http://foreverfamlies.byuedu/xml/articles/marital_intimacy.aspx=print.xsl
t&pub.html   3/23/06

ABUSES in relationships; sexual abuse

The **Abuse** in any relationship is one of the toughest things to deal with. A person has to look at the **abuse** in the **relationship**. There are different kinds of relationships of course. The **paramount question** is?
- How bad is it,
- What can be done about it?
- How does a person deal with the impact of **abuse**?

We are going to take these **ABUSES;** of **sex** and then the degrees of the **abuse** of course.

I know a person will know when it's becomes **physical abuse;** the problem is when they don't do anything about it. The person in this situation has to be able to define the **physical abuse** that also can relate to sex problems, and identify the reason they are fighting about sex, we know this when a person feels abused. When the assaults take place they are always glad when they are over, but one of the symptoms is living in consent fear all the time. There is an unholy way in which a person takes advantage of a person.

I find this to be true in most cases of **abuse** in relationships. There is a problem when they don't know *who they are*, and *where they are going* from day to day. There is a real danger at this point. Another thing I want point out we know they are being dominated, controlled, and they feel isolated. They can lose their identity as a person and low self-esteem sets in, they feel inadequate within themselves.

The person has to deal with the other person's anger and disapproval, and even worse they are trapped. These traumatic experiences build up with each episode, they get to where they can't think for themselves, and can't make their own decisions. They can't stand up for themselves, or stand on their own two feet; they feel they have no rights in the **relationship**.

This can happen to a (male or female). These are some of the trade marks in a bad marriage **abuse** is the evidence in the relationship. A person feels inadequacies, insecurities and the need for love keeps them in the **relationship**. Their childhood influences are entangled in their need for love.

Sexual Abuse.

A driving force is characterized by the need to be loved, and the need for love is one of the basic needs and drives, and it can lead to **sexual** and **porn abuse**. This can take on many forms of desire such as **sexual addictions**, wanting someone else, and the need can take on different forms of love and lust is one of the down falls in America, this happens in many ways and is expressed in **sexual desires**.

I believe these are some the most reveling characteristics of a (man or women) characterized **by their sexual miss behaviors**. These acts of **sexual domination** usually come short of abuse in some cases, and can border on **sexual abuse** If the other person does not consent to the sex and why they didn't. This again is very reveling; there are many reasons why a person is conditioned to **sexual-behaviors**. They are usually brought about from a family back-ground of **abuses**, cultural back-grounds, and even religious beliefs about sex.

Where does a person draw the lines in their relationship? There is something wrong when a person is afraid of what the other person may think when they don't consent, in some cases it hurts the other person and again, what is the reason they don't want to consent? The act of **sex** should come under the guidelines of smoothing the other person and feeling closer to each other there is a need evaluate their feelings for each other.

Then on the other hand the other person maybe overly friendly to the point of flirtation, which is a **sexual over tone**. Sometimes it makes them feel good to know that someone else likes their looks. The point I'm making does that person carry it too far, like when it is to the point it borders on **sexual attractions.** If that is the case they have crossed the line and even worse when comes to the point of lust. This could be one of those cases where a person has crossed the line of proper conduct. I know most people are protective and responsible. The Bible says "to look on a women is a sin" this can come in the form of making a remark about or looking at a lady walking down the street. I have seen a group of men do this all too often.

This is one of the basic needs is feeling good about one's self, it starts showing up as early as kinder-garden the attraction to the opposite sex. The need to love and be loved can drive a person to doing things that their own convictions would not approve of and yet some get into an affair.

A person can do some pretty crazy things to get attention, especially when in their early teens, and as young adults, especially when the love and sexual needs are very high not knowing how to meet those expectations and desires. There can be an opposite affections, and I will not go into that at this point. It will cause a person to do things and accept people into their lives that are not right for them. The excitement of a new love and romance is one thing, but the excitement and challenge of an affair is another. There are other factors to deal with.

Example: When it goes past the normal love for another, when it leads to lustful desires. It is a little like the animal instincts, when the person cannot control their natural needs and desires of the flesh. This is more likely happen to men, but it takes "two to tango". It is sad when a person gets caught up in an extra marital affair. This happens a lot during the "mid-life crisis", and in some cases it can get out of control. I hope I have not carried this example too far.

Never-the-less, a person tends to want to be loved, the excitement of a move can turn a person on while it may turn another person off and there are some people who go from one romance to another, and do this after they get married, sex should be wholesome and good for the relationship.

I found this to be very true in my life. How does a person deal with the impact of a problem or crisis in a relationship? Then on the other hand how does it affect the person and people in the relationship, as a person it is a very important to **ask questions**? How a person reacts to their **sexual needs**. When there is sexual misconduct it affects both lives in a relationship.

The one who is in the affair and how they deal with an affair, many want to keep the affair and their wife at the same time, what is going to happen to that relationship if it continues. Sometimes this leaves a person feeling helpless during the affair. This does not take anything away from their responsibility away from why they had the affair, and I think this is the key when the person who has been affected by the affair has to look at the affair very seriously, honestly and as objectively as possible as they decide what to do about the affair.

To sum up the **affair question,** do what is right for each other, and get **key answers to these questions as to why**. What should a person do to help this person if they have had more than one affair, it has to be dealt with as an abuse, and dealt with in a positive way. I know of those who have an affair and the spouse doesn't care, and in some relationships both do it. Those that don't like the affair will probably need help in reaching the right decision, and how to go on with *their* life, there is help out there for those who need support and professional help.

Some are more sexually driven and in many cases the sexual needs are not the same. Let me say this some relationships are based on sexual desire and when the sexual desire wanes over time the relationship suffers.

Sexual Addictions
Overcoming Sexual Addiction in Marriage   Pages 1-2 [14]
Dr. Barry Leventhal for *Two Becoming One*

"The problem is so prevalent we have had to invent a new phrase for it: *sexual addiction*. Men and women, young and old, are being swept into the compulsive behavior of sexual addictions at an alarming rate. A recent survey of adults, ranging from ages 18 to 59, reported that 40 percent of women and 30 percent of men suffer from some form of sexual dysfunction. And one of the fastest growing dysfunctions in America is sexual addiction. It is estimated that sex addiction affects 3 to 6 percent of our population. Not surprisingly, this sexual epidemic has also lodged itself in the Church as well. From youth pastors to seasoned pastors and missionaries, among both men and women, pornography has invaded our sanctuaries, classrooms, and bedrooms. Whole ministries, as well as marriages, have reaped the whirlwind of this scourge and have gone down in destruction. Those involved in marriage counseling are aware of the devastation sexual addiction can cause.

But what can we do to prevent sexual addictions from invading our lives?

Or, if we have been infected with the disease, how can we find the healing and deliverance from this sexual onslaught? Once again, we need to go back and recapture the basic biblical realities of God's perspective on human sexuality and how it has degenerated into its present state of affairs. Jesus promised that if we would abide in His Word, we would become His disciples and that we would "know the truth, and the truth would set [us] free" (John 8:31-32).

First, all addictions, and sexual addictions in particular, are a judgment from God."

http://www.learnathome.comlfamily/1 1 89690.html   8/24/2004

Summary of sex in the marriage

Let me give you an idea of what I mean when I say marriage is good? We have discussed how men and women are different in their sexual despairs, I want explain why that is good. The women expects a man to live up to her expectations and that means a man has to do things she expects of him, when he does that it pleases her and she wants to be proud of him and please him. A man should take advantage of this knowing what she expects, some don't want to do that and that makes the women unhappy. I recommend you read this book it helped me understand that primus, "Men are from Mares and women are from Venous." The summary of that book says "When a man goes into his cave leave him alone until he is ready to come out and when he does he will be open and talk. The women is just the opposite she talks when she is in trouble, but she doesn't want him to solve her problem she wants him to love her, his mistake is when he tries to solve her problem, she wants him to listen and show her he cares/loves her she will come up with own answers just give her time." The goal of a man is to make her the queen in his life and she will make him feel like a king is his home.

The same is true men are usually the strength in the marriage if not there is usually problems for the most part, women are emotional and the women depends on the man for stability. I have found over the years some married couples say they begin to think alike because they understand where each other is coming from, now they know each other's boundaries; one or the other will become the dominate person. The other one accepts it, they become a part of each other, they become of one mind, if not by the mid-40s to 50s and the children are grown if they have not grown together one of two things happen they live in the same house, but they live separate lives from each other doing their own thing or divorce if that does not happen they will still have their arguments.

At this point *you* maybe living with forgiveness that does not mean *you* have to live with that person, yes unless they are willing to change and in some cases people separation. I know of couples that go back together after a separation and renew their marriage and they are happy. The idea a couple has time to think it through and change their mind. It is not a matter of love as much it is how much you love each other and are both of you are willing to change. In some cases its matter of an affair or giving up an affair. The main thing is solving the problem and going on with your life. I know of those who have waited over five years and they got back together. I know of one lady who sat a place at the table every day until her husband came back. I hope your marriage has a balance of power with both of you enjoying each other.

First and for most *you* must make peace with *yourself*, others, and put God first, then with *your spouse and family*, and only then can *you* go on and have a happy marriage. If you confess your sins to God, He well forgive,

I John 1:7-10 (KJV), and so should *your partner*.

V-7 "But if we walk in the light, as he is in the light, we have fellowship one with another, and the blood of Jesus Christ his Son cleanseth us from all sin."

V-8 "If we say that we have no sin, we deceive ourselves, and the truth is not in us."

V-9 "If we confess our sins, he is faithful and just to forgive us *our* sins, and to cleanse us from all unrighteousness."

V-10 "If we say that we have not sinned, we make him a liar, and his word is not in us.

Some words of wisdom from the Song of Solman Proverbs 10:12 (KJV)
12 Hatred stirreth up strifes: but love coverth all sins.

Read the rest of John chapter 10 "a wise man and a foolish man; look at how the mouth of a foolish deceives and betrays him or her." My dad said, "love covers a multitude of sins" but not every sin.
Companion Verses to look at;

Matt. 22:37-40; John 13:34-35; John 13:9-13; John 15:12-17; I Cor. Chapter 13; Rom. 13:8-10; Eph. 3:18-19.

The man's place in the marriage relationship

- The man is the head of the wife and home,
    1) As Christ is the head of the church **Eph. 5:23** "For the husband is the head of the wife, even as Christ is the head of the church: and he is the saviour of the body."
- The man should be the spiritual leader,
    1) If the man is not right with God, then his relationship is probably not right with his wife and children.
- The woman's place in the marriage relationship,

I don't expect everyone to look at these statements in the same way, they are very good guidelines in the relationship, it is also true the wife should set a good example in the relationship, if she is not right with God it will show up her relationship with her husband and children. I think the hardest thing is to life up to those teaching and it will show up in how the children follow in their parent's footsteps, if they have laid a poor foundation for their children's relationships it will show up in their conduct in their marriage and in the home.

Prayer is the key that opens the door to heaven but love unlocks a person's heart.

If you have a bad relationship let God be a part of the changes in *your* marriage, but it will give you away if you don't repair the things in your life, it should change your heart. It will change *your* love when you pray for that person, it is hard to pray for someone in the right spirit and not love them that does not mean *you* will like everything they do.

Philippians 4:6-7
V-6 "Be careful for nothing; but in every thing by prayer and supplication with thanksgiving let your requests be made known unto God."

V-7 "And the peace of God, which passeth all understanding, shall keep your hearts and minds through Christ Jesus."
1) Take hope in a new beginning
2) Be aware of old mistakes
3) Throw out the old ideas that don't work, and create new ones
4) Don't be afraid to try new ideas

May God bless *you* and *your family*? This is one of those cases where I hope when you read and study this information on relationships and marriage will help you and your spouse. I will pray for each of *you* and *your family*.

Here are some other studies that we will go through if the marriage does not work.

- God – can He help a person "I can do all thing through Christ which Strengtheneth me."

Sense a person may not like what they are dealing with; they need to take time out of *their* busy schedule set down and talk with their children. If you are in an argument wait until one or both of you have combed down, I want *you* to have an idea what *you* are in for in *your marriage*. Studies show there is a 50% chance for a divorce in marriages whether *you're* a Christian, or non-Christian. We want to prevent a divorce and the other contributing facts leading up to divorce?

They have created a real problem within the family, there has to be a certain amount of parental control because of the children. Especially if they don't want to destroy the emotional stability of the children! But, in most cases they are under mind by the circumstance that caused the problem! In some cases the parents are so bitter they don't realize what they are doing to the children. They are more concerned about getting even, this is one of the ways of getting-even by using the children, and make them pay for the suffering and pain they caused.

The two fold part of this study is how a person deal with the opposite views, "are you saying what do you mean", when it comes to the other person's wants and needs, that is a very good question because that is the why I want you to deal with your problems now rather than later. You should be able to come some kind of agreement.

There are other issues like how they are going to raise their children. Two people don't always see things in the same way for instance the number of children and how many boys and girls they want and how we are dealing with the children's want and need. This is not always easy to know what the "RIGHT THING" is for their children. Now think with me and follow my line of thinking, OK.

MARRIAGE – FAMILY & ADDICTIONS

Marriage ABCs.

Marriage how does your marriage measure up?

A = Abandon Selfishness
B = Bestow Praise on One Another
C = Call Home if Running Late
D = Dream a Lot of Dreams Together
E = Enjoy Learning New Discoveries About One Another
F = Flowers Say I
G = Grins are Life Giving
H = Hands are for Holding
I = Invest Your Time, Talent and Treasure on Your Marriage
J = Journey Together
K = Know How to Have Fun Together
L = Love is a Decision
M = Make Time for Being Alone Together
N = Negativity is Death Dealing in Any Relationship
O = Obliterate Jumping to Conclusions
P = Plan for Passion
Q = Quit Quarrelling – If it's Over 48 Hours old, Let it Go
R = Remember Those Special Days, e.g. Anniversaries
S = Share Feelings on a Daily Basis
T = Take Lots of Pictures and Create Great Memories
U = Unity Creates Joy
V = Vacations are Not Luxuries – Take Time to Re-Create
W = Write Love Letters to One Another
X = Xmas is a Time for Building Traditions, Not for Creating Tension
Y = Yearn for a Great Marriage, Not Just a Good One
Z = Zestfulness Breeds Excitement

Do you have any to add?"

http://marriage.about.com/library/weekly/aa070697.htm 7/20/04

Meeting the couple and introducing myself, and then getting acquainted, and let them know that counseling is a good way for every couple to really get to know themselves and their spouse. I will start with their dating & engagement in the first session. There is much more to be leaned in the next six sessions. There is a lot to know about a good marriage relationship.

If you get the first step right in choosing the right marriage partner that is great, but if not you may have difficulty in adjusting to the marriage. Because a person can be attracted to a person for the wrong reasons, and the consequences are usually devastating to one or both persons; it will affect the relationship sooner or later in the marriage.

NEW BEGINNING II, THE AFFECTS OF DIVORCE

Chapter 7

The Real Hurt & Pain:

PREPARING BEFORE AND AFTER DIVIORCE

I kissed a (Prince or Princess) & they turned out to be a __?
In the real world a person doesn't always get a (Prince or Princess).

In this study we will deal specifically with **divorce** and the results of a **divorce**. There are things I learned as I look back over my divorces I felt like I had kissed a princess when we married. The good, bad, and the ugly pretty will describes each **divorce;** I wondered what happened the princess I married. Things got pretty bad and then they got ugly before the divorce and that was the reason for the divorce there was nothing nice after the divorce, I guess all of that is a part of the divorce.

Then how to deal with the **divorce** is where I want to start. I will tackle this difficult subject of our modern society. My advice to anyone they will need counseling before and after a **divorce,** you may need a counseling service that looks out for you, a counselor cannot help both you if there are major problems. I recommend two different counselors in some cases and then have them meet with both counselors jointly so no one takes advantage of the situation/**divorce**. Divorce, separation and failed relationships are one the most devastating circumstances a person may have to deal with outside of a death.

There are so many multiple marriages in today's society. I don't know of anything that can leave a person, family and children so mentally and emotionally crippled, and leave so many scares. The utter sense of failure and rejection is so common in those situations. The whole family has to deal with the divorce and its effects on the family and home. The children also feel the effects because they are emotionally involved. They feel all the pain and guilt associated with the problems involved with divorce.

The relationship and marriage can start so wonderfully and feel so right! The cheer joy and happiness that once was, is now gone, the expectation of a happy marriage is gone. At one time they thought this was the person they would spend the rest of their life with. How could this happen, how could they have been so mistaken about this person, then the hurt, anger and bitterness that sets in, then usually divorce.

I am going to deal with this in two ways.

One is how I dealt with the divorces in my life and how it affected my children. Then how I look at divorce, you will be able to see how I dealt with it in my life story "Facing the real me, Run John Run". Then you may want my Biblical view on divorce (Booklet).

I would like to call this the LAME DUCK scenario for my own reasons. In my case divorce was a self-infected wound that I had to deal with and how I have dealt with them over the years. This situation is created by two people for whatever reasons. I have chosen to deal with the details in my life story rather than in my study guides I do make some references to help make a point, but I go into a lot of the details in the personal section of my biography "the real hurt and pain," I can't ignore those facts even if I wanted too and I didn't understand all many of the problems before the marriage, you may wonder why?

I marry three widows and one had been married before and all of the marriages end up in a divorce. Why? There has to be some common emotional tie to each one of these widows, does that mean there was something drastically wrong before the marriage, yes, and was there something drastically wrong with me? Yes, and I know it now, I really cared for them, but could not understand their feeling because I was not a widowed person or had not lost a loved one. I am going to be as honest as I possibly can with myself and you, as I look back on these circumstances. I could never live up to their view of the death of a person. I think of it like this, I felt like I had shoot myself, I could feel their pain because it was hurting me and the pain is there, but the real pain was in the fact I didn't know how to deal their pain, everything I said or done seem to make thing worse.

The question is how am I going to deal with these pains and I wondered why I ever married these ladies in the first place? I certainly am not going to shoot myself, but I felt their pain because it was hurting them, then why was divorce a solution.

I don't know that I handled any of my marriages or divorces very good. I would not be happy with myself if I felt good about divorce. There were drastic situations, and untimely each was a death at an early age; none of them were able to deal with what happened. There were drastic reactions taking place in each of these people before the marriages and did that actually but a contributing factor the divorces. I hope I have made good assessments as to why these were contributing factors I will show you how I related to each of these as I go on with this study.

I am a normal guy or am I "I'm a lame duck," I fall for a sad story and each of them had one worse than the other, I'm a guy that wanted to help them and I thought I could help them because I'm a minister, that is one of reasons I got involved, was I the answer, no, I made a serious mistakes in marring them, now that I look back. I thought I could help them pick up the pieces. I remarried and thought I was ready to go on with my life; I hope you can see a person running around hurting hoping I could help someone who hurting worse than me and I was hurting in different way at the same time. I almost became an emotional and physical cripple because of all this. Let's deal with the healing of the heart first. OK!

Divorce

I have tried to show you how I dealt with these two problems. One is how I dealt with the **divorces** in my life, and then how I looked at **divorce**. You will be able to see why **divorce** caused me to feel like failure and also why I call this the LAME DUCK theory, for my own reasons. They were bad marriages for many reasons I became a statistic in the divorce rate.

MARRIAGE – FAMILY & ADDICTIONS

Divorce Rate: Divorce Rate in America
50% of all marriages in the America end in divorce."

"**Age at marriage for those who divorce in America**

AGE	WOMEN	MEN
Under 20 years old	27.6%	11.7%
20 to 24 years old	36.6%	38.8%
25 to 29 years old	16.4%	22.3%
30 to 34 years old		

The divorce rate in America for first marriage, vs. second or third marriage
50% percent in first marriages, 67% in second and 74% in third marriages end in divorce, according to Jennifer Baker of the Forest Institute of Professional Psychology in Springfield, Missouri. According to enrichment journal on the divorce rate in America:
The divorce rate in America for first marriage is 41%
The divorce rate in America for second marriage is 60%
The divorce rate in America for third marriage is 73%

The divorce rate in America for childless couples and couples with children

According to discovery channel, *couples with children have a slightly lower rate of divorce than childless couples.*

Sociologists believe that childlessness is also a common cause of divorce. The absence of children leads to loneliness and weariness and even in the United States; at least 66 per cent of all divorced couples are childless."

http://www.divorce.org   1/18/2012

That sets the stage for **Divorce** I think it is kind of like a self-inflected wound because I couldn't see the danger it feels like a stab in the heart. This situation is usually created by two people not just one, and there are lots of reasons for a divorce. I have chosen to deal with this subject because it is a part of life and for those who have had to deal with it. I got mixed up because I did not think divorce was the end, and I was caught up the dilemma of dealing with my divorces, in this frame of mind; why do people go through a divorce. This usually happens during "the development years" that is when it happened in my case and that is why I put it this study.

In the course of each marriage I thought there was nothing wrong with me, the next marriage would the right one, but I would like to ignore that fact there are problems in any marriage, I believed everything would turn better if I tried harder. That was a false impression within my thinking, and the way I thought about life.

Although I can't change what happened, or go back even if I wanted too. I did learn a great deal about myself during and after divorce. I thought there has to be something drastically wrong with me! I didn't know why or what I had done wrong to cause each divorce? I am going to be honest as possible as I make some assessments of myself.

The real pain of **divorce, separation** and **failed marriages** are some of the most common problems families face, you may have a family member who is **divorced,** and there is family involvement. It is not like someone going to a ball game or movie. The emotions can get out-of-control when there is screaming and yelling, that should only happen at a sporting event, or be emotional and crying over a movie. The pain and emotion of those situations may affect lives prenatally, but the impact of divorce affects the whole family. They are short lived unless *you* are the one it is happening to. The fact that *you* are involved, when *you* are personally involved makes all of the difference in the world, doesn't it!

It is that personal involvement that brings about emotional stress as a person begins to deal with thought of divorce, and a person identifies themselves as a divorcee.

What happens when a person goes through a divorce, we are going to deal with the demands of a divorce and the pressure they go through. There is a problem when someone expects a person to do something or tells them to do something they don't want to do is that enough of a reason to get a divorce? This is a part of life and yet it put demands on a person and their relationship, consequently this creates some of the ups and downs in a marriage. A person may not want to do I will discuss some of those reasons as it relates to relationships, and even your job, etc.

Now let's deal with some of the different details when it comes to divorce? The demands put on a person going through a divorce can be over whelming, no one really wants to deal with the messy details of a divorce. There is a breaking point in any situation or problem how a person deals with the divorce is very important because they are people they loved.

(Illustration) I thought a new marriage with a new person would mean a successful marriage and bring about happiness; the same is true in relationships. For the most part the marriage and relationship was better at times, but when the relationship didn't work I was more confused than ever. I wanted a successful marriage more than anything because I had failed before. Sometimes this is a driving force in people remarrying.

There are patterns of behavior in every individual and people don't change because they marry another person, if we're not careful little things become big problems. Divorce maybe the only way out for some people, I'm not here to judge or criticize what is right or wrong in your life that is between you and them, and how you see God in all of it.

That is just one thing I want to address in this study. No person wants to be looked down on or belittled. This is a very sensitive area from both sides I'm going to try to present both views of each other's problems. I want them to step back and take a look at each other's motives and insecurities.

The 10 Most Common Causes of Divorce / Marriage and Separation Advice   Page 1-5[16]

"It's fair to say that there is no one cause for any divorce. There are often several factors, sometimes many. But those who interview couples and try to analyze why their marriage failed have come up with several reasons named as common causes of divorce. Here they are in no particular order:

1. **Communication.** If you think of a ship and its crew or a sporting team and its players, you'll understand how important it is to communicate with everyone involved. Things need to happen when sailing and commands must be clear, timely, and acted upon. In a game of football or baseball, it's essential that players on the same team communicate with one another in order to run their plays. The way to win in all these examples is to communicate properly and to do so whenever it is necessary. If there's a problem in your marriage and you try the silent routine or the "bury your head in the sand" response, you are most likely heading for divorce.

2. **Money.** How many marriages end in divorce because of money? Married couples certainly but so do business partners, siblings, traders, and customers. The love for money is supposedly the cause of all evil and it's definitely the cause of arguments, fights, and court actions. One spouse spends money without telling their partner. One spouse loses their job and the combined income falls and they can no longer buy certain things. The problems boil down to money or having none at all. Couples who are relatively successful with their finances are less likely to argue and thus head towards divorce. **NOTE:** If you are suffering money problems or are considering bankruptcy, possibly you should consider a FREE Bankruptcy Evaluation today.

3. **Cheating.** It doesn't matter who is involved, for how long and why, because infidelity causes pain and suffering to parties involved. Some marriages are able to survive infidelity but many don't, which is why it is known as one of the leading causes of divorce. Of course, there are couples who are faithful to each other but still divorce.

Therefore, if you're tempted to stray, understand that cheating can cause a giant chasm in a relationship.

4. **Wrong expectations.** Children can suffer greatly from their parents having the wrong expectations. They are promised a treat - be it a visit, an outing, or a present - but the parent is unable to fulfill the promise. Expectations are dashed. The same can be true of some marriages. One partner thinks the world of their spouse and wants to live happily ever after. But we are all human, we all have faults. Don't see your partner as the perfect person? Be prepared to discover faults which you either didn't know about or thought would never cause a problem. Be hopeful and confident but don't allow your expectations to reach heights which mean they are never realized.

5. **Commitment.** A marriage is a partnership and it takes two people to make it work. If both partners don't care about the relationship, then their marriage will certainly die. Even if only one partner doesn't commit wholeheartedly to the marriage, the marriage can still be undone. Both partners need to commit and it almost always means making sacrifices, which is what commitment is all about. Without a solid support for the partnership from both partners, divorce could very well be a possibility.

6. **Addictions.** Sadly, alcohol and drugs are an ever-present part of today's society and many married people get caught up in substance abuse. So often the beginnings are seemingly harmless. A few drinks or a sampling of a drug. Once the addiction takes over, a person's life is often in turmoil. If they are married, they will have difficulty living with each other. If your partner is involved in alcohol or drug abuse, professional help is often the best way. And the sooner the better.

7. **Sex.** Of course the intimate and physical side of a marriage is important and yes, problems in this area can cause stress and lead to divorce. But as people get older and, hopefully, mature, they realize that personal happiness is not centered only on love-making. Having children, being healthy, successful, and growing together as a couple are just as important. Any couple experiencing difficulty with their love life can seek professional help.

8. **Mid-life crisis.** The exact definition of this phenomenon varies from person to person but in men it usually means a desire to change job, location and/or lifestyle. They think their life is getting to the stage where they need a new challenge. And it's possible they may but such an abrupt and seemingly selfish determination can have a big impact on their partner. Massive change may be scary or unnecessary to the spouse. The turmoil from this new lust for life can be the cause of many a divorce among couples who have been married for many years.

9. **Little things.** It seems hard to believe that a partner's snoring is the cause of a marriage failure but it may be true, at least in part. Not being able to get enough sleep can be enormously stressful but you would think a loving partner would find another bed or bedroom or seek professional help. However, if a marriage is under strain for another reason such as money troubles, a small thing like snoring could be the straw to break the camel's back.

10. **Society.** The rules regarding divorce today have changed dramatically. Separation for as little as a year with the sole grounds in many countries being the desire that one or both partners want a divorce. Some argue that marriage is still an institution which needs commitment from both parties and that divorce is far too easy. The fact that you can file for a divorce online and never attend a court only adds to this argument. Divorce is easy. But that's what society has determined and so, for better or worse, that's what we're stuck with. It may not all be bad. And it's certainly just one of the many causes as to why people get divorced."

http://divorceguide.com/free-divorce-advice/marriage-and-separation-advice/the-   1/18/2012

I hope you have looked at this information about divorce and it will help people make good decisions. I know I've lived through situations I thought they were unbearable at the time.

There is a fall-out from divorce the children of **divorce** are a product of **divorce**. They usually have to deal with it because it affects their home; they have friends or classmates that are dealing with **divorce**. They may have to live with or at least they will learn about **divorce** from their friends, and how they relate to their problems and they will learn from others going through a divorce.

In the situation of **divorce** they may have different parents, ½ brothers and sisters, or step brothers and sisters, who live in the same house with a step parent. When there are visitations in these cases of **divorced** the children may have to deal with different stepparents as they visit one of the parents.

This has left the family with some real problems. I don't know of anything that can leave person, family, and children so mentally crippled, and emotions to deal with when there is a **divorce**. Even the children feel guilty. They are devastated by all of this as they should be. The utter sense of failure and rejection is so common in all of their lives. The mom and dad, grandparents can feel like they have failed as parents and grandparents.

Everyone is emotionally involved, and it is personal. They feel all the pain and guilt associated with **divorce**. It is hard to remain objective. People also take sides because this becomes a family matter, and of course the children and grandparents will take sides.

Recipe for a happy marriage Fact or Fiction   Page 1 – 5 [17]
18 Shocking Statistics About
Children and Divorce

"I've compiled these statistics about children and divorce "I'll believe it when I see it" type of people who don't accept anything as true unless it's from a credible source or it's been PROVEN in a convincing study.

If you are NOT one of these people, you need to read this anyway.

These days most people accept divorce as a way of life, completely unaware of the damage they are doing to their children. Tell your friends, acquaintances and co-workers to read these shocking statistics about divorce and children. It may help save a child's life down the road. (And no, I'm not figuratively speaking either….just keep reading to find out what I mean.)

1. Half of all American children will witness the breakup of a parent's marriage. Of these, close to half will <u>also see the breakup of a parent's second marriage</u>." (Furstenberg, Peterson, Nord, and Zill, "Life Course")

2. Among the millions of children who have seen their parents divorce, one of every 10 will also live through **three or more** parental marriage breakups. (The Abolition of Marriage, Gallagher)

Forty percent of children growing up in America today are being raised without their fathers. (Wade, Horn and Busy, "Fathers, Marriage and Welfare Reform" Hudson Institute Executive Briefing, 1997)

4. Of all children born to married parents this year, fifty percent will experience the divorce of their parents before they reach their 18th birthday. (Fagan, Fitzgerald, Rector, "The Effects of Divorce On America)

The EMOTIONALLY Damaging Statistics about children and divorce

5. Studies in the early 1980's showed that children in repeat divorces earned **lower grades** and their peers rated them as **less pleasant to be around**. (Andrew J. Cherlin, Marriage, Divorce, Remarriage –Harvard University Press 1981)

6. Teenagers in single-parent families and in blended families are three times more likely to need psychological help within a given year. (Peter Hill "Recent Advances in Selected Aspects of Adolescent Development" Journal of Child Psychology and Psychiatry 1993)

7. Compared to children from homes disrupted by death, children from divorced homes have more psychological problems. (Robert E. Emery, Marriage, Divorce and Children's Adjustment" Sage Publications, 1988)

These statistics about children and divorce are pretty shocking, aren't they?

The DEATH of a parent is LESS devastating to a child than a DIVORCE. (Even *I* wouldn't believe this if I didn't see the statistic myself.)

The PHYSICALLY Damaging Statistics About Children and Divorce

8. Children of divorce are at a greater risk to experience injury, asthma, headaches and speech defects than children whose parents have remained married. (Dawson, "Family Structure and Children's Health and Well Being" National Health Interview Survey on Child Health, Journal of Marriage and the Family)

9. Following divorce, children are fifty percent more likely to develop health problems than two parent families. (Angel, Worobey, "Single Motherhood and Children's Health")

10. Children living with both biological parents are 20 to 35 percent more physically healthy than children from broken homes. (Dawson, "Family Structure and Children's Health and Well-being" Journal of Marriage and the Family)

11. Most victims of child molestation come from single-parent households or are the children of drug ring members. (Los Angles Times 16 September 1985 The Garbage Generation)

12. A Child in a female-headed home is <u>10 times</u> more likely to be **beaten** or **murdered**. (The Legal Beagle, July 1984, from "The Garbage Generation")

This is what I mean when I said *"these statistics on divorce and children could save a child's life someday."* Did you read #12? A child raised by his/her mother is <u>10 times more likely</u> to be beaten or murdered.

The Long Term Effects and Statistics About Children and Divorce

13. A study of children six years after a parental marriage breakup revealed that even after all that time, these children tended to be "lonely, unhappy, anxious and insecure. (Wallerstein "The Long-Term Effects of Divorce on Children" Journal of the American Academy of Child and Adolescent Psychiatry 1991)

14. Seventy percent of long-term prison inmates grew up in broken homes. (Horn, Bush, "Fathers, Marriage and Welfare Reform)

Problems Relating to Peers

15. Children of divorce are four times more likely to report problems with peers and friends than children whose parents have kept their marriages intact. (Tysse, Burnett, "Moral Dilemmas of Early Adolescents of Divorced and Intact Families. Journal of Early Adolescence 1993)

16. Children of divorce, particularly boys, tend to be more aggressive toward others than those children whose parents did not divorce. (Emery, "Marriage, Divorce and Children's Adjustment, 1988)

Suicide Statistics About Children and Divorce

17. People who come from broken homes are almost twice as likely to attempt suicide than those who do not come from broken homes. (Velez-Cohen, "Suicidal Behavior and Ideation in a Community Sample of Children" Journal of the American Academy of Child and Adolescent Psychiatry 1988)

High School Drop Out Statistics About Children and Divorce

18. Children of divorced parents are roughly two times more likely to drop out of high school than their peers who benefit from living with parents who did not divorce. (McLanahan, Sandefur, "Growing Up: What Hurts, What Helps" Harvard University Press 1994)

I can't stress how important it is to know all the facts before you get a divorce. Your child's life is in your hands. If you're seriously considering divorce and you haven't attempted to**save your marriage**, I've just given you 18 reasons why it's at least worth a try to keep your family together."

http://www.marriage-success-secrets.com/recipe-for-a-happy-marriage.html   1/18/12

I bet there was someone who said their marriage will never last.

There has to be a certain amount of communication about who is wrong, now let's talk about the children after the **divorce**. There is a certainly two sides in any situation and there is a certain amount emotional insatiability in any situation. In some cases the parents are so bitter they don't realize what they are doing to their children. They are more concerned about getting even, and discrediting their x spouse. The children are in the middle one of the ways of getting even with the x spouse, is by using the children to make them pay for the suffering and pain they caused.

Here are some the major events in my life; at the age of 13 I became a Christian, 18 graduated from high school, I graduated from Bible College at the age of 22 then a Youth Ministry. At the age of 25 I marry for the first time, and go through a divorce in the same year and at the age of 29 I remarry again, I still continue with youth work. Then we have 3 children and she has 3 children at the age of 39 a second divorce I'm not through yet I marry again at the age of 42 and I am divorced at the age of 53.

I have numerous health problems to deal with along the way. I had very religious back ground in the first part of my life. I don't think this was abnormal beginning at the time in which I lived, as time goes on my life changes, and also the views of society changes. The changes I go through fit in as society changes over the years. There are some very interesting questions to be answered as I go into my life experiences.

I'm the normal every day person other than being divorced, numerous health problems along the way, and lived through them. I lived to tell how my life was saved from heart problems. I think that will add a little spice to my life experiences as we go on. Other than that, there is nothing special about my life. I have never amassed a great fortune nor was I a great athlete, a great Spiritual leader or a great author either. There are some special things that happen to me as I talk about these experiences. This is probably the most important thing I do not regret any time spent raising my kids and helping teens find their way in life. To each one I owe them a doubt of gratitude for being a part of my life because they are what I am all about. If I have done anything that merits any praise that is the work I have done with these young people.

I did not get to see my girls as much as I would have liked they grow up in another town. I would like say I think a family is the greatest experience in the world. I am a signal **divorced** person since 1993, and have lived alone sense then I have spent a part of my life in Florida.

After the divorces I have had time to get over the bitterness of a past marriage, people tend to carry over their feelings into the next relationship as I did.

That brings me to talking about my twin daughters who were four (four is a good age for children going through a **divorce**, they are not old enough to accept the blame, and not old enough remember being a family, and children can accept someone new into their life at a very easily age). There is a sense of wanting and needing a mother and dad, a family unit, at that age, they feel a strong need for both parents, but in some cases it doesn't happen that way. I also have a daughter who was eight at the time of the **divorce**. She felt it more than the twins. (Eight and up **divorce** is much harder for them). My oldest daughter took it very hard; we have had several talks about what happened in the past few years. Now she sees what happened and why, now she has a family of her own, and I think that has helped her in understanding the divorce, and by the age of eight children will have formed most their own opinions, core values, and standards, they've been taught.

The children are the ones' that suffer and pay the biggest price for **divorce** problems. They take it just as personal sometimes even more personal than the parents. They even take sides for the most part because they have their set of core values and prejudices based on their life experiences. They even pit both parents against each other to get their own way. One thing about people and children they do tend to transfer blame to someone else it is someone else's fault, another thing they that happens they feel someone should pay for their hurt and pain. It shows up in a rebellious attitude at school and in the home.

This comes into play because they need the security and the peace of a home. They are torn between two people they love. They need a stable atmosphere to grow in, a home, and loved by both parents. This can help them to deal and adjust to the **divorce**.

This will turn out to be a syndrome such as insecurities, trust, but they are more likely to get over the **divorce** or separation as they get older, and have their own relationships to deal with. They are more likely to be able to forgive, but they are going to have a greater need for love and understanding if this is going to happen.

I was talking to someone I'd known a few years back, she had stopped to eat lunch where I was working, I had not seen her in about 10 years. Her daughter and my step daughter had played basketball together. I ask her about some families we had known back when I was involved in raising my stepchildren. I had either coached her daughter, or the team she had played on. In the summer our kids played ball with her kids.

As I was talking with her I asked about the kids and her parents, three of the parents we knew had either separated or divorce because of an extra martial affair.

One out of every 4 marriages, 25% end-up in divorce because of extra martial affair according to most statistics. The family that once was is now dealing with a **divorce**, the kids are torn apart over the love for each parent, and in one instance the kids don't speak to their mother, or at that the time. I know how sad this can be because of the battles are over child custody, I've been there, a big problem is over visitation.

I have gone through several divorce classes, group sessions, and gone to seminars on divorce to become a whole person. In the process I have learned a lot about myself, and that is why I wanted to change some of the things, I wanted my next marriage to last I will be glad to tell a person more about the reasons I **divorced**.

I don't have all the answers, nobody does, but I do know what it takes to have a good relationship, I have taken courses on relationships in my Master's and Doctorate studies. The reason I have done this is to help myself and others to understand why there is hope after a divorce. I want people to have love and passion for each other, and to learn to communication with each other. I want both to be commitment to the marriage. I don't believe in **divorce**, and yet it happened. For that reason I don't want to carry any excess baggage with me anymore; that has led me into helping others.

I want to bring up some miss conceptions about divorce.

I will be clear as I can about the matters of **divorce**, I believe it takes "true love for each other and commitment to each other if it is going to last", my heart goes out to those who are having marriage problems and dealing in their relationship, "commitment to loving that person will last", but only if your committed to each other no matter what.

I have brought up the separation and **divorce** because that is what is happening in so many lives. I'm not afraid of the subject, and have talked about it because the subject should be covered by some who has gone through **divorce**. I would really like to talk about things that are relevant and what people are dealing with, I have talked about my divorces hoping it will help someone else.

You see I am family man at heart and love my family. How are *you* going to deal with the problems as *you* go through a **divorce** are *you* going to be able to put the past behind *you*, knowing that a new relationship brings new problems, it is very important to solve the old problems before going into a new one.

I have looked at my divorces, and failed marriages. This is a strong case and point, what is wrong with the picture of a failed marriage?

How can a person's remarriage be different from the last one? In my case I have gone through divorce classes and other seminars, I want to help *you* by giving some other studies on counseling before getting a divorce.

Look at some of these reasons before you get a divorce?
First and foremost divorce is the dissolution of a legal marriage. It is not an annulment, which is the ending of a marriage by having it declared 'void'. Although it must be noted that even in cases of annulment child support, alimony and property distribution laws may still apply.

Look at your state laws, each state has its own laws, this is a general definition.

Let us be clear divorce is not a party it will likely be a traumatic experience, difficult and emotionally trying. Much more when kids are involved. Children will forever be impacted by a divorce no matter how civil because it involves them? Was it something they did? Just remember everyone in your family is impacted when you divorce. It does not end there.

According to national statistics you will have to get along with less money and a reduced lifestyle compared to what you were previously accustomed to, are you sufficiently scared yet? You should be because it is a serious decision that will impact your life more than any decision you will probably ever make (unless you get married and divorced again you may continue that pattern if you don't get some kind of help).

Sociological studies indicate a profound impact in a variety of important areas including your economic, social, physical and mental well-being. Yes, you may very well end up a wreck after a divorce. But, you will not be alone. We'll get into that later almost 70-percent of children coming from divorced families consider divorce and contribute to their own marital problems to their parent's divorce, compared to only 40-percent of children from non-divorced families.

Is Divorce Worth It?
With all that, why would anyone want to get divorced? Despite all of the above horrors, there can be a light at the end of the tunnel, or there will be a train wreck?
In my humble opinion: a divorce is a better option than living in an abusive marriage and this goes for everyone in the household. That should be one guide when it comes to deciding on the path of **divorce**. You will be doing both you and your spouse a favor in that regard and even your children, since it is presumed they are unhappy when Mom and Dad are unhappy.
Just take the time to reflect deeply on what I've just said up to this point, in considering a **divorce** and why you need to plan for changes in *your* future.

- Is your reason for wanting a divorce something that can be worked out and improved? Is it because of the bad times you and your spouse have been dealing with?

- Remember, far too often, many spouses make the mistake of thinking that their next marriage will not have problems, which the previous one did. Not so fast.
- All marriages have their ups and downs.
- Each marriage comes packaged with a whole new set of bills, in-laws, gifts, vacation plans.
- You get the picture. The point is not to discourage you from choosing this course, but merely to make you think deeply about it.
- It is a life-changing and important decision.
- You need to give it the serious consideration it deserves.

If you ultimately decide to pursue a divorce or maybe you have no other choice since your spouse has demanded one, let us then consider that window of opportunity to look at what went wrong.

Will divorce really solve your problems? Will it provide a way to a better life? Here is an opportunity for those who have weighed the consequences, and still feel that divorce is the only course of action, divorce can be an option. Below are the greatest reasons in which most people feel justified in ending a marriage.

Why do people get divorced?
Drugs and alcoholism

Uncontrolled person, abusive and binge drinking the same goes for any addictive substance, be it cocaine or prescribed pain killers. Keep in mind if you truly loved your spouse at one time - you owe it to them to try to help them with their problems, but you can only suffer for so long without it causing a breakdown. In the case of an addiction or drug abuser they will have to "want to change". If you don't see that desire, then you are wasting your time. This may come when *you* can't change a destructive situation, then you must seek a change to benefit yourself and the rest of your family. In this case **divorce can bring some peace** and quiet to your life.

There are times when a person ends-up with a relationship that has to do with such things as: Sexual-addictions/Adultery plus other situations that relate to addictions, plus others I have not discussed at this point.

There are so many people that have to deal with these problems on an everyday basis. I put all these into one group category for the purpose of personal identity and whether they are considered social disorders. There is a direct correlation between Co-dependency is can lead to being an enabler in Addictions, and the result is abuse, and that is why I have put them together in this case. They are personal and social problems at the same time, but being realistic there are people and families involved, in some cases they are thought of as metal illness and they are in some cases.

Today sexual-addictions and pornography are thought of as social problems. Let's spend a little time on these prevalent miss-conducts. I have addressed to them before in different sections of this book, but I address the subject, and define the results of these addictions. There is usually a correlation between the hurt and pain they cause, and the actual act.

There is usually Co-dependency in Addictions and the next level of social behavioral problems has to do with the effects of drugs in a relationship. They usually apply to the co-dependency syndromes associated with a person who enables the person to stay on the addiction, and they abuse the enabler. They can't let go of the addiction, a person can become dependent and it is a problem when the other person becomes the enabler and in some cases both may be addicted to drugs. It can even become a dependency on a substance. I know it's hard to believe that sexual-addictions can fit into this category. This can result in abusive actions and it may bring about harm to a person's own physical well-being, they can harm the mind and body. While affecting and doing damage to other metal processes.

How many relationships are affected by Sexual-addictions / Adultery when they become addictive, how do people deal with those addictions, there are ways, I have discussed up this point. There are people that have to deal with these problems on an everyday basis week end and week out. There is a direct correlation between Co-dependency/Addictions/Abuse they are social problems in a sense and in some cases it can result in physically illnesses.

Physical abuse

If you are involved in a physically abusive relationship then run, don't walk, to the nearest law office and get yourself a good lawyer. When it comes to physical abuse, no one deserves such treatment: they are you're worst enemies and you are letting control you! Compounding physical abuse is usually a level of mental and verbal assaults that lead one into a sort of paralysis, which can cause one to wonder if they are to blame. Don't fall into this trap. You will surely be making a move to a better your world through divorce. The sooner you do so, the sooner you can start enjoying life again while being treated with the respect and the dignity you deserve.

Verbal/Mental Abuse

In some ways, insults and put-downs are just as bad over the years it can be every bit as debilitating as physical abuse. No one deserves to be put down, insulted ripped into screeds; there is a perceived lack of good communication, there are flaws or in ability to discuss things. As a spouse you are entitled to the dignity and self-respect, and nobody has a right to attack those aspects of a person.

Financial Recklessness

Finances are a major reason why some marriages fail and it mostly has to do with spending habits. Strong marriages are when people are on the same page when it comes to the money spent and your budgets are clearly defined and understood. This does not mean that both spouses should get full access to the cookie jar at all times, it just means that whatever system is in place must be understood by both spouses. Perhaps one spouse has a personal savings account for spur of the moment purchases. That, in itself, is okay. It is just when suddenly eight thousand dollars is missing from the joint checking or savings account, one spouse was saving the money for a family vacation next spring tempers can flare given enough time such matters can lead to **divorce**. Go see a credit counselor first and clearly outline how you and your spouse are going to deal with the money and retirement.

What if a husband won't get a job?

I am not going say that it is the role of the husband has to work while the woman stays at home in some case it might be ok if the husband is handicapped in some way, but generally speaking the provider needs to provide for the family, they need to wear the paints when it comes to the family. The same applies if the main provider is a woman. You can't provide from the sofa. A chronically lazy spouse will eschew every chance to be employed, this can be disastrous to the spouse that works hard, sweat and tears to make a living. You married into a partnership, not into a one-sided relationship. Make sure (his or her) reluctance is not merely caused by depression. If it isn't and they are loafing and are wholly ingrained in an uncorrectable behavior, consider a **divorce**.

Divorce Planning & Preparedness do you need to get a lawyer?

You don't always have to get a lawyer, check with the court house or library in your state they may have all the legal documents you need. The divorce process can be over whelming or you may need a trusted and trained professional to help you navigate these difficult waters. Keep in mind that you are going to be taxed mentally, physically, financially, spiritually and emotionally, perhaps in other ways you are not thinking of right now. The last thing you need to do is worry about the legal ins and outs of the divorce process. Ask trusted friends for recommendations. Find an attorney you instinctively trust and can feel comfortable with stick with them to the end. Remember one thing about lawyers they are in it for the money the longer it takes the more money they make.

We are not saying you have to break the bank account, although you might. But, a few pennies here and there are not going to do you any good if you get taken to the woodshed by your spouse's professional attorney. When I say they are not cheap, I mean in quality as much as in price.

Unless there is a real fear of physical abuse, don't get in hurry to get into another relationship because you need time to heal. Talk it over with your lawyer and remember that you are entitled to a place just as much as your spouse. Be cordial about it, but remember, this is not the time to give away the house, literally.

What I have just said may seem ridiculous blunt, but look at it this way. A divorce can easily develop into a revenge contest, which often will be just what the lawyers want as you try to destroy each other; it is destructive for both parties, especially if you have kids. Yes, your spouse may fight nasty, but taking the emotions out of it, it makes it easier to deal with the blows. The idea is not to ruin your spouse, but let them get on with their life. In time both of you to settle your differences among yourselves. You may see that divorce was the right course of action for everyone involved. But, even if the other spouse plays dirty, keep your cool by remembering what you are going through it is the better choice for all involved and you will be less emotional about it. This will help when you go to court.

Actions speak louder than words and both speak volumes in the presence of a (JUDGE). A great piece of advice is not to say or write anything that you would not want read aloud in a court room. So, be careful about nasty messages you might leave for your spouse's answering machine or email. You might see that answering machine message played back to you in court. The same goes for e-mail. Don't send any threatening correspondence; refrain from communication with your spouse except for picking up the kids or taking care of the house and dog. Act like the judge is standing right next to you when you communicate with anyone and you should be okay.

A key to putting up a good fight in the court room is to have as much documentation as possible and that means hauling stuff down to your local UPS store and making copies. A rule of thumb is to copy bank account records and print-offs, mortgage statements, medical bills, investment accounts or anything related to your valuable assets. Your lawyer will need them to help *you* win your battle.

Guess what, if both of your names are on the credit cards and you no longer have them, and your spouse does, anything (he or she) puts on them is your responsibility as much as it is theirs. We don't care if it is the Netflix membership, contact them and have your name removed or the account shut down completely. The last thing you need is to do is stop an account and finally close it.

Make a detailed list of everything that is of value and even debts. Take pictures of assets and or DVD's stuff if you can. The more ways you can document assets the better and this will surely help when it comes to dividing up everything.

You can't bring your lawyer too much information, pay attention to assets of sentimental value. They may be low in financial value; they are oftentimes the most value to you. Family photos are a prime example. Make copies of everything you want.

Don't forget about the financial aspects of stocks and retirement benefits. They are valued as assets; you will have to pay capital gains on them. The tax asset is really not worth much but 4-1- K's are. Someone will need to look at the capital gains, pick which assets you want to retain and keep that in mind.

Finally, preparing for a divorce, have the strength of friends and family to support you. You will need their emotional support more than anything as the dissolution of a marriage can be draining in every area of your life. Not to mention the hurt of a divorce, the final realization comes when *your* dream was never realized. This will bring pain of its own. Line up your friends and lean on those you can trust.

What is marriage a war?

"I was married," this anecdote is true in a sense of how bad divorce can get.

Funny, perhaps, but it does underscore what a bad marriage is like, some would say it is similar to serving a tour in 'Nam' or a stint in the forgotten war such as Korea. Seriously, nothing is like the real war that goes on before a divorce, but a worthy comparison is merely an exaggeration. Hopefully you will never have to experience a real war, which may make your divorce seem like a day at the beach comparatively speaking.

Nonetheless, many will describe a divorce as a battlefield, though it may seem like it. However, let me humor you with this analogy: when the war is over they are going home, they are on the chopper going back to the land of free. Look at it that way, but wait a second a lot can happen before you get on the chopper back home you are so close to freedom not really. This means you better understand how the ride home works. You have your freedom was it worth it?

The following chronology order gives a general idea of how bad things may get in the typical divorce process. Your divorce may be a little different because there are differences among state laws or because of specific issues between you and your spouse and how your children deal with the divorce. For example, arguments over where your kids will live and who is going to pay for the college savings account can make the process more complicated. Your attorney can help you understand exactly how your divorce will fit into this chronology. Herein I will emphasize a very important aspect of the divorce proceedings - your attorney works for you and should clearly explain every step of your divorce.

A good tip is to check your State's web site (most of them have them now) and you should be able to glean the nuances of your States laws regarding a no fault divorce and what you have to do. The process below is in generality, there might be 50 different variations to the steps below. Still, it generally works as outlined below. This may attest you in the way it may go.

The Divorce Proceedings
The Plaintive

To start the divorce, one of the spouses gets a lawyer, who writes up a petition (also known as a complaint). This is a legal document that says why the spouse wants a divorce and how (he or she) wants to settle financially. It also will detail custody aspects and other issues relevant to the divorce. A divorce of a marriage might have lots of issues to be resolved. Then again, every divorce is different and there will be something uniquely frustrating about yours. Count on it.

Papers are filed

The lawyer files the petition or complaint with the court in the local jurisdiction. Sometimes this is in Family Division court or will be named something similar. A critical aspect is that the either the lawyer or the court will ensure the petition/complaint is served on the other spouse, together with a summons that requires that spouse's to responded in official legal sounding language.

The served spouse has to answer within a certain time (usually about four weeks) as to their official response to the complaint and what they want to do about it. The answer (or response) says whether or not they served spouse agrees with the petition/complaint. If (he or she) doesn't answer the petition/complaint, the court regards that the spouse agrees to the terms. So, if you happen to be on the receiving end of the divorce papers, whatever you do, don't pitch them in the trash can answer them immediately. The response says how the served spouse would prefer to deal with divorce decisions and this is often where all hell will breaks loose, especially if the divorce comes as a surprise.

Trial by a judge

The couple exchanges documents, and other information about issues such as property and income and the kids. By examining this information, the couple and the court can decide how to divide up the property and how to deal with child support and alimony. This can be very emotional so relax and let your lawyer work out the details.

Sometimes, the couple can voluntarily resolve all their issues through mediation or settlement. Some states require that divorcing couples go through this process in an effort to avoid the divorce judicial-process.

If a settlement is reached, the settlement agreement is shown to a judge at an informal hearing. The judge will ask a few basic questions and whether each party understands and chooses to sign the agreement and that nobody was made to sign it or was not there when they were said to have signed-such-a-document.

If the judge approves the agreement, the Judge gives the couple a divorce decree that shows what they have agreed. If he or she does not approve to it, or then the couple does not reach an agreement, the case will go to trial such as 'Kramer vs. Kramer' (a movie with Dustin Hoffman regarding divorce).

At the trial the attorneys will presents evidence and arguments for each side, and the judge decides the unresolved issues, including child custody and visitation, child and spousal support, and property division. Once the judge has reached the decision, the judge grants the divorce and you have to live with it for the better or worse.

Would you like to appeal?

Either spouse can appeal a judge's decision to a higher court. It is unusual for appeals to be overturned by another judge or decision when it comes to divorce. Also, keep in mind that settlements usually cannot be appealed if both spouses agree to the terms so this makes it problematic that an appeal would actually work. In short, take it is a bitter pill if you have to take a judge's decision, but you will have to take the judge's ruling.

Example of not getting a divorce

My mother was never sure about getting a divorce; dad had some mental problems that went back to his childhood. He grew up with the legend of his grandpa, who settled his problems with two shoot-outs. He was born in the mid-1850s where people did such things.

When there was a problem between him and mom he would get out the gun and say I am going to kill both of us. She would give in, thinking he would kill her at the same time, or anyone who would help her. I believe it was personal between him and mom. Mom would back off from leaving him, in reality he got his own way, and that was his primary objective. Who knows how far he would have gone to get his own way. Growing up in the home he never did anything like that, but he always got his own way, he was never challenged by any of us, but we did know he had such feelings.

We see this happening in today's society, where a man kills his wife and then himself. This is a form of mental abuse, and the fear of what a person will do. In a given situation any person might do anything to save their life. In this kind of situation a person is fearful of what another person might do. Is this a good reason for a divorce yes, and they should seek protection first?

There are places for a woman to go to be protected, most states and cities have a "women's shelter".

I went through with a divorce because my mother didn't, so you see my back ground caused me feel divorce is an opinion because of what my dad did to my mother. My daughters have a different view of divorce because of what they went through.

There are many reasons for divorce, and good reasons not to divorce and some do not chose to go that route.

Excessive devotion to in-laws
You married him or her for better life not their drunks, but you have live with the in-laws.

Invariably there are many other reasons to get a **divorce** and this is just a summation of some of the more common ones. The underlying factor in all of these reasons is an infringement upon yourself dignity, well-being, and the right to be in a happy marriage. For whatever reasons, if it causes you to be unhappy and it cannot be worked out through counseling and after considerable effort from both spouses, the divorce could be a window for getting your life back. But, again, I stress it is a serious decision and it will involve pain no matter what benefit you will gain. If there is abuse, verbal abuse, physical or drug abuse, then the pain of divorce will probably be worth it. You owe it to yourself to fight for your well-being and self-respect.

For better or worse the decision has been made

So you have come to the conclusion it is time to end the marriage. Let me remind you once again there are consequences to live with. Having come to that conclusion, it is time to consider how you should plan and execute the **divorce**.

I will emphasize that you will be inclined to want the divorce over with as fast and as painless as possible. However, this thinking can be counterproductive and cause longer lasting pain. It may even add to the painful years it takes to put this difficult chapter behind you. In retrospect you don't want to find yourself thinking if only I could take back the decision, took the time to plan the divorce. The other is preparation it will save you heartaches in the long run; first begin to think of your divorce process in the long term. This way, when the going gets tough - and it will. The guidelines below will show you how to get started.

Healing Your Heart After Divorce   Pages 1 – 2 [18]

"Healing after divorce involves rebuilding your life on your own terms. Begin taking care of yourself again. Just think.........you can arrange the house to your liking......dress to your tastes........even cook the foods he detested. It's exciting choosing your life's direction and doing the things that you refrained from in order to please him.

Start With A Clean Slate. One of the most healing things that you can do is to remove his "stuff" from your life. Why not let him have his favorite recliner, especially if it was never to your liking. Give him all his memorabilia from high school, family, sports and hobbies. All these things really hold no meaning to you, and their presence can bring back painful memories. Start your new life with a clean slate.

Evaluate Your Friendships. Part of this process may mean re-inventing your friendships. Some of your married friends may not feel comfortable with you right now. It's as if your divorce threatens to cause problems in their marriage. They may be jealous of your new found freedom. Try not to take offense. In time, they may come around to accepting the person you are now. Meanwhile, stick with the friends who willingly support your healing and are there for you when you need to rant, rave, and cry. Having a shoulder to lean on can save your sanity at times.

Joining a support group will give you the chance to talk to other people healing from the wounds of divorce. Having a support system can help you cope with the inevitable stress you will face. You can check the paper or your church for any divorce recovery programs being sponsored. The United Way is also a good source or information on support groups, and can also help you locate a shelter if you need one. Click here to look up your local United Way. You can also check out Parents without Partners and Divorce Care for local chapters:

You can also get addition support and information on healing the wounds of divorce by reading: Single Again: A Guide for Women Starting Over. It is an excellent guide to attaining a satisfying lifestyle after divorce or widowhood. For more information on the emotions that you may be face when healing from your divorce, check out the following sections:"

http://www.womensdivorce.com/healing.html   3/9/06

Don't be afraid, may I confess my problem is being very careful because I'm a very loving, compassionate, emotional personal about a relationship. I spent about year in "DivorceCare"

Because I liked the way it was set up and handled. Here is an opening statement from their website:

DvorceCare: Divorce Recovery Support Groups   Page 1 of 1 [19]

"There aren't many people around you who understand the pain of your divorce or what a separation has caused you, even your family, and your friends don't understand. That is the reason for DivorceCare. It's a series of support groups and seminars conducted by people who understand what you are experiencing. Most importantly, you'll learn how to deal with the pain of the past and look forward to rebuilding your life.

There are thousands of groups meeting throughout the US, Canada and in 20 other countries. The **Group Finder** page will help you find a group meeting near you. DivorceCare groups are sponsored by churches. The groups are nondenominational and open to all.

There are two parts to each weekly DivorceCare session. During the first 30-40 minutes of the meeting, the group watches a videotape featuring top experts on divorce and recovery topics. These tapes contain valuable information about recovering from divorce and are produced in an interesting-to-watch television magazine format.

Following the video, the participants spend time as a 'support group,' discussing what was presented on that week's videotape and what is going on in the lives of the group participants."

For more information call 800-489-7778 • International callers dial 919-562-2112

Church Initiative • P.O. Box 1739 • Wake Forest, North Carolina • 27588-1739 • info@divorcecare.org"
http://www.dovorcecare.com/   8/09/07

As you can see I have been through divorce and after the last divorce I knew I had to deal with the healing in my life. I went through an anger stage and went through anger management classes to help get past the anger stage.

How can I know what *you're* thinking because I've been there? I am happy with the decision I've made to get my life back on track, I don't like leaving things unfinished so I did something about my life. There are a lot of web sites on divorce recovery, and I hope you can find some support during and after the divorce.

I have discussed ways to deal with **divorce**, and what can happen during and before, I believe I have been honest, and will continue to do that. I have gotten past the divorce stigma, and put the past behind me, and I am ready to settle down, ready for the right person, I only want a beautiful marriage with a Christian woman and let God be a part of the marriage. My first thought and concern is for a person's happiness.

I believe two people in love should take their time, and get to know each other before and after the marriage. I think a couple should have things in common and be able to settle their differences, if they don't get a long, and if they argue or fight as a couple they won't be happy in the marriage. I believe that is the back-bone for relationships.

I know I am repeating over 65% of remarriages end up in another divorce and almost every remarriage there are two sets of parents with half and even step brothers and sisters. I have been in those situations.

I have seen the time when grandparents and parents do not divorce and they stay together no matter what. Then I lived in the time when divorce was not the answer to every marital problem. It would be nice if our society could protect children from marital problems, but we can't. Now we live in an age of confused adults because they have seen all this transpire as they grew-up and now they are adults. They are trying to work this out in their lives and so are the children. Today, there is a lot more information and counseling along these lines.

I am of the opinion it is a start in the right direction, I believe there is hope in this kind of openness in today's society and I have spent a lot of time in this study with the hopes of helping people understand their life in a better way. I think I have a better understanding of myself and my inner self. I am satisfied that this is the best way to go about helping you and your children deal with divorce.

What do you think of this subject in relation to your relationship?

The experiences in a person's life can make or breaks them, but that molds the life of a child in many ways. You can have two children from the same parents and they are likely to have two different personalities and views on life. There are different views depending on whether a person is a boy or a girl and as they date and marry, some stay single longer looking for the right person to come along.

My life is going to reflect views from both sides of life because I've been single and married. I believe most young people have choices to make in their life and relationship.

All of the guys I knew were married and had good jobs early in life marriage was the driving force in their life in the 60's and 70's it should have been. The time in which I have lived has had an influence on my beliefs. I found this brings about some in decision when a person is not fitting into the age + stage in their relationship. I have done some research along those lines and talked with young people why they married and at what age. This is one of the questions I ask them? What were your priorities when you decided to marry and why, I got different answers depending whether they are a male or female?

Most of the young people I know today do not want to settle down until they get older. When young people pass that stage of restlessness in their teen years, they are in no particular hurry to settle down and raise a family. They are care free, they have their life in front of them and that is their priority, they have established a way of life and a pattern has formed.

The opposite is true with some young girls in high school they believe marriage is the answer to their problems. Why do they want to marry, the driving force in these young girls is to find the right person and getting married after high school. Others who want to go to college have different view as they get older their priorities change because a career is more important for them. They become more like the young men who wanted a career before getting married and having children is not a priority in their 20's. Starting a family is much more important as people get order and out of college, they are in no big hurry at any stage of their life to settle down.

People have the ideal in mind when it comes to love and love is supposed to make a person happy. Then the ideal person is supposed to come along and everything is going to be great for the rest of their lives.

Of course that is a story book ending, and children start out with these fairy tales make believe that adds to the equation of love and marriage.

There is the sharing in a relationship and who is going to share their dream? Don't ask me who that should be, because the ideal man and woman has not happened yet. All I know is two people should share equally in the responsibilities if the marriage is going to work. Each one has their own needs and they need to respect each other's needs. To me marriage is like this, "It is like a bed of roses". It can be beautiful, but "you have to watch out for the thrones" especially in a second marriage.

I have counseled with people with bad relationships, divorced, or dealing with people who have broken up, separated, people who needed help and those who wanted a change. There are services and programs to help people.

I practice living life to the fullest, I exercise, I'm into a health and fitness program, and do that so I can be mentally and psychically healthy, and I'm in good shape I have a great life, I also believe these qualities will add to any person's life.

As you can see I have done all those things to bring about healing in my life. I went through an anger management class to help get past the anger stage.

I have discussed ways to deal with **divorce**, and I believe I have been honest with you. I believe two people in love should take their time, and get to know each other. I believe that is the back bone for relationships.

You are responsible for assessing the degree of depression or other symptoms so that you can decide whether to do marriage counseling. Individual counseling for psychological problems usually damages *the troubled marriage* because the counselor becomes the advocate for the individual client and disturbs whatever tenuous balance of power existed prior to counseling. However, if the client is seriously depressed, marriage counseling may not be what is needed at that time to protect the client. I thus recommend that the client pursue individual counseling (usually with a different therapist so that the depressed client and I will not form a special bond that impedes future marital counseling) until the depression is under control. Then the couple should return for marriage counseling with me.'

If the depression is not severe, I usually treat the couple for marital difficulties and include individual counseling within the marriage counseling. The difficulty is keeping clear who the client is—the marriage or to individual. Confusion can make counseling unfocused and ineffective.

NEW BEGINNINGS III, SINGLE PARENTING, ADOPTION, & BLENDED FAMILIES

Chapter 8

SINGLE PARENTING:

Presenting the problems in single parenting

All parents harbor fears when considering a divorce, but the next step is to look at how single parenting is going to affect the children. This concern is intensified by the developmental, social, and economic costs for the children of divorce. Do not underestimate the traumatic nature of divorce for the children, but over the past twenty years a lot has been said and done to help children going through a divorce. If parents can work with the strengths of their children, many of the day to day struggles can be avoided and the-long-term-consequences-minimized.

Children are resilient, they have an even greater capacity than parents to adapt to changes in their lives, perhaps because they have less fixed ideas of what life will or should bring. There are a number of problems when it comes to dealing with remarriages now they have two sets of parents, to care about them, and can be relied on to be there in good times and bad. No parents whether married, separated, or divorced should do anything to threaten this basic foundation of a child's-emotional-growth-and-development.

If children are treated with the respect most-of-them will cooperate with adults rather than act out against them. Divorce can threaten a child's sense of trust, especially when parents try to make themselves look good. A divorce can turn their children's world apart and could turn their world upside down, parents need to be careful to tell the truth in order to maintain credibility in the months and years to come. When a child learns their parents are not perfect, the parents are the one who lose, not only their willingness to trust their word, but perhaps their ability in their adult life, to trust-anyone.

Children are tremendously adaptable and flexible after-all their whole life is about change. But, unpredictable problems imposed on them problems and can make them feel very vulnerable. Last minute cancellations of an eagerly awaited parental visit, or missed telephone calls are not readily forgiven. If parents know of a change in plan it is inevitable, children appreciate a call and an apology before the event rather than an expensive present as an afterthought. If you need to make changes where your children are concerned, where they go to school, involve them in the planning so they can be active participants. When children can see the funny side of situations, be careful they may be covering up their true feelings, and don't be offended when your kids laugh at a situation they may to do that to cover up their true feelings, whether you burn something or a parent can't do the math homework. Laugh at yourself, they will feel at ease, it is only natural to laugh, stay good natured about the situation. A sense of humor will go a long way in making life more-enjoyable. Children are remarkably accurate in assessments of their parents, especially if one or the other is deceitful, unfaithful, or when it becomes substance abuse, or physically abusive. It is painful enough for them to see the imperfections in their parents. They do not need those faults thrown in their face by the other parent. Bad communication about the other parent, setting up loyal choices, or using your children to spy on their ex will not enhance their opinion of a parent, and in the long run dishonesty will lead to resentment-and-distancing. In most cases the need for support is another aspect after a divorce, sibling relationships often become closer as they share their emotionally changes in the family situation. Children also want to feel needed by their parents rather than feeling in the way. Parents should avoid making excessive demands on their kids, but support them. When requests for help are fair, children will often willingly undertake new responsibilities at home to help a struggling parent. They often feel proud of this new role. However, after the divorce the child become independent or become a parent's helper, or a best buddy this can be an inappropriate, or when parent's expectations become-a-burden.

Given half a chance children will ask questions. However, if their questioning is stopped by false reassurance or embarrassed silences they will retreat into their own world of fantasy, and become less available to participate in solving real day to day problems with you. They need to have the right kind of friends it is essential in their childhood growth and devolvement. Peer groups can be supportive and provide the buffer zone for children. There needs to be stability in their lives in the months following a divorce. Encouraging new relationships and activities is productive, even if these cut into the time you and your children have together. Sometimes divorce provides an opportunity for one parent or the other to establish a stronger bond with their child through a joint hobby or interest, whether it's photography or fishing. Alternatives, if neither parent has time to spare, enrolling the children in a new sport or art activity may introduce them to other children and other interested adults during this time they need outside resources sports, and hobbies.

All of these are understandable. There will be times when things get unbearable and tough getting through this is a tough time for any adult, and we know in our hearts that our children suffer when-they-are-in-distressful-situation.

If that isn't enough, there is solid research that shows parenting judgment gets compromised when they are in such distress. We might pretend to be superwoman or superman to their kids, but in the middle of this…parents do feel it too! Some of the many daily things they are used too were taken for granted…it is just not so easy to do. They don't have the same energy or time. They don't have the same clarity of thinking or they don't have the same emotional strength. (You don't really need a psychologist-to-tell-you-that?)

Over the years as a Clinical Psychologist' I have worked with divorced families, I have spoken to parents and the children need healthy relationships, I see the mistakes other parents have made, I point out the ones they may not see. Many parents are blinded as to the impact of their decisions. Others feel lost, and that is familiar…the deer-in-the-headlight look.as they struggle just to get through each day. Others were more aware of their predicament, and I describe it like a ship lost at sea. In the midst of this, many even asked, "Why don't they have a divorce manual for parents? I-could-really-use-that-one.

They truly felt they had to make a difference I have seen anger and dysfunctional children in dilemmas of getting through a divorce they don't seem to understand their parent's mistakes and some think they caused it. I have also seen remarkable strength, courage and wisdom in children; I am grateful for-my-experiences.

It is with these experiences and many hours counseling I am trying to teach parents how to make a positive difference. I use this information and teach parents how they can do a terrific job despite all of the many challenges they face…day to day. It is true there is no parenting manual for getting through a separation and divorce! You can't substitute love and caring parents to remind all of us of the importance of making decisions that hold those values… how will this decision affects their kids and this is a reminder of the passion it takes to keep people on track.

You Deserve More! Your Children Deserve More!
Parenting-solutions/kids-first   Pages 1 – 2 [20]
The don'ts in parenting"

- Most parents don't intend to express their anger in front of the children, but they do.
- Most of parents don't intend to ever speak disrespectfully of the other parent to their children, but many do.
- Most parents don't intend to undermine the other parent or to argue with the other parent in front of their children, but they do.
- Most parents don't intend to (unknowingly) suggest it's wrong for your child to express your love and excitement for the other parent when they do something right, but many do.
- Most parents don't intend to build walls, healthy child-focused discussions how-ever difficult builds happiness.
- Most parents don't intend to make their anger to show in a child's anger, but it ends up that way.

- Most parents don't intend to put their children in adult roles (because it's upsetting for dad or mom), but they do it all the time.
- Most parents don't intend to have their personal biases blind their judgment about what's going to serve their children, but they do.
- Most parents don't intend to become soft in their parenting so that children get the wrong message, but many do.
- Most parents don't intend to set up two entirely different homes with two entirely different sets of rules and two entirely different sets of expectations, but some do.
- This is only the beginning. Despite good intentions, and a desire to do the right thing, children often end up being caught in the middle of these common types of mistakes made during the separation and divorce.

Even one of the above situations can be emotionally harmful to your child

If one parent can't control (his or her) reactions toward the other parent and to the new situations as a result of the separation or divorce, the child may become the unintentional victim of added stress and anxiety. Children are smart learners and they sense when their parents are sad or in trouble, and to top it off they worry about it, they tend to feel their parent's pain.

Here's the tough part: If it's not clear already, **you first have to manage your own emotions**, and get them under control and out of the way of your judgment in parenting to co-parents. If you don't address this, and you just can't see the damage of your own self-absorbed decisions, and how can the children bring about life long changes that are necessary.

Next, you likely need to learn to be a co-parent…during and after the divorce…than while you were together.

This means discussions about schedules, rules, shared responsibilities and working together (when-possible).

As you go through the co-parenting struggles (trying to do the right thing), differences arise in opinions over parenting issues. Significant differences become huge obstacles at times, to peaceful solutions. How do you resolve those differences? You need a definitive tested and proven guide, such as the "Terrific Parenting Through Divorce" E-book, so you don't have to re-design the wheel every time you sit down to have a discussion. Many people have been down this path, and we know these decisions are common…and what are some of the common mistakes that have devastating consequences for children and families. You can avoid those common mistakes by mastering the information in this chapter.

Finally, any weaknesses in your general parenting approach will become amplified and they will reveal (the weak links in the chain, first don't bend under stress). So it often becomes necessary to add to your parenting skills and help them have a better understanding of how to-shape-and-nurture-their-behavior.

Okay…try to work your way through all this WHILE still struggling with your own anxiety, sadness, guilt, shame, frustration, anger or disappointment. It's tough…"
http://www.terrificparenting.com/parenting-solutions/kids-first.htm?=CMv1980OC640.   8/10/08

Children & Divorce   **Pages 1 -5 [21]**

"While Children of Divorce Do Not Always Experience Problems, There are Significant Negative Differences In Teen Births and High School Dropout Rates Between Children Whose Parents Have Divorced and Those Whose Parents Have Remained Together.

	Two-Parent	Divorce
High School Dropout Rate	13%	31%
Teen Birth Risk	11%	33%

- 73% of children receive a high school diploma and another 12% receive a General Equivalency Diploma (GED). Nevertheless, of the 15% who do not receive a high school diploma, children from divorced families are about twice as likely to drop out of school as children from two-parent families. The differences between these two groups of children are even larger when GEDs are excluded and only high school diplomas are used as indicators of school success. Thus, living in a divorced household increases the risk of dropping out of school, but it is not the primary source of school failure.

The Differences in Outcomes Relate in Part to Differences in the Parents and the Amount of Parental Conflict

- Parents who will later divorce are more likely to have experienced pre-break-up difficulties such as alcoholism, drug abuse, physical and emotional abuse, disagreements about gender roles, and other incompatibilities than those who maintain their marriages. These factors clearly affect children and create marked differences in children's outcomes.
- Also, parental conflict plays a key role in children's well-being. Indeed, parental discord can be more disruptive to children than parental absence through divorce.
- Pre-separation conflict--rather than parental separation itself-- may account for much of the statistical differences between children whose parents have divorced and those whose parents stay together. According to data of the National Survey of Children, the experience of parental separation in and of itself has only modest, statistically non-significant effects when measures of children's prior well-being are taken into account.
- In fact, high conflict in intact homes has been found to produce effects that are similar to and as strong as those associated with marital disruption. Indeed, over time, children in intact but persistently high conflict homes show more deleterious effects than

do children who have experienced divorce but go on to live in a relatively conflict-free post-divorce situation.

- Thus it is not surprising that the effects of marital disruption on children vary according to the level of marital conflict that existed before the divorce. The effects of divorce are found to be more negative if the amount of conflict that precedes the divorce is greater. A high level of post-disruption conflict also aggravates and prolongs the negative effects of divorce.
- Part of the reason for this is that parents engaged in conflict are less consistent in the discipline they provide, have disrupted bonds of attachment with their children, serve as models for negative behavior in their children, and/or place their children under emotional and cognitive stress.

For Affected Children, However, Marital Disruption Has Some Immediate Effects

- In the period immediately following marital breakup, the custodial parent's ability to be a good parent often declines. Many custodial parents, distressed and overburdened, become less supportive and more inconsistent in disciplining their children. In addition, household routines are frequently interrupted, resulting in irregular meals and bedtimes.
- This particularly effects children in the year following the divorce. These effects are in attention somewhat over time, especially if the divorce is followed by the establishment of a unstable conditions, conflicts in the situation and when it includes participation by the non-custodial parent (if this does not involve concomitant conflict).

The *Intermediate* Effects of Divorce in Children *Health*

- Children experiencing the disruption of their parents' marriages tend to have poorer emotional adjustment, including being more anxious, than children not undergoing this experience.

- 14% of children with divorced parents needed psychological help in 1987, according to their parents, and 13% reported that their child actually saw a psychiatrist or psychologist in the past, compared to only 6% and 5.5% respectively, for children in two-parent families.
- Children living with formerly married mothers had a 50% greater risk of having asthma in the preceding 12 months.
- Children from disrupted families showed an increased risk of accidents, injuries and poisoning, and elevated scores for health vulnerability in comparison to those living with both biological parents. The predicted risk of injury was about 20% to 30% greater for children from disrupted marriages than for other children.

Academic Achievement
- Children with divorced parents are more likely to exhibit signs of early disengagement from school than children from intact families.
- Marital disruption is accompanied by increases in truancy and more negative attitudes toward school. Marital disruption appears to be associated with behavioral and affective changes, rather than with changes in more cognitive phenomena like aspirations and grades.
- Children of divorce report lower educational expectations on the part of their parents, less monitoring of school work by both their mothers and fathers, and less overall supervision of school and social activities than children from intact families. The change in parenting practices is strongest for father's monitoring of school work, which reflects the fact that most children live with their mothers after a divorce.
- One possible reason for lower academic achievement is a diminution in income in the custodial parent's household. For example, income differences account for between 30 and 50 percent of the overall difference in high school graduation rates among children from two parent and single parent households.

- Part of the income effect is that a decrease in income frequently leads to an increase in residential mobility. In turn, residential mobility is associated with lower school achievement. Thus, residential mobility and the accompanying disruption of social ties are potentially important mechanisms underlying the lower school achievement of children from disrupted families.
- Moreover, children who move frequently do not receive specialized educational services, nor do they receive the individual attention they may need from teachers in order to identify gaps in their knowledge.

Behavioral Problems
- Children experiencing the marital disruption of their parents' exhibit a disproportionately high range of negative behavioral problems. They can be more oppositional, aggressive, lacking in self-control, distractible, demanding of help and attention, overly dependent, to exhibit anti-social, depressed/withdrawn, or impulsive/hyperactive behavior problems, and to be troublesome at school, and disobedient at home and school.
- In one study, the observed proportion reported to have received professional help for emotional or behavior problems in the preceding year varied from 2.7% for children living with both biological parents to 8.8% for children living with formerly married parents.
- Reduction in family economic resources and standard of living as a consequence of divorce is partly associated with these disruptive and antisocial behaviors especially in boys. Children may be affected by the losses either directly through lower income and assets, or indirectly through maternal stress caused by the economic hardship.
- Following divorce, boys' reveal a disproportionate increase in substance use, which is significantly greater than that of boys with continuously married parents and that of girls from disrupted homes. Girls from disrupted households do not have a proportionately greater increase in substance use than girls with

continuously married parents, although disrupted girls show more frequent substance use before and after the divorce.
- Divorce appears to be particularly hard on adolescents. Children who experienced a parental divorce during adolescence were more likely to be involved in substance use and to report problematic substance use than were children who experienced no divorce or a divorce during their preadolescent years. Adolescents from disrupted families also reported lower psychological well-being, lower self-esteem, lower sense of mastery, higher strain with parents, and more substance use than their counterparts from continuously married families.

Long-Term Effects of Parental Divorce
- The effects of marital discord and family disruption on children are visible 12 to 22 years later in poor relationships with parents, high levels of problem behavior, and an increased likelihood of dropping out of high school and receiving psychological help. Disruption-related problems were at least as evident in adulthood as they had been in adolescence. In the case of mother-child relationships, a significant effect of divorce was evident in adulthood, even when none had been found in adolescence.
- The younger the child at the time of divorce, the greater the likelihood of long term effects. Parental divorce in early childhood (before age 6) poses more long-term risks to a young person's social and emotional development than does parental divorce at later ages.
- Poor relationships with parents are particularly striking during the young adulthood of children with divorced parents. Nearly twice as many young adults in disrupted families (30%) had poor relationships with their mothers as those whose parents remained married (16%). In addition, nearly two-thirds of young adults in disrupted families had a poor relationship with their fathers, compared to 29% of those whose parents had not divorced.

- This is particularly true of mother-daughter relationships. In young adulthood, 29% of women with divorced parents had poor relationships with their mothers compared with 14% of women from non-disrupted families. By contrast, among young men, the proportion with poor relationships with their mothers was roughly the same in divorced and non-divorced families: 19% and 20% respectively.

Gender Differences in the Effects of Marital Disruption
- Boys and girls have strikingly different reactions to a parental divorce. This is especially true during middle childhood and adolescence. Boys are more likely to respond with conduct problems and acting out at home and in schools, whereas girls are more likely to respond with depression and 'over controlled' behavior.

Boys and Divorce
- Although boys from divorced families seem more likely than girls from these families to show consequences such as behavior problems and high school dropout, these differences do not imply that boys are especially vulnerable to the effects of disruption. Rather, the differences can be accounted for by marital disruption and the interaction of gender (boys are generally more prone to these difficulties than girls).
- Boys' self-esteem declines more after divorce than girls'.
- Marital disruption is also associated with declines in socially acceptable behavior for boys, but not for girls.
- The experience of marital disruption lowers boys'--but not girls'-- mathematics and reading performances. However, the adverse effect of divorce for boys' math performance is largely offset when they break-up means the termination of a high-conflict relationship.
- Boys from disrupted families have higher high school dropout rates (28% to 20%) and behavior problems scores (23% to 14%) than girls from disrupted families.

- Boys from divorced homes displayed poorer performance than intact-family males on mental health measures, while there were no differences in these same criteria between divorced- and intact-family girls. Children of divorce, especially boys, evidenced higher frequencies of dependency, irrelevant talk, withdrawal, blaming, and inattention as well as decreased work effort and higher frequencies of inappropriate behavior, unhappiness, and maladaptive symptoms.
- However, some of this effect can be alleviated by parental contact. Divorced-group boys who maintain contact with the father perform better on several mental health measures than those who do not have regular communication.

Girls and Divorce
- Girls' difficulties occur prior to the marital separation and do not change substantially after the divorce, while boys' difficulties increased subsequent to the divorce, especially for substance use.
- Girl's reading achievement is not significantly affected by parental divorce, even when pre-disruption characteristics are considered. But, it is also possible that girls manifest distress in ways that are more difficult to observe, such as by becoming more anxious or depressed or exhibiting over controlled good behavior."

http://www.clasp.org/publications/children_and_divorce.htm 8/04/07

Children of divorced parents are more likely to end their own marriage.

Main Category: Psychology / Psychiatry News   Pages 1 – 5 [22]
Article Date: 28 Jun 2005 - 2:00 PDT

"Children of divorced parents often bitterly vow not to repeat the same mistakes. They want to avoid putting themselves and their own children through the pain that comes from the dissolution of a marriage. But, according to University of Utah researcher Nicholas H. Wolfinger, these children's aspirations face unfavorable odds.

'Growing up in a divorced family greatly increases the chances of ending one's own marriage, a phenomenon called the divorce cycle or the intergenerational transmission of divorce,' says Wolfinger, assistant professor in the University of Utah's Department of Family and Consumer Studies.

Wolfinger has spent a decade studying the marriages of children from divorced homes in America. These children are more likely to marry as teens, cohabitate and marry someone who is also a child of divorced parents. And they are also one-third less likely to marry if they are over age 20.

Wolfinger's new book is devoted entirely to the divorce cycle. 'Understanding the Divorce Cycle: The Children of Divorce in Their Own Marriages,' published by Cambridge University Press, contains important information for those interested in divorce and its repercussions and for policy makers-who-determine-family-and-divorce-law.

'Divorce is an important topic because it has so many consequences for well-being,' writes Wolfinger, also an adjunct assistant professor in the university's Department of Sociology. 'Its transmission between generations adds a whole new dimension by perpetuating the cycle of divorce. The divorce cycle, in short, can be thought of as a cascade. Ending a marriage starts a cycle that threatens to affect increasing numbers of people over time, a sobering thought in an era when half of all new marriages fail.' Wolfinger's research also suggests that if one spouse comes from divorced parents, the couple may be up to twice as likely to divorce. Spouses who are both children of divorced parents are three times more likely to divorce as couples who both hail from intact families.

Besides observing the marital stability of the offspring of divorced couples, Wolfinger's 180-page book provides perspective on how parental divorce affects offspring marriage timing, mate selection, cohabitating relationships as well as historical trends in the divorce cycle. Wolfinger also explores the divorce reform movement in America and argues in favor of no-fault divorce laws, arguing that a return to an age of tough divorce laws would recreate the social conditions that used to make divorce harder on children.

'One reason children from divorced families get divorced more often is because they have a tendency to marry as teenagers,' Wolfinger reports, adding 'the older you are when you marry, the less likely you are to get divorced. It's good advice for everyone.'

On the other hand, the more transitions children experience while growing up, the more they will experience as adults, Wolfinger notes. 'What is the hardest for kids is how many disruptions they experience -- the up-and-down cycles. Many will have stepparents, and some will see their new families dissolve. A disruption occurs any time they lose a parent -- except from death. That's different, and doesn't have the same negative effects on children. Whereas divorce is ambiguous. Children wonder whether the divorce was their fault or who is to blame. And they wonder 'Is he coming back?' Wolfinger writes, 'It is certainly good news that people are less likely to stay in high conflict marriages than they used to.' However, 'ending a low-conflict marriage may hurt children as much as staying in a high-conflict family,' and the odds of divorce transmission are actually highest if parents dissolve a marriage after little or no conflict.

'The most interesting finding,' Wolfinger says, is that 'some of the negative consequences of growing up in a divorced family, including stigmatization, are less severe because divorce has become more common.'

Ultimately, Wolfinger shows that the divorce cycle can primarily be attributed to the lessons children learn about relationship skills and marital commitment, and secondarily to the effects of parental divorce on offspring marriage formation behavior and educational attainment. Wolfinger's research is based on the National Survey of Families and Households, which included detailed information on family background for 13,000 people, and the General Social Survey, which surveyed 20,000 people over a 30-year period."

Nicholas H. Wolfinger, University of Utah Department of Family and Consumer Studies
nick.wolfinger@fcs.utah.edu
801-364-3283

Ann Bardsley, University of Utah Public Relations
abardsley@ucomm.utah.edu
801-587-9183
University of Utah
http://www.ucomm.utah.edu
http://www.medicalnewatoday.com/articals/2614.php8/11/07

Questionnaire IX 14, Critical Situations?
(√ Check those that apply)

1. If your children have experienced open conflicts and at school, most of which remain unresolved?   Yes ____ No ____
2. You (or your spouse) are having difficulty controlling your reaction to the things after the divorce? Yes ____ No ____
3. Do you often feel that the separation or divorce is too much stress and emotional energy or do you feel the need to give in when there is conflict?   Yes ____ No ____
4. You are worried about what to do, when to do it, and how to do it, often leads to repeated delays in taking action, or to hesitate in your parenting and discipline?   Yes ____ No ____
5. Do you feel like you are in some kind of competition for the best parent award, and you don't want it to become game?
                                            Yes ____ No ____

Your children...
  • Pretend nothing is wrong despite their changes?
6. Is there uncertainty in present that makes you feel the in effective or unworthy...and do your children feel the effect of it too?
                                            Yes ____ No ____
7. Is there too much of your time and energy spent on events that are out of your control, and often in your future...does this leave you exhausted and afraid?   Yes ____ No ____
8.   Yes ____ No ____
  • Are you overly affectionate and need excessive reassurances?
                                            Yes ____ No ____
  • Emotionally over whelmed?   Yes ____ No ____
  • Have your kids begun to take sides? Yes ____ No ____
  • Has their behavior deteriorated?
                                            Yes ____ No ____
  • Do they seem unusually angry or saddened?
                                            Yes ____ No ____
9. Do your children feel they live two different lives, can you see

that you are headed in that direction…if you do how can you change things. Yes ____ No ____
Explain Why: _____

The effects on divorced children

Some children go through their parents' divorce with relatively few problems or no permanent negative effects that means the two parents work together. However, if one or more children feel the effects of the divorce can be because of a traumatic experience other than the divorce. Changes in a child's living arrangements may cause lost time with their kids, education and lifestyle can trigger the body's fight-or-flight response – anger or fear. But when a child cannot adequately express or mentally process those emotions, the child may feel extremely powerless and have personal feelings and reactions based on the traumatic impact of a new life.

Trauma is determined by the child's *experience* of the event, not simply the event itself. Different children in the same family may have a dramatically different emotional reactions to the numerous changes related to divorce. Your attitude can shape your children's attitude. Your emotions and actions can either expose your children to unnecessary emotional pain or help them develop a positive attitude.

I think my children came out of our divorce very well, that does not mean there were no problems, but they had a healthy attitude about life. I have discussed all this with them sense they have married and are on the own. As dad I had a different role, I was there for them when they needed me. I never ran down their mother, but we have talked openly about her and the divorce, and why we divorced. No that does not mean I tell them everything that happened. Each one has a different view of the divorce, and they understand and they don't blame me for the divorce. It was a troubled marriage from the beginning, and I will not take time to go into the details because I have already done that earlier chapters.

Now let's see if we can find some good things to help you with your children after the divorce.

Profiling challenges conflicts in divorced children

Parents of both the children avoid or become ambivalent over the children, can happen after the stress of a difficult marriage and/or divorce, turn to their children for emotional support. The children may offer it, and become enmeshed in their parent's emotional feelings some are more sensitive to emotional distress while others care less. Alternately, they may reject the parent who is emotional and try to disconnect themselves from the family as much as possible.

The key to understanding how children adjust to divorce is the issues with the parental conflicts. Children need supportive co-parenting; this means that parents must cooperate well to see that the children's needs are met. The children do not need parents who fight and argue with each other, or in front of the children.

For example, criticizing the absent parent in front of the children, or offering the condemning comments, you're just like your father/mother. Since the custodial parent has expelled the absent parent from their life for reasons brought out in the divorce, at least in the child's mind it stands to reason that the child too could have problems relating to the conflict brought into the family.

Previous studies show that parental interactions after the divorce were marked by anger and conflict. The conflicts drop significantly after the first two years for most divorced families, but in some cases the level of stress after two years remains very close to the level of distress soon after the divorce. Witnessing conflicts between the parents is very disruptive to children's adjustment. Children exposed to conflict are more likely to have behavioral and emotional disturbances, suffer social and interpersonal problems, and show impairment in their thought process and reasoning processes. Numerous studies have shown prolonged marital conflicts affects the child for years, as opposed to short-term conflict in times of short-term stress, it is a very good predictor of the child's behavior problems in the future. The prediction of miss behavior *grows* after the divorce; that is to say, parental conflict are more likely to lead to emotional and behavioral problems after a divorce. When conflicts escalate to physical levels, the children are 500% to 600% more likely to have severe behavioral problems, and those who are abused are-more-likely-to-be-bullies.

Why do conflicts cause problems, even verbal conflicts produce these kinds of conflicts? Children are exposed to all sorts of emotions during conflicts, such as anger, apathy, and alienation. Children are like sponges in some ways and easily soak up the emotions around them, especially when the arguments center about them, their behavior and their need for help. They become overwhelmed and confused, and may feel a need to side with one parent and intervene trying to stop the arguing. This is more likely when arguments quickly escalate from small quibbles to huge fights. The adrenaline levels are elevated, their heart rate increases, and their blood pressure rises. As noted, when depression or alcohol is used reaches clinically significant levels..

When alcohol and drugs are a part of the problem there is an emotional adjustment because there are more conflicts, the children are unable to adjust. Parents are unable able to maintain consistent structure in the children's lives, children do respond to their parent's rejection, resentment, and confusion. When parents argue over child-rearing issues, and when they reach an agreement parents need to come to a compromise, children show much less anxiety, insecurity, and- when parents are able to do that.

The key element in the children may be when the problem started before the divorce. The amount of conflict before the divorce is in direct correlation to the problems after the divorce. These parental conflict serves as a general stressor to a child's environment and can threaten a child's sense of security.

I am talking about the conflicts and difficulties that lead to the divorce. However, they are usually set in motion well before the family actually separates, and when this disruption does occur, the events that follow have been described as the "crisis period", characterized by dramatic changes in the children's day to day lives. Adolescents experience conflicts in families are more likely to demonstrate antisocial tendencies, commit delinquent acts, and don't do well in school.

Still another concern is the effect that a highly violent household may have on a child's formation of (his or her self) and in further relationships with others. In some cases children often model or do the opposite and become over achievers while others have behavioral problems. Therefore, an aggressive husband may influence the male children to be aggressive and act like they are under-control, or externalize their behaviors by being rude. In turn, many female children witness aggression toward their mother's; others may form ideas of submissiveness to others and let them control them. Some become disobedient in their relationships as well males formulate unhealthy sexual roles, while others feel they are victims.

These studies do prove a point the state of the marriage has a lot to with how children do in school, why? Because if there is less conflict in the marriage, couples that don't get a divorce do better, but if it translates to, too much stress in the family, then there is usually a divorce. Especially young children offer and enhance marital stability, but do create stressors, and everyday drudgery are often more than a parental relationship can withstand.

These average stressors alone can create some chaos, turmoil and eventually lead to marital strain, discord and divorce. This can set off a chain of negative events and transitions that are psychological behaviors in the children, and may be more of a problem than the physical separation of parents. If there is too much stress it impairs a parent's ability to effectively raise their children. Thus the parent's psychological state of mind makes it more difficult, at times it can lower their ability to support their children needs, and negatively impacting a child's overall well-being. Many couples believe they should not divorce no matter how much conflict there is in the household, the divorce would be so strenuous on their children. Some divorce for other reasons some are more likely to stay together for the "sake of the children" than dissolve a marriage and there is a lot to be said for that argument. If the parents can cut out the conflict, child or children will be much better off staying with the marriage.

While critical decisions are made by couples to stay together for what they may perceive as the "best" option, the fighting, stress and chaos needs to stop. If it continues or worsen in the household and has not improved over extended period of time and if the result causes complications in the children's mental health and stability, the children really need to be the number one consideration as an option.

This continued chaos can in fact cause more stress and harm to a child's well-being than the actual divorce that many parents have tried to avoid. The effect of parental conflict can be more harmful to children than parental absence through death and divorce. There is evidence as well that proves being exposed to a high degree of conflict between married parents places children at risk for a variety of problems similar to those caused by the divorce itself.

I have presented data and views supporting the stress caused by chaos and conflict prior and after the divorce itself. I have presented the different ways that children are affected before and after the divorce itself and the effects of bad relationships, the potential threat of divorce may affect a child's adjustment and mental well-being, the effects that a divorce may have on a child's later marriage and their own family.

Past evidence supports these findings a child who is well adapted, self-confident, and secure in who they are and when they are raised in a two parent home as opposed to a single parent household. This is a logical thought as children do benefit from receiving support from both parents whether they are divorced or not. What is not included in this line of thinking, in order for a child to excel and completely benefit from a two parent household these families must prove to be "harmonious" and have a well-rounded marriage.

A summary of single parenting after divorce

Regardless how you look at your relationship there is hope and it will improve the child's outlook on life they will be healthier over time. Especially in relation to the child's custodial or residential parent, usually a mother's poor parental skills will do more harm than a dad's poor parenting skills both have an effect on the child. Also divorce erodes the children's effective ties with their fathers more than their mothers, and children that spend time in a single parent home are considerably more likely to keep in close contact with their residential parent rather than their non-residential parent.

Most divorcing parents are understandably concerned about the custody status and how to deal with it. It is good for children to define how the major decision-making has responsibilities that will need to be addressed, where they will live and stay when they visit the other parent. However, what primarily impacts the children's lives is not their custody status, but the schedule of time that they spend with each parent, that is the nuts and bolts of it. They should have a say in the time and how much time depending on the age of a child. Teen scheduling will largely depend on what they are involved in. Think of it as a blueprint for the children's custodial care, planning document should be a much more comprehensive than the typical visitation agreement. A successful parenting plan needs to incorporate sufficient details to ensure children will not experience ongoing arguments and conflicts between their parents about the arrangements they are putting in place.

Helping Children Adjust to Divorce Pages 1 - 7 [23]

(...) "While some researchers see a grim outlook for many children of divorce, they also recognize that children are not necessarily headed for a life of hardship and unhappiness. Most children are resilient and go on to find happiness and success both at home and at the workplace. In her longitudinal study lasting 25 years, Dr. Mavis Hetherington (2002) compared divorced families with intact families:

Twenty-five percent of youth from divorced families in comparison to10% from non-divorced families did have serious social, emotional, or psychological problems. But most of the young men and women from my divorced families looked a lot like their contemporaries from non-divorced homes. Although they looked back on their parent's breakup as a painful experience, most were successfully going about the chief tasks of young adulthood: establishing careers, creating intimate relationships, building meaningful lives for themselves. (p. 7)

So a healthy majority of children – three-quarters – went on to lead happy and healthy lives after experiencing the divorce of their parents. Studies show that about 90% of children raised in intact homes lead generally happy lives. The 15% difference is significant, indicating that children are at a greater risk following a divorce, but the great majority become happy, healthy, and functioning members of society.

Children's Reactions to Divorce by Developmental Stage

Children experience and react to divorce differently depending on their age. As a parent, you can better help your children adjust to divorce if you know what to expect in each age range. Below are key developmental milestones of children and recommendations from experts about how to help children of each age as they experience divorce (Debar; Gable, 2002; Knudson-Martin, Christopher, & Duncan, 1997; Long & Forehand, 2002; Marten, 1994).

Infants

Infants are highly sensitive to their parents' moods and emotional states. If their parents are in distress, infants may be more irritable, fretful, and anxious. They may lose their appetite, change their sleeping patterns, and change other routines. As a parent, you can help by maintaining a consistent routine, being loving and affectionate, and responding physically and emotionally to your children.

Toddlers

Toddlers notice the absence of a parent but can't comprehend the meaning behind the absence. They may have difficulty separating from the parent who no longer lives in the home, crying more and clinging. They may regress to infant behaviors of thumb sucking or needing diapers. They may also show more anger and have trouble sleeping. Toddlers need you to be reassuring and nurturing. Be understanding if they regress to infant behaviors. Be consistent and stick to routines.

Preschoolers

Preschoolers don't understand what divorce means, but they realize that one parent is not living at home. They may feel angry and may blame themselves for the separation. They grieve over a parent's absence and may develop elaborate fantasies of reuniting their parents. You should make sure your children understand that they are not responsible for the divorce, and they will always be loved and taken care of. Regular and predictable contact with both parents is important.

Early Elementary

At this age children begin to understand that a divorce means their parents won't live together and don't love each other as they once did. Most feel a sense of loss. They often feel rejected by the parent who is absent. They tend to worry about the future. They may show physical symptoms such as headaches, stomach aches, and difficulty sleeping. Be sensitive to signs of depression such as a withdrawal from long-time friends and favorite activities, fears about the future, and feelings of rejection. Be open with children this age about the changes caused by the divorce, encourage your children to talk about their feelings, and be a good listener. Reassure your children that divorce is not their fault. Keep a consistent routine. Plan specific times for your children to be in contact with both parents. Reinforce that the divorce is a final decision.

Preteens and Adolescents

Children this age understand divorce but do not want to accept it or the changes it brings. They may feel angry and abandoned. Adolescents may show extremes in behavior. Some become moralistic and the "perfect angel" child. Others become rebellious and troubled, getting involved with drugs, alcohol, or shoplifting. Teenagers often worry about whether they will be able to form meaningful relationships in the future. They may worry about taking on adult responsibilities and being forced to grow up too soon. You need to talk openly with adolescent children about *their* feelings and concerns, but not about difficulties between you and your ex-spouse. Make sure your child's responsibilities are appropriate to their age and that they are not being compelled to grow up too quickly. Be a consistent parent and stay involved in your child's life.

Becoming an Effective Post-Divorce Parent

How well you as a parent manage conflict and become an effective co-parent after divorce has a tremendous impact on how well your children fare after divorce (Knudson-Martin et al., 1997). To encourage quality parenting, some states have passed legislation that allows judges to mandate educational programs for divorcing parents. These programs teach parents about children's common reactions to divorce, about how to move forward after divorce, and about how to keep the best interests of children in mind. They also teach communication skills and conflict management so that divorcing parents can minimize divorce battles. Even if your state does not require you to attend such a program, it would be wise to find a course in your area and enroll.

Ideas for Reducing the Impact of Divorce on Children

Research shows that many of the harmful effects of divorce can be lessened when parents make a concerted effort to keep the best interests of their children as their first priority. Here are some ideas that can help children adjust to divorce:

- **Practice positive parenting.** According to researchers Hetherington and Kelly (2002), 'Parenting is not only the most important but often the sole protective social factor in a very young child's life' (p. 126). Much of the negative effects of divorce are mediated by good, quality parenting (Hetherington & Stanley-Hagen, 1999). 'Children need parents who are warm and supportive, communicative, responsive to their needs, exert firm, consistent control and positive discipline, and monitor their activities closely' (Hetherington & Stanley-Hagen, 1999, p. 134).

- **Maintain a stable routine.** According to Tiber, (2001), 'Children adjust better when parents can keep as many things as possible constant in their lives' (p. 19). Providing a sense of structure and stability is essential for children's well-being (Ricci, 1997). They feel more secure when they have consistency and predictability in their lives. Continue routines such as bedtime rituals, reading books together, and celebrating birthdays and holidays. Make every effort to keep your children in the same school and neighborhood (Duncan, 1999).

- **Help your children share and deal with their feelings.** Children of divorcing parents experience a wide range of emotions, including fear, sadness, anger, guilt, rejection, and loneliness. Your children will need time to mourn their lost family and adjust to new circumstances. Outbursts of anger, such as tantrums and shouting, are normal. Encourage your children to talk about their feelings by acknowledging their feelings and empathizing with them. Offering solutions is not always necessary. Just hearing your children out can be helpful. For very young children, talking about feelings is difficult. They might communicate more easily by drawing a picture.

If your children don't want to talk to you, encourage them to talk with someone else, such as a teacher, family friend, or another family member, such as an aunt, grandmother, or grandfather (Benedick& Brown, 1995; Marten, 1994; Parents Without Partners).

- **Reassure children that the divorce is not their fault.** Many children believe they are the cause of their parents' divorce. Often they think that if they had behaved better or done better in school, Mom and Dad would still be together. Bussel reports that 'children who place some of the blame for the divorce on themselves tend to be more poorly adjusted' (cited in Amato, 2000, p. 1281). Reassure your children that the divorce is not their fault. The decision to divorce is made by adults, not by children. Parents should never blame a child for a divorce. You should also be careful that family matters are not discussed within hearing of children. If a child overhears conversations, he can easily misinterpret what is said. When telling your child about the divorce, and in all conversations thereafter, be sure to choose your words with sensitivity and care (Long & Forehand, 2002).

- **Practice positive discipline.** Positive and consistent discipline is essential for raising healthy children. The guilt that some divorced parents feel sometimes causes them to indulge their children, which can compound the harmful effects of divorce. Children thrive under loving, positive discipline, so be sure you set proper limits and provide guidance. Be clear about what behavior is acceptable, what is not acceptable, and what the consequences are for non-compliance. Consistently impose consequences. Also, listen to your children and work together as you set limits and make compromises when you disagree. Be sure you recognize good behavior and praise your children often. Use discipline to teach, not to punish (Long, 2002). When your children misbehave, separate the deed from the doer, allow your child to experience the consequences of his or her actions, and practice forgiveness (Marston, 1994; Benedek & Brown, 1995).

- **Keep both parents involved.** Shared custody usually serves children best, as long as parents can negotiate and get along. Parents who are constantly in conflict, however, make shared custody miserable for children. Whatever the living arrangement, each parent should encourage involvement of the other. Work as a team to ensure that the needs of each child is met. While this might be difficult, remember that your children didn't make the decision to divorce, and it is your obligation to make sure the effects of that decision caused the least hurt possible. Studies show that "the longer the time since the divorce, the less involved the noncustodial parent is in his child's life" (Long, 2002, p. 83). To keep this from happening, each parent should keep the other informed about each child. Instruct schools to send information to both homes. Research indicates that non-residential fathers are more likely to continue both contact and child support when they feel they have their share of control over decision making (Hetherington & Stanley-Hagen, 1999).

- **Help children maintain positive relationships with both parents.** Children want both their parents. When your child wants to spend time with the other parent, don't see it as rejection of you but as a healthy desire to stay connected to both Mom and Dad. Encourage your children to enjoy time with the other parent. When they come back, encourage them to talk freely about what they did and share in their happiness when they had a good time. Help your child acknowledge birthdays and special occasions for the other parent. If you support the parenting of the other partner, you'll make it easier for him or her to have a good relationship with your children. (Ricci, 1997; Duncan, 1999; Marston, 1994).

- **Don't put your child in the middle—allow him to love both parents.** Your children want to love both Mom and Dad. "If your children know you both, and have lived with you both, then they love you both" (Ricci, 1997, p. 140). Don't put them in a situation where they have to choose between you or your ex-spouse. Asking your child "Do you want to live with me or your daddy?" puts him in a no-win situation, because by choosing one parent he is forced to reject the other.

- **Don't use your child as a go-between.** Don't send messages to your ex-spouse through your child or ask your child for information about your ex-spouse. Keep adult communications direct between adults. You and your ex-spouse should communicate directly with each other rather than through your child (Morgan & Coleman, 2002). Control your emotions and restrain yourself from saying negative things about the other parent in front of your child. If your child complains about his other parent, encourage him to talk directly with that parent (Long & Forehand, 2002; Knudson-Martin et al., 1997).

- **Allow your child to be a child.** Children need their parents to be the grownups. While some responsibility is good for children, they should not be expected to counsel you, comfort you, make meals for the family, or be your sounding board about important decisions. Take stock of the responsibilities that you have given your child, and make sure the tasks are appropriate (Ricci, 1997). Parents are supposed to support their children, not the other way around. Don't burden your child with information that she is too young to handle, don't expect her to take on adult responsibilities, and don't depend on her as though she were a peer (Long, 2002). Rely on friends and family of your own age and maturity. "Asking a child for an opinion is important on some issues. " (Ricci, 1997, p. 138).

- **Spend time with your child.** Spend one-on-one time with each child regularly (Marston 1994). While time demands are tremendous for single parents, spending focused time with each child is invaluable to their growth and development. Be an "ask able" and approachable parent. Let your child know that he can always come to you with any concerns he may have. Tell your child often that he will continue to be loved and taken care of (Benedek& Brown, 1995; Long, 2002; Welker, 2002)."

Additional Reading
Ahrons, C. (1994). *The good divorce;* New York: HarperCollins.
Long, N., & Forehand, R. (2002). *Making divorce easier on your child: 50 effective ways to help children adjust.* New York: McGraw-Hill.
Ricci, I. (1997). *Mom's house, dad's house: A complete guide for parents who are separated, divorced, or remarried.* New York: Simon & Schuster.
Teyber, E. (2001). *Helping children cope with divorce.* San Francisco: Jossey-Bass.
Websites http://parentswithoutpartners.org

References
Amato, P. R. (2000). The consequences of divorce for adults and children. *Journal of Marriage and the Family, 62*, 1269-1287.
Benedek, E. P., & Brown, C. F. (1995). *How to help your child overcome your divorce.* Washington, DC: American Psychiatric Press.
DeBord, K. *Focus on kids: The effects of divorce on children.* Retrieved July 5, 2002, from North Carolina Cooperative Extension Service: http://www.ces.ncsu.edu/depts/fcs/human/pubs/effectsdivorce.html.
Duncan, S. F. (1999). *Families facing divorce.* Retrieved July 2, 2002, from Montana State University Extension Service: http://www.montana.edu/wwwpb/pubs/mt9514.html.
Gable, S. Helping children understand divorce. Retrieved July 5, 2002, from:http://muextension.missouri.edu/xplor/hesguide/humanrel/gh6600.htm#momdad.
Hetherington, E. M., & Kelly, J. (2002). *For better or for worse: Divorce reconsidered.* New York: W.W. Norton & Company.
Hetherington, E. M., & Stanley-Hagen, M. (1999). The adjustment of children with divorced parents: A risk and resiliency perspective. *Journal of Child Psychology and Psychiatry, 40,* 129-140.

Knudson-Martin, Christopher, J. & Duncan, S. F. (1997). *Parenting through divorce: Helping your children through your divorce.* Bozeman, MT: Montana State University Extension Service.

Long, N., & Forehand, R. (2002). *Making divorce easier on your child: 50 effective ways to help children adjust.* New York: Contemporary.

Marsten, S. (1994). *The divorced parent: Success strategies for raising your children after separation.* New York: William Morrow.

Morgan, M., & Coleman, M. *Focus on families: Divorce and adults.* Retrieved July 2, 2002, from University of Missouri-Columbia, Department of Human Development and Family Studies: http://muextension.missouri.edu/xplor/hesguide/humanrel/gh6601.htm.

Parents Without Partners. *Practical parenting...tips to grow on.* Retrieved July 5, 2002, from: http://www.parentswithoutpartners.org/Support2.htm.

Ricci, I. (1997). *Mom's house, dad's house: a complete guide for parents who are separated, divorced, or remarried.* New York: Simon & Schuster.

Simons, R. (1996). *Understanding differences between divorced and intact families.* Thousand Oaks: Sage.

Teyber, E. (2001). *Helping children cope with divorce.* San Francisco: Jossey-Bass.

Waite, L. J., & Gallagher, M. (2000). *The case for marriage.* New York: Broadway Books.

Wallerstein, J. S. (1991). The long-term effects of divorce on children: A review. *Journal of the American Academy of Child and Adolescent Psychiatry, 30*, 349-360.

Welker, J. E. *What parents can do to help children adjust to divorce.* Retrieved July 5, 2002, from Ohio State University Extension Fact Sheet: http://ohioline.osu.edu/hyg-fact/5000/5160.html.

NEW BEGINNGS III, THE ROLE OF STEP PARENTS

Chapter 9

STEPPARENT'S AND ADOPTED PARENTSROLE

My personal profile as a stepparent

I have been a stepparent I will start with the role of a stepfather because I married a women with three children; their father had died at the age of 28 from a heart attack. This does not make it any easier, because she had children I was a stepfather. The early adjustments went fine, because I had never had children before I didn't have any hang-ups. The boy was 13 and we got along very well, he even called me dad. The old girl 11 she didn't know what to call me at first, hay or hi. The youngest was 4 at the time and I was dad right off the bat. The mother helped set the role of each child.

About a year late we have our first child, a girl, then the twins came about four years later, I always thought of them as a brother and sisters to my children. But, the older boy and girl marry and are on their own after a few years. That left the 4 year old to grow up as one family. They have all married now, and the relationships are not as close over the years for two my girls have little to nothing to do with their older half brother and sister, but one of my daughter's still keeps in touch with one of the half-sisters and I still keep with the three of them on face book.

The second time I became a stepparent, we married and she had a 5 year old boy and a 3 year old girl, and he called me dad from the start because he wanted a father in his life. I will say the girl was much like the older daughter in the previous marriage, she never called me dad and that was ok. They had visitation every other weekend, and I think it caused a bigger problem for their mother. She had some anxiety when the kids went to visit their dad. She always bought them a gift when they came home; I think she carried it a little too far. My kids came once a month because of the distance.

I stayed out of the role of a disciplinarian in the second marriage, because I was not their father. I was active in their life in every other way. Coached little league and basketball, went to school functions, and teachers meeting.

In the first marriage I was the disciplinarian because I took on the father's role with her kids and my girls. There are a couple reasons they did not have dad, and both sets of kids lived in the house. One set of parents which set the stage for the family.

The second marriage my kids came for visitation, when there was a problem my kids never did anything right, in her eyes it was always my kids fault if there was an augment among the kids. But, for the most part it caused problems on the weekends they were there. My kids didn't really like her because she picked on them for whatever reasons, and I didn't blame them when they got into trouble they came to me; it was my time to be with them and I loved our time together. I am not going into any more details because that is not necessary other than to let a person know firsthand what divorced families go through.

Now let's look at some web sites and see if this does fit into what others have to say about being a stepparent. Both marriages lasted about eleven years, after a few years the honey noon is over, after ten years the problems are real problems.

A Stepparent's Role   **Pages 1 – 2 [24]**

"As a stepparent, you may face difficulty fitting into the new family. Since you may be viewed as an 'outsider,' you may encounter surprisingly stiff resistance to your inclusion in the family, in the form of unexpectedly powerful and negative feelings such as jealousy and resentment, as well as your own confusion and sense of inadequacy. Your role in the family, especially early on, is ill-defined and you may end up trying out several different roles before finding one that fits. While the lack of a definition can be stressful and confusing, it also gives you the freedom and latitude to determine a role all of your own.

It's important that you and your spouse decide together the best way for you to be involved as a stepparent. In many families, stepparents take on a role that is less 'parental.' For example, when my stepfather entered our family, three of the children were grown and two were teenagers. Pete took on the role of playmate and skill teacher, introducing my brother and me to tennis and woodworking. However, if our family had consisted of younger children, a more nurturing involvement on his part would have made more sense.

Experts agree the most important thing is to establish a relationship with your stepchildren that is mutually satisfying. Here are some suggestions for doing just that.

• Give yourself and your stepchildren time to get to know one another. Relationships develop slowly, so allow lots of time for bonds to form. Spend time getting to know each stepchild one-on-one without competition from biological parent-child relationships. It's natural for stepchildren to resist this at first. During that one-on-one time, do things that you both enjoy.

• Hold realistic expectations for yourself. Resist the myth of instant love. Don't expect that you will automatically love your stepchildren or that they will love you. If love develops, super! But aim for mutual respect. You may fall victim to rejection and displaced hostility from your stepchildren. Thus, you may occasionally feel as if your stepchildren don't like you, which may make you hesitant and uncomfortable. Try assuming an "as if" position, where you act toward your stepchildren as if they really cared for you. Try not to take their displaced reactions too personally. Remember that you come into the family after the children are likely to have experienced many losses. It will take time for stepchildren to warm up to someone new.

• Don't expect stepchildren to call you 'Dad' or 'Mom.' Instead, let the children decide on what to call you. Some children choose to call their stepparent 'Father Bill' or 'Mother Julie' or some other term that is comfortable for them. However, most children, except those who were very young when the stepparent entered the family, call their stepparent by their first name.

- Share skills and interests you have that might interest your stepchildren. These abilities and aptitudes will distinguish you from the other parents and reduce the likelihood that you will be viewed as competing with the biological parents. For example, in my family my stepfather taught us tennis and entered us in tournaments. We played and watched a lot of tennis together. He was also a master woodworker.
- Leave the disciplining role to the biological parent, and support the parent in this and other areas behind the scenes. As respectful relationships form, the time may come that you can successfully share this role with your spouse. It is quite appropriate that the biological parent allow the stepparent to participate in decisions and activities surrounding discipline as the stepparent-stepchildren relationships develop. If you and your spouse have difficulty coming to an agreement on discipline and parenting, take a parenting class together. Forge an approach that fits your family's needs.
- Stepparents have little or no legal responsibility for their stepchildren. The biological parent is wise to give you legal permission to act when necessary, especially in the case of an emergency.
- Show interest in and involve yourself in a nonintrusive way in stepchildren's activities, interests, and accomplishments. Attend concerts, praise specific achievements, and do other things that show you care and are proud of your stepchildren. Be involved in school, religious, sports, and other activities with the family.
- Look for ways to send messages to stepchildren that you trust them. For instance, allowing teens to borrow your car for a date might be a nice way to build a connection. And the favor will probably not be forgotten.
- Don't play favorites. You will almost certainly have closer, stronger feelings for your own children than your stepchildren. But if you want to build connections with your stepchildren, you must

separate your actions from your feelings. Treat your stepchildren with the same respect and consideration you show your own children, even though real caring has not yet developed.

- Don't attempt to replace or compete with the absent parent and never badmouth him or her. As one stepfather put it, 'If stepparents try to set themselves up as equal parents, they set themselves up for failure.'
- Find groups supportive of stepfamilies. Communities may have an ongoing stepfamily support group, or one could be organized. Support groups bring people together who share similar concerns to encourage and learn from one another. If a support group is not available in your area, the Stepfamily Association of America (**www.stepfam.org**) can provide assistance to you to help you organize a local chapter. Contact them at (800) 735-0329. (…)"

http://www.foreverfamilies.net/xml/articales/step_stepparents_role.aspx?&publication=short   8/05/2007

Step-parents **Pages 1 – 3 [25]**
Stepmothers (and Stepfathers too)
Copyright 1998 by Douglas Darnall, Ph.D.

"If you decide to marry a parent with children, there are some things you have to accept as a reality. It is part of the baggage parents bring with them into the marriage. To begin with, children will want to spend time alone with their parent without your presence. Many times the parent will want to put their children's needs before yours. Standing the background is a biological mother or father. She or he could have very strong feelings about you that have nothing to do with you as a person or stepparent. The biological parent could be jealous of your time with the children, fear your discipline, hate their ex, and distrust your motives. However unfair or unjustified these problems appear, you and your spouse have to deal them while trying to not get the children caught in the middle.

Child support is important. Stepparents should not in anyway interfere with visits and child support responsibilities. It must be remembered by all, that parents are more likely to pay child support if they have an ongoing active relationship with their children.

Step-parents:

- Stepparents must move slowly with the stepchildren. Remember most of the time the children didn't ask you to be there. You are intruding into their world, a place of familiarity and security.
- If you are having problems with the stepchildren, discuss these problems with your spouse privately, not within earshot of the children. Keep in mind that children are nosey and will listen through the walls.
- Regardless of your feelings about your biological counter-part, don't make derogatory comments about the other parent to the children. This is alienating and damaging to the child and your relationship with the child. The child will usually want to defend the targeted parent but will avoid saying anything because that's easier than confronting you. Children live by a simple principle, went uncomfortable, avoid. Don't be fooled by their silence. You will probably not hear their thoughts. They will have opinions and feelings about what you say. You just won't know what they are thinking.
- Your stepchildren still need time alone with their biological parent. Don't always feel like you have to be involved with what they are doing.
- Until the children know and accept you, don't be overly demonstrative with their parent. Kids watching the two of you cuddle and kiss can be embarrassing and 'gross' (That's what the kids tell me).
- A biological parent's feelings will be influenced by what the children say about you. Kids, like adults, are quicker to complain than say good things, especially if they believe their mother

doesn't want to hear about what a wonderful person you are to them. Don't be overbearing when communicating with the biological parent. Be pleasant and maintain self-control over your feelings. If there are important issues to be discussed with the biological parent about the children, biological parents rather than you should have these conversations. Perhaps after a period of time and you develop a good relationship with the biological parent; you can become a more active participant. I have found that many problems with stepmothers when the stepmother becomes overbearing, tries to take control while the father passively sits by and says nothing.

- Do not expect to just take over the management of the house and set the rules when you move into your new spouse's home. Rules and expectations about each family member's responsibilities must be discussed and negotiated. If a new stepparent moves in like a bulldozer and plans to rebuild the family structure, (he or she) is heading for big trouble with both the stepchildren and new spouse. Stepparents must move slowly and be sensitive to everyone's feelings.

- Children should not be expected to keep your secrets. Assume that whatever you do in your household, they will tell their biological parent. After all, what is it to you, it is your house so both should care about it?

- Your stepchildren come from a very different world than what you are familiar with. They were possibly exposed to different values. Don't go into this step parenting thing with the idea that you know best and you are going to remake the children into what you think is best. First of all, you don't have this right and secondly, you will be heading for disaster.

Stepparents and new romantic partners can all get caught up in the problems between two warring parents. This creates a perfect breeding ground for alienation because significant others frequently believe they have to take a side. Stepparents can be a tremendous source of support and love for their spouse and the stepchildren

without getting caught up in these issues. What is best for children is when stepparents and biological parents treat each other with mutual respect and concern for the children. Parents who are able to keep parent/stepparent conflicts from the children will have a better overall adjustment to the divorce and new family. Patience is a must for the successful stepparent."
http://www.parentalalienation.com/stepparents.htm   8/20/07

Parents On A step-Parents   Pages 1 – 2 [26]

"My parents divorced when I was five, and I acquired step-parents, step-sisters, and a half-brother -- making me an oddity in the 1950s. Today, the step-family is fast becoming the normal family unit.

People are often in their second or third marriages, with children from previous unions, plus biological children from their current marriage.

I talked with Jean McBride and Mary Robertson, marriage/family therapists, who offer workshops and counseling for divorced and remarrying families.

According to them, today's statistics show that 50 percent of first marriages end in divorce; 80 percent of divorced or widowed people remarry within three to five years -- and those unions can be vulnerable to divorce without therapy intervention.

However, Jean and Mary emphasize the positive behind these depressing figures. Divorce is often best for all parties. No longer is there a stigma attached to the step-family; in fact, there is greater acceptance of all types of family units. The wicked step-mother portrayed in fairy tales is more of a myth than reality -- the step-family scenario can be quite successful.

Advice for Step-Parents

- Education yourself on what being a step-parent means; it is different from the role of a biological parent. Join a support group or

read books on the topic. Recommended is 'Step-Family Realities' by Margaret Newman. Contact the Step-Family Association of America, out of Lincoln, Nebraska. Step-parents themselves, the group offers a newsletter, catalogue of books, conferences and on-call counseling. Call 402-477-STEP.
- Work on your relationship with your spouse -- for the couple is the architect of the family. Discuss expectations and problems that arise.
- Introduce children to a possible mate gradually during dating. After marriage, realize that it will take time (from 18 months to two years) for children and adults to get acquainted and adjust. After all, it was the adults who fell in love with each other, not the kids.
- Be flexible and understanding in your expectations, demands and time. Situations can be even more complicated with two sets of step-parents, step-children, and half-brothers and sisters. Biological parents and children need time together, as well as the newly formed family unit. Responding to individual needs is even more important when mates bring adolescent children to a new union. The teenager's goal is for autonomy, at the same time that a new family requires greater togetherness to bond.
- Make your mate's job as step-parent as easy as possible. Remind children that he/she should be treated with respect. Remember that the biological mate has the primary responsibility. A step-parent shouldn't be a co-equal with the biological parent in terms of discipline; this could be a set-up for failure. But the step-parent can be empowered to deal with situations when necessary. Use a family conference to establish house rules and avoid power struggles. The babysitter model works well in terms of discipline. The biological mate can state to children, 'Your step-dad will be in charge while I'm gone'. And the step-parent can state, 'This is the house rule.' or 'Your mother wants your homework done before you watch television.'
- Realize that as a step-parent, you can play a special role as a mentor and friend. But don't try to replace the biological parent or put the child in the middle of parental quarrels. Even if the biological

parent is dead, he or she still holds an emotional place. It's important to say, 'I can't be your dad, but I care about you. I am here for you as your step-dad, if you need me; and I want to be your friend.'

Wouldn't it be nice if all children were born with an easy-to-use foolproof set of instructions? Instructions that were updated on a daily basis from birth to age ninety? Until that instruction set is created, we have the next best thing."

Parent-To-Parent is a bi-weekly column that appears in the *Coloradoan* newspaper of Fort Collins, Colorado. It is written by **Pam Wynne Fellers** who is a local free-lance writer and mother. These articles deal with everyday parenting problems and offer practical suggestions and solutions that can tried in your own home."

Parent to Parent: On Being a Step-Parent / EpiTwo@aol.com
***Pam Wynne Fellers** is a local free-lance writer and mother. This information originally ran in the Parent to Parent column she writes for **The Coloradoan**, a daily Fort Collins, CO newspaper.*
http://www.fornet.org/ParentToParent/PFellers/par_step.htm

Blended families is another extension of the divorce and we will deal that in the next chapter.

The duties and obligations of the dependent child are transferred to the enabler, where the step parent's role is to provide support within the family.

The step parent is an enabler too, they can help smooth out the rough edges created by the divorce and makes everything appear OK on the surface. In the case of the step parent to let them spend time with them when she needs a break, help clear up some of the problems, and instructed the children to assume of their mother's duties. They can help protect the children and compensated for the loss of a spouse, in effect enables both parents to work out their differences. For that reason, the parent is often referred to as the codependent

Anger is possible the most common emotion children harbor in reaction to parent's divorce. When children learn that expressed anger is wrong, expressed anger is often veiled with false smiles. Anger:
- Betrayal
- Disputes
- Mixed messages
- Broken promises
- Destruction of personal belongings
- Over and over children say they have no sense of personal ownership of the divorce.

Fear and anxiety being afraid and terrified of what is happening at the time. Couple with violence and psychological, physical abuse, and sometimes sexual abuse, impending doom is the silent companion. Many have been slapped, hit or thrown around more than once.

Fear
- Apprehension and fear become normal reactions for children in unpredictable situations.
- They may be afraid that Mom will not be able to take care of them and lose their home.
- Worry that someone will hurt them.
- Fear their friends will not understand why their parent got a divorce.

The seesaw back and forth between the families is enough to elicit More anxiety.

Guilt is often because they are unaware of the problems and they blame themselves for causing their parent's problems.

NEW BEGINNGS III, BLENDED FAMILIES

Marjory says "she has four parents now"!

Chapter 10

BLENDED FAMILY'S

When people consider divorce as a way out and this maybe the best reason to stay married, this is problem most face when they remarry a parent with children are you thinking of how this is going affect the new marriage.

I going to spend time trying to help **blended families** set up some plans of action and how you can work with others, we have information on blinded families. I think the previous web sites verify what has happen in my life as step parent. To a child who has gone through a divorce or death, they become a part of a stepfamily. In the story of Cinderella it seems to be one conception of how there is difference in the way her step mother treated her. The Brady Bunch is a real drama of two families having problems and working them out for the good of the whole family. Actually, neither situation tells the whole story. In a blinded or stepfamily, one or both partners have been married before or it could be because of a death which I dealt with on the mother's side. Each has lost a spouse through divorce or death. One or both of them have children in my first and second marriage I didn't have any children before the first marriage. They have fallen in love and decided to remarry. The second has a new family that includes children from a previous marriage.

Today, at least one-third of all children in the U.S. are expected to live in a stepfamily before they reach age 18. The blended family is becoming more of a norm or while others deal with the loss of loved one. They find a newfound situation and the new challenges of two different family and new commitments to a family situation. This is often a heart-wrenching transition; stepfamilies face many lifestyles, adjustments, and changes. Fortunately, for those who are able to work out their problems and live together successfully.

But it takes careful planning, open discussions about each person's feelings, positive and negative attitudes, mutual respect and patience. The children are the ones' who do as much adjusting as the parents. Most parents are prejudice toward their child or children which can create problems for the new couple I have been there and know about those feelings. If they have not considered the problems involved before they will need to as the two families become one family.

Blended families # 1   Pages 1 – 3 [27]
"How to Raise Children in a Blended Family and Keep Love in Your Marriage

Letter #1

Introduction: Blending families in second (or third) marriages is one of the greatest causes of divorce. Very few of these marriages survive five years. However, I have witnessed many couples who have learned to beat the odds and create a wonderful, love-filled marriage. The secret is in following the **Policy of Joint Agreement**. (Check out my column, "**You Believe What? How to Resolve Conflicts of Faith (Part 2)**." It is also on the subject of Blended Families.)

Dear Dr. Harley,

This is our second marriage for each of us. We each have two children, all of whom are older teens except one. We seem to constantly disagree on simple child rearing issues, i.e. cleaning the room, household chores, curfew, etc. My largest complaint is that since we have blended our families, it seems my children have had to make the most adjustments while my husband's children just seem to run wild when they are here (they live with their mother most of the time). My husband is always very critical of my children and their 'conformance' to house rules yet his seem to make their own rules. While I have tried to stress that no two children are reared the same, he continues to punish them for seemingly minor infractions. This is causing a great deal of distrust among all of us. Is there anything we can do to rebuild trust between us? I am beginning to question my faithfulness to someone so unwilling to compromise.

D.K.

Marriages with blended families tend to be very unsuccessful, one of the greatest predictors of divorce. You have first-hand experience to see why this is the case. It is common for each spouse to put his or her own children's interests first. It is often in an effort to compensate for the trauma children experience when there is a divorce. But when the children's interests are first, the interests of the other spouse and the other spouse's children are found somewhere down the list, and that's a formula for marital disaster.

However, in cases that I have witnessed, these marriages can be saved if both spouses are willing to follow my Policy of Joint Agreement (Never do anything without an enthusiastic agreement between you and your spouse). In effect, whenever you follow this policy, you put your spouse's interests first, where they should be. (Read my **Basic Concepts** section if you have not already read it, with special attention to the **Policy of Joint Agreement**.)

Dear D.K.,

Following this policy means that neither you nor your husband act to reprimand or discipline any child until you have reached an enthusiastic agreement about it. At first, you may not agree about much of anything, in which case you are not to discipline the children (they may do whatever they please). But as you practice applying the policy, you and your husband will begin to establish guidelines in child-rearing issues, and agreements will start to form. Eventually, you will agree on how to discipline your children in a way that takes each other's feelings into account, and your marriage will be saved.

Child rearing is a huge problem in blended families, but it's not the only issue in your marriage, I'm sure. Regardless of your conflicts, however, you'll find that you can resolve them all when you have learned to negotiate with the Policy of Joint Agreement.

Here are a few guidelines that will help you negotiate an enthusiastic agreement:

1. Set ground rules to make negotiations pleasant and safe:

a) try to be pleasant and cheerful through your discussion of the issue,

b) put safety first--do not threaten to cause pain or suffering when you negotiate, even if your spouse makes threatening remarks or if the negotiations fail,

c) if you reach an impasse, stop for a while and come back to the issue later.

2. Identify the problem from the perspectives of both you and your husband. Be able to state the other spouse's position before you go on to find a solution.

3. Brainstorm solutions spend some time thinking of all sorts of ways to handle the problem, and don't correct each other when you hear of a plan that you don't like. You'll have a chance to do that later.

4. Choose the solution that is appealing to both of you. And if your brainstorming has not given you an answer that you can enthusiastically agree upon, go back to brainstorming.

The reason you argue is that you are incompatible -- you have not learned how to act in the interest of both of you at the same time. But if you follow the Policy of Joint Agreement and use the guidelines for negotiation that I have just described, you will find yourselves in greater and greater agreement. Eventually, your marriage will turn out better than you could have ever hoped.

If you don't follow this policy, however, you will eventually make each other so miserable that you will lose your love for each other and divorce, like most marriages with blended families. This process has already begun. Stop it before it goes any further."

Letter #2

Dear Dr. Harley:

I have enjoyed reading the information you have on the net and I downloaded just about everything. So much of it pertains to the problems my husband and I are having now, unfortunately, when I show it to him, he is not very receptive. I have tried the things you have suggested, but I just get the cold shoulder. We are both in the conflict/withdrawal stage right now and refuse to listen, understand or see things from the other person's point of view. We've been married 2 1/2 years, 2nd marriage for both of us. I have 2 children, 12 and 14 and he has 2, 19 and 17. My kids are really good, but my husband is unforgiving when they forget to shut off a light or fail do one of their chores. His children on the other hand have been in trouble with the law, were involved in teen-age pregnancies and more. But their behavior seems to be irrelevant. I am constantly on the defensive because he refuses to see the good side of my children. He is always right there to point out what they do wrong. Any suggestions on how I can break down this barrier? Our marriage was great at first, but it has become intolerable. Thanks so much!

Dear A.L.,

Your husband disciplines your children in a way that does not take your feelings into account, and that is the core of your problem: He does not follow the **Policy of Joint Agreement**. Granted, the children probably irritate him, and his discipline is his way of expressing his annoyance. But the way he goes about it drives a wedge between you and him.

You have undoubtedly expressed your resentment about the way he handles the discipline of your children in harsh terms. And that has probably made him feel taken for granted, that you don't care about his feelings, and that you may have married him just to have someone to help you raise your children. I'm not sure of the details, but I can tell you there are times it seems like you need the "Wisdom of Solomon" to resolve the conflicts of blended families. But unless something changes soon, you and your husband will be divorced, or at least wish you were.

In some marriages like yours, where there does not seem to be a way to follow the Policy of Joint Agreement, I have recommended a separation until the children are grown, or until you can both learn to follow the policy in the way you both treat your children. In this separation, you and your husband talk to each other every day, at least by telephone, see each other regularly, and have sex together. You may find that this kind of separation can bring you and your husband back together again emotionally, restoring you to the state of Intimacy. When you start feeling better about each other, you may want to try living together again, this time making an effort to follow the Policy of Joint Agreement.

In some blended families that I've worked with, the children of one spouse upset the other spouse so much that they simply cannot live together while the children are still in the house. Even after they return to the state of Intimacy, they still find living with each other's children to be intolerable. When that's the case, the marriage has not ended, but the children and the upset spouse simply remain separated.

What I'm suggesting is a drastic measure, but since I do not have all the facts, it may not be the right thing to do at this time. Keep in mind, however, that saving marriages of blended families is probably the most difficult situations a marriage counselors face, and often requires drastic measures. It's difficult because people in that situation tend to put their children's interests before their spouse's interests as a result, they are unwilling to follow the Policy of Joint Agreement."
http://www.marriagebuilders.com/graphic/mbi5008_qa.html8/20/07

Profile of emotional involvement in the children of blinded families

There are things a person can do to help a blinded family, and how to deal with things that will hurt in raising the children. Sometimes it is hard to look at a situation and know if it is good or bad because of the emotionally involvement. I have always gotten emotionally involved and yet I am an internal optimist. I always see some good in a bad situation or relationship. I created some of my own problems, but on the other hand there was some good that came out of my situations and problems. I hope you will be able to say the same in your situation.

Then some were out of my control and yet I contributed to the demise of the problems. There is a saying "Control the things that you can control and leave the things alone that you can't control and have the wisdom to know the difference". There are at least three kinds of situations that a person may have to deal with. One is the kind that you create for yourself, and the other kinds are situations and the ones you can't control. That is where someone else or something else has created a situation or problems for you. An illness, death, and many other kinds of things are out of the hands of a person. Then, there are many kinds of problems brought on such as a divorce, the list can goes on and on, but I will show you how this relates to any situation including blinded families.

There is no one who can be totally prepare themselves for every problem. I'm going show you what I'm talking about. We can look any situation, and some seem to have the answers for every problem. There is no one who seems to be more difficult when a person's emotions get out of control, or when it comes to the loss of a loved one or divorce, there are answers for any of those situations!

That is when you are pretty will out there on your own, and it is hard to reach out to someone at that this point in their life, but people do and one of them is a remarriage. When you make that decision to take on a new mate, usually you are taking on a family. I have had to deal with all of these situations in my life and some good came out of all them, but it wasn't easy taking on a new partner, I felt it was right at the time.

There is one thing to remember at this point while dealing with the problems in a new family. This is a good time to look for the "silver lining"; it may take some time before that to happen. I was very strong, but fragile at the same time, I lost my prospective at the time, I couldn't see any good I still remember those bad feelings of another divorce. I did learn as I go through these different experiences of divorce so will you and your children.

Because of these divorces I have had step children I have learned to have a sensitivity for what others are going through. I have lived in and through the same situation and I understand what people are dealing with, be realistic about the situation I always try to look at both sides of the story.

Step Children

It is interesting sense some kids are unruly and uncontrollable. Perhaps your spouse has let their children grow up unruly and don't mind, and who routinely spends more time with her own children, which you help provide for by exploiting the fact they have unruly children. Perhaps you are not allowed to discipline her children while she disciplines yours, what if they are little monsters running roughshod over the step parent, who feels bad because they left their father for you (or vice-versa).

- Rules need to be established and couples need to be respected each other's children: that includes you. If you don't have both sides in the household being treated the same that needs to be dealt with before it tars up the family.

- However, there could be another problem when it comes to the children in a blinded family she may or may not want another child under those conditions, wanting more children should been agreed on before remarriage, now a reversal of a previous decision has come up or maybe it wasn't planed there is going to be another member to the family. For instance, if you had children in a prior marriage and decided together that you both did not want more children, a house and a dog was enough, but suddenly a year or two later, your spouse wants to have child. A four bedroom house, this does happen, it can be grounds to keep in mind: if you never talked about having kids prior to the marriage, then ask why it is no big deal now? What is the reason for changing their mind, why do they want the change now?

- Kids will not understand what is happening and may even come to vilify one parent over the other. Whatever you do, tell the kids specific reasons why you are having another child in the family and don't say insulting hurtful things about your mom or dad during the pregnancy. Jus explain that it is for the best interest to stay out of it and that both of you are going to deal with-it. Also, don't try to win them over to your side with gifts and money or other trips. Kids are more attuned to this sort of emotional bribery then you might think. Take the high road and don't insult your spouse. Instead, be nice, but not manipulative toward their children. They may hate you now, nonetheless, but in time there will be a greater chance they will come to understand.

- There is a possibility they felt that way before, but never let their true feelings be known about any situations. They may have felt they could get their way, this could be about anything, after being married for a while they may feel better about a situation of the past now they can get their kids to agree to new things hoping they will be able to work things out.

In the next chapter we discuss children of alcoholics the confusion brought about by inconsistency and unpredictability are the hallmarks of alcoholism that repeal children into the cyclone of confusion.

- Alcoholics are notorious for mood swings, making and breaking promises during drinking bouts.
- Children often find themselves walking on egg shells and desperately trying to second-guess parents in order to do what they want at the time of drinking.
- Especially difficult for preschoolers, who need consistency to learn how to venture out socially, show their feelings and know right and wrong, plus the good and bad?
- There are ethical morals of good and bad
- There are laws of legal and illegal

NEW BEGINNINGS IV, HOW ADDICTIONS EFFECTS THE FAMILIY

Chapter 11

ADDICTIONS IN RELATION TO THE FAMILY

Addictions Alcoholism-Drugs-Pills-Smoking
Substance abuse
1) Profile the types of "Help and Healing"
2) Addiction centers and group therapy
3) Drugs, Brain, and Behavior – The Science of Addiction – Addiction and Health.
4) Treatment for Young Adults Troubled Teen Drug Use and Alcohol Rehab
5) Profiling alcoholism
6) Four personal examples of alcoholism, by the author.
7) Person profiling of the four cases of drinking alcohol.
8) Is alcoholism a social issue or a disease?

The Effects of Drugs

Addictions cover a vast spectrum from the physical-well-being a person from minor's who are on drugs and become addicted, to dealings with serous to severe problems of addictions in adults. Now let's look at some:

Symptoms – disorders may be cured and treated, and dealt with in many ways depending on the severity of the addiction.

They can be freighting if a person doesn't know how to deal with the uncertain feelings that makes them insecure about their predicament, situation, and addiction. But, for the most part knowledge and understanding of the problem and situation will help, and the genetics, the makeup (character) and background is a key to opening the vast unknowns in person's life.

This can lead to many different kinds of cure-alls.

Substance abuse

1) when their genetic parents have been on drugs or alcoholics there is an unhealthy dependence on drugs and alcohol.
2) when there is an usual defensive behavior patterns that leads to an addiction.
3) when they are usually helpless in controlling or quitting behavior patterns.
4) in some cases shyness and self-consciousness aide in their dependence and co-dependences on addictions.
5) another misconception is it makes them feel happy and self-confident.
6) another down side is usually depression and unhappiness afterwards.
7) another downside is the dependency and it takes more and more all their time.
8) last is the money it takes to support the habits of alcohol and drugs.

Substance abuse help &treatment centers and programs.

1) depends on the determination of the person and how bad the addiction is?
2) well-power and personal well-being will help.
3) they must decide to quite the drugs or alcohol.
4) most programs advocate admitting to the problem.
5) self-awareness and admitting the need for help.
6) it may involve personal counseling and/or group support.

Addictions Alcoholism-Drugs-Pills-Smoking

I have covered some of the things about addictions when I dealt with relationships and marriage. Now I want to deal with the treatment of addictions. We have also dealt with other addictions and the effects on a person and how **sexual addictions** can affect the marriage? There are so many people that have to deal with these addictions every day of their life. The real problem is those who live with them and how it affects their love for the other person.

There are ways to solve these problems concerning addictions. How does a person build and repair their life and relationships after they get off of their addiction is important? Again they usually live with the status quo, the do nothing attitude, or maybe in this case they can't help themselves, it will never get better under those conditions. When all else fails they can't get rid of the addiction. Addictions usually start out innocent enough they say they can take them or leave them; when it happens over a period of time they get hooked, sometimes they don't realize they have become addicted. Another thing to look for is how much real damage has been done because of the addiction.

One day they may say to *themselves* and wonder what has happened and they can't help *themselves*. They become over whelmed, and they can't control their addiction. They may take other people for granted, that will affect a relationship, or job. The person is to blame at this point like a lot of other problems they usually think it is someone else's fault. At this point they may not be able to use good judgment. One course of action is our **SOS LIFE ENHANCEMENT STUDIES** book may be of help.

These addictions are considered <u>Social-Problems: Alcoholism - Drugs-Pills – smoking - sexual-addiction and others</u>. These are some abuse factors in an addicted person they may not be able to deal with their inner feelings. The addicted person differently has more ups and downs, more than that these social diseases can be devastating to deal with. These people know they are dealing with a terrible disease, but they feel they can't help themselves, when a person lives through these terrible times, it becomes a part of the process in order to change them, every person suffers until they decide to do something, or do something to change things.

Addictions have become known as mental illness! It can destroy some of the brain cells, and creates a mental in balance. They can't cope, and they rely on drugs and alcohol to get them through the day. There are all kinds helps they usually don't take advantage of the help because they have become dependent on them.

Personal will-power will help:
1) They must decide to quit the drugs or alcohol.
2) Most programs advocate admitting to the problem.
3) Self-awareness and admitting they want help.
4) It may involve personal counseling and/or support groups.

Drugs, Brain, and Behavior – The Science of Addiction – Addiction and Health   Pages 1 – 4 [28]

"Drugs are chemicals. They work in the brain by tapping into the brain's communication system and interfering with the way nerve cells normally send, receive, and process information. Some drugs, such as marijuana and heroin, can activate neurons because their chemical structure mimics that of a natural neurotransmitter. There is a similarity in the structure of the receptors and allows the drugs to lock onto and activate the nerve cells. Although these drugs mimic brain chemicals, they don't activate nerve cells in the same way as a natural neurotransmitter, and they lead to abnormal messages being transmitted through the network(...)

Other drugs, such as amphetamine or cocaine, can cause the nerve cells to release abnormally large amounts of natural neurotransmitters or prevent the normal recycling of these brain chemicals. This disruption produces a greatly amplified message, ultimately disrupting communication channels. The difference in effect can be described as the difference between someone whispering into your ear and someone shouting into a microphone.

How do drugs work in the brain to produce pleasure?

All drugs of abuse directly or indirectly target the brain's reward system by flooding the circuit with dopamine. Dopamine is a neurotransmitter present in regions of the brain that regulate movement, emotion, cognition, motivation, and feelings of pleasure. The overstimulation of this system, which rewards our natural behaviors, produces the euphoric effects sought by people who abuse drugs and teaches them to repeat the behavior.

How does stimulation of the brain's pleasure circuit teach us to keep taking drugs?

Our brains are wired to ensure that we will repeat life-sustaining activities by associating those activities with pleasure or reward. Whenever this reward circuit is activated, the brain notes that something important is happening that needs to be remembered, and teaches us to do it again and again, without thinking about it. Because drugs of abuse stimulate the same circuit, we learn to abuse drugs in the same way.

Why are drugs more addictive than natural rewards?

When some drugs of abuse are taken, they can release 2 to 10 times the amount of dopamine that natural rewards do. In some cases, this occurs almost immediately (as when drugs are smoked or injected), and the effects can last much longer than those produced by natural rewards. The resulting effects on the brain's pleasure circuit dwarfs those produced by naturally rewarding behaviors such as eating and sex. The effect of such a powerful reward strongly motivates people to take drugs again and again. This is why scientists sometimes say that drug abuse is something we learn to do very, very well.

What happens to your brain if you keep taking drugs?

Just as we turn down the volume on a radio that is too loud, the brain adjusts to the overwhelming surges in dopamine (and other neurotransmitters) by producing less dopamine or by reducing the number of receptors that can receive and transmit signals. As a result, dopamine's impact on the reward circuit of a drug abuser's brain can become abnormally low, and the ability to experience any pleasure is reduced. This is why the abuser eventually feels flat, lifeless, and depressed, and is unable to enjoy things that previously brought them pleasure. Now, they need to take drugs just to bring their dopamine function back up to normal. And, they must take larger amounts of the drug than they first did to create the dopamine high - an effect known as tolerance.

How does long-term drug taking affect brain circuits?
We know that the same sort of mechanisms involved in the development of tolerance can eventually lead to profound changes in neurons and brain circuits, with the potential to severely compromise the long-term health of the brain. For example, glutamate is another neurotransmitter that influences the reward circuit and the ability to learn. When the optimal concentration of glutamate is altered by drug abuse, the brain attempts to compensate for this change, which can cause impairment in cognitive function. Similarly, long-term drug abuse can trigger adaptations in habit or nonconscious memory systems. Conditioning is one example of this type of learning, whereby environmental cues become associated with the drug experience and can trigger uncontrollable cravings if the individual is later exposed to these cues, even without the drug itself being available. This learned 'reflex' is extremely robust and can emerge even after many years of abstinence.

What other brain changes occur with abuse?
Chronic exposure to drugs of abuse disrupts the way critical brain structures interact to control behavior - behavior specifically related to drug abuse. Just as continued abuse may lead to tolerance or the need for higher drug dosages to produce an effect, it may also lead to addiction, which can drive an abuser to seek out and take drugs compulsively. Drug addiction erodes a person's self-control and ability to make sound decisions, while sending intense impulses-to-take-drugs.
(…)

For more information on drugs and the brain, order NIDA's Slide Teaching Packets CD-ROM series or the Mind Over Matter series at **www.drugabuse.gov/parent- teacher.html**. These items and others are available to the public free of charge.

What are the medical consequences of drug addiction?

Individuals who suffer from addiction often have one or more accompanying medical issues, including lung and cardiovascular disease, stroke, cancer, and mental disorders. Imaging scans, chest x-rays, and blood tests show the damaging effects of drug abuse throughout the body. For example, tests show that tobacco smoke causes cancer of the mouth, throat, larynx, blood, lungs, stomach, pancreas, kidney, bladder, and cervix. In addition, some drugs of abuse, such as inhalants, are toxic to nerve cells and may damage or destroy them either in the brain or the peripheral nervous system.

Does drug abuse cause mental disorders, or vice versa?

Drug abuse and mental disorders often co-exist. In some cases, mental diseases may precede addiction; in other cases, drug abuse may trigger or exacerbate mental disorders, particularly in individuals with specific vulnerabilities.

What harmful consequences to others result from drug addiction?

Beyond the harmful consequences for the addicted individual, drug abuse can cause serious health problems for others. Three of the more devastating and troubling consequences of addiction are:

- **Negative effects of prenatal drug exposure on infants and children.**

It is likely that some drug-exposed children will need educational support in the classroom to help them overcome what may be subtle deficits in developmental areas such as behavior, attention, and cognition. Ongoing work is investigating whether the effects of prenatal exposure on brain and behavior extend into adolescence to cause developmental problems during that time period.'

- **Negative effects of second-hand smoke.**

Second-hand tobacco smoke, also referred to as environmental tobacco smoke (ETS), is a significant source of exposure to a large number of substances known to be hazardous to human health, particularly to children. According to the Surgeon General's 2006 Report, The Health Consequences of Involuntary Exposure to Tobacco Smoke, involuntary smoking increases the risk of heart disease and lung cancer in never-smokers by 25-30 percent and 20-30 percent, respectively.

- **Increased spread of infectious diseases.**

Injection of drugs such as heroin, cocaine, and methamphetamine accounts for more than a third of new AIDS cases. Injection drug use is also a major factor in the spread of hepatitis C, a serious, potentially fatal liver disease and a rapidly growing public health problem. Injection drug use is not the only way that drug abuse contributes to the spread of infectious diseases. All drugs of abuse cause some form of intoxication, which interferes with judgment and increases the likelihood of risky sexual behaviors. This, in turn, contributes to the spread of HIV/AIDS, hepatitis B and C, and other sexually transmitted diseases.

What are some effects of specific abused substances?

Addictive stimulant found in cigarettes and other forms of tobacco. Tobacco smoke increases a user's risk of cancer, emphysema, bronchial disorders, and cardiovascular disease. The mortality rate associated with tobacco addiction is staggering. Tobacco use killed approximately 100 million people during the 20th century and, if current smoking trends continue, the cumulative death toll for this century has been projected to reach 1 billion.

- **Alcohol** consumption can damage the brain and most body organs. Areas of the brain that are especially vulnerable to alcohol-related damage are the cerebral cortex (largely responsible for our higher brain functions, including problem solving and decision making), the hippocampus (important for memory and learning), and the cerebellum (important for movement coordination).

- **Marijuana** is the most commonly abused illicit substance. This drug impairs short-term memory and learning, the ability to focus attention, and coordination. It also increases heart rate, can harm the lungs, and can cause psychosis in those at risk.
- **Inhalants** are volatile substances found in many household products, such as oven cleaners, gasoline, spray paints, and other aerosols, that induce mind-altering effects. Inhalants are extremely toxic and can damage the heart, kidneys, lungs, and brain. Even a healthy person can suffer heart failure and death within minutes of a single session of prolonged sniffing of an inhalant.
- **Cocaine** is a short-acting stimulant, which can lead abusers to 'binge' (to take the drug many times in a single session). Cocaine abuse can lead to severe medical consequences related to the heart, and the respiratory, nervous, and digestive systems.
- **Amphetamines**, including methamphetamine, are powerful stimulants that can produce feelings of euphoria and alertness. Methamphetamine's effects are particularly long lasting and harmful to the brain. Amphetamines can cause high body temperature and can lead to serious heart problems and seizures.

(…)

- **Prescription medications** are increasingly being abused or used for nonmedical purposes. This practice cannot only be addictive, but in some cases also lethal. Commonly abused classes of prescription drugs include painkillers, sedatives, and stimulants. Among the most disturbing aspects of this emerging trend is its prevalence among teenagers and young adults, and the common misperception that because these medications are prescribed by physicians, they are safe even when used illicitly.
- **Steroids**, which can also be prescribed for certain medical conditions, are abused to increase muscle mass and to improve athletic performance or physical appearance. Serious consequences of abuse can include severe acne, heart disease, liver problems, stroke, infectious diseases, depression, and suicide.'

For more information on the nature and extent of common drugs of abuse and their health consequences, go to NIDA's Web site to view the popular **_Research Reports_**, **_Info Facts_**, and **other publications**.

Can addiction be treated successfully? Yes. Addiction is a treatable disease. Discoveries in the science of addiction have led to advances in drug abuse treatment that help people stop abusing drugs and resume their productive lives.

Can addiction be cured?

Addiction need not be a life sentence. Like other chronic diseases, addiction can be managed successfully. Treatment enables people to counteract addiction's powerful disruptive effects on brain and behavior and regain control of their lives.

Source: The Journal of Neuroscience, 21(23):9414-9418. 2001

Does relapse to drug abuse mean treatment has failed?

No. The chronic nature of the disease means that relapsing to drug abuse s not only possible, but likely, with relapse rates similar to those for other well-characterized chronic medical illnesses such as diabetes, hypertension, and asthma, which also have both physiological and behavioral components. Treatment of chronic diseses involves changing deeply imbedded behaviors, and relapse does not mean treatment failure. For the addicted patient, lap back to drug abuse indicate that treatment needs to be reinstated or adjusted, or that alternate treatment is needed.

Source: McLellan et al., JAMA, 284:1689-1695, 2000.

What are the basics of effective addiction treatment?

Research shows that combining treatment medications, where available, with behavioral therapy is the best way to ensure success for most patients. Treatment approaches must be tailored to address each patient's drug abuse patterns and drug-related medical, psychiatric, and social problems.

How can medications help treat drug addiction?

Different types of medications may be useful at different stages of treatment to help a patient stop abusing drugs, stay in treatment, and avoid relapse.

- **'Treating Withdrawal.** When patients first stop abusing drugs, they can experience a variety of physical and emotional symptoms, including depression, anxiety, and other mood disorders; restlessness; and sleeplessness. Certain treatment medications are designed to reduce these symptoms, which makes it easier to stop the abuse.
- **Staying in Treatment.** Some treatment medications are used to help the brain adapt gradually to the absence of the abused drug. These medications act slowly to stave off drug cravings, and have a calming effect on body systems. They can help patients focus on counseling and other psychotherapies related to their drug treatment.
- **Preventing Relapse.** Science has taught us that stress, cues linked to the drug experience (e.g., people, places, things, moods), and exposure to drugs are the most common triggers for relapse. Medications are being developed to interfere with these triggers to help patients sustain recovery.'

How do behavioral therapies treat drug addiction?

Behavioral treatments help engage people in drug abuse treatment, modifying their attitudes and behaviors related to drug abuse and increasing their life skills to handle stressful circumstances and environmental cues that may trigger intense craving for drugs and prompt another cycle of compulsive abuse. Moreover, behavioral therapies can enhance the effectiveness of medications and help people remain in treatment longer.

How do the best treatment programs help patients recover from the pervasive effects of addiction?

Getting an addicted person to stop abusing drugs is just one part of a long and complex recovery process. When people enter treatment, addiction has often taken over their lives. The compulsion to get drugs, take drugs, and experience the effects of drugs has dominated their every waking moment, and drug abuse has taken the place of all the things they used to enjoy doing. It has disrupted how they function in their family lives, at work, and in the community, and has made them more likely to suffer from other serious illnesses. Because addiction can affect so many aspects of a person's life, treatment must address the needs of the whole person to be successful. This is why the best programs incorporate a variety of rehabilitative services into their comprehensive treatment regiments. Treatment counselors select from a menu of services for meeting the individual medical, psychological, social, vocational, and legal needs of their patients to foster their recovery from addiction.

- *'Cognitive Behavioral Therapy*. Seeks to help patients recognize, avoid, and cope with the situations in which they are most likely to abuse drugs.
- *Motivational Incentives*. Uses positive reinforcement such as providing rewards or privileges for remaining drug free, for attending and participating in counseling sessions, or for taking treatment medications as prescribed.
- *Motivational Interviewing*. Employs strategies to evoke rapid and internally motivated behavior change to stop drug use and facilitate treatment entry.
- *Group Therapy*. Helps patients face their drug abuse realistically, come to terms with its harmful consequences, and boost their motivation to stay drug free. Patients learn effective ways to solve their emotional and interpersonal problems without resorting to drugs.'

For more information on drug treatment, NIDA offers a selection of free treatment manuals and guides for practitioners, including

Principles of Drug Addiction Treatment: A Research-Based Guide) and *Brief Strategic Family Therapy for Adolescent Drug Abuse*.

Leading the Search for Scientific Solutions

To address all aspects of drug abuse and its harmful consequences, NIDA's research program ranges from basic studies of the addicted brain and behavior to health services research. NIDA's research program develops prevention and treatment approaches and ensures they work in real-world settings. In this context, NIDA is strongly committed to developing a research portfolio that addresses the special vulnerabilities and health disparities that exist among ethnic minorities or that derive from gender differences."

Bringing Science to Real-World Settings

- National Drug Abuse Treatment Clinical Trials Network (CTN). The CTN 'road tests' research-based drug abuse treatments in community treatment programs around the country (...)"

U.S. Department of Health and Human Services. Questions? See our Contact Information. *Last updated on Wednesday, May 16, 2007.* http://www.nida.nih.gov/scienceofaddiction/health.html   8/29/07

Treatment for Young Adults Troubled Teen Drug Use and Alcohol Rehab   Page 1 of 1 [29]

"Young adults struggling with alcohol and/or drug addiction have many options available to them for treatment of their substance abuse. As information is empowerment, Young Adult Drug Treatment makes available information on both alcohol abuse and drug use for parents, educators and teens. Please take the time to read our articles on drugs and alcohol and **contact us** if you have further questions on your young adults road to drug and alcohol addiction recovery.

Breaking the Cycle of Drug and Alcohol Addiction

Childhood can and should be a time of wonder and discovery, when parents nurture, protect, and care for the precious gifts of life they have brought into the world. But for **children of alcoholic parents**, life often is filled with shame, suffering, and fear. These children may find themselves trapped by the same disease that affected their parents and grandparents unless there is outside intervention from caring adults in their lives.

Breaking the Cycle of Drug and Alcohol Addiction

Childhood can and should be a time of wonder and discovery, when parents nurture, protect, and care for the precious gifts of life they have brought into the world. But for children of alcoholic parents, life often is filled with shame, suffering, and fear. These children may find themselves trapped by the same disease that affected their parents and grandparents unless there is outside intervention from caring adults in their lives.

According to the Substance Abuse and Mental Health Services Administration (SAMHSA), part of the U.S. Department of Health and Human Services, children of alcohol-addicted parents can suffer from physical illness and injury, emotional disturbances, educational deficits, behavior problems, and alcoholism or alcohol abuse later in life. Perhaps most troubling, however, is the fact that children of alcoholics (COAs) are two to four times more likely to become problem drinkers and continue the addictive practices of their parents with similar devastating consequences.

(SAMHSA) Administrator Charles G. Curie urges every adult to learn about the needs of COAs and the simple actions they can take to help COAs develop into healthy adults.

'We know that COAs are at greater risk for substance abuse problems in their own lives. But we also know what to do to help them avoid repeating their family's problems. We can break the generational cycle of alcoholism in families.'

That's good news for the millions of children in the United States who live in households in which one or both parents have been actively alcohol dependent in the past. Experts say COAs can be helped, whether or not the alcohol- abusing adults in their families receive treatment. Adult relatives, older siblings, and other adults who have contact with COAs at school, in the community, through (faith-based organizations), and through health and social services agencies do not need formal training or special skills to be caring and supportive.

To help a child of an alcoholic, one must take that first step--show care for a child with an alcoholic parent. Since research shows that one in four children lives in a family with alcoholism or alcohol abuse, many adults will not have to look far to find a child to help.

Curie said, 'Perhaps the best way adults can help COAs is to provide them with accurate information about alcoholism to help them develop the skills needed to cope with their day-to-day challenges.' He added, 'Accurate information helps COAs understand that alcoholism is a disease that has nothing to do with them--they are not to blame for the disruptions and other problems happening at home. It clarifies and validates their reality and shows them the choices they can make to be safe and healthy.'

According to the National Association for Children of Alcoholics, the life skills that COAs need often are learned outside the family and can be gained through educational support groups and healthy relationships with others, especially adults who show they care about the children. By providing these children with experiences in which they have opportunities to succeed, COAs can learn to respect themselves, which in turn helps them cope with their situations.

Almost every community has resources to help make a difference in the lives of COAs. Services such as educational support groups and counseling are widespread across the country. Free publications, including *"It's Not Your Fault and You Can't Help It,"* available from (SAMHSA's) National Clearinghouse for Alcohol and Drug Information, offer important insights and resources for adults who want to help.

Abuse of Inhalants Among Young Adults

Initial use of inhalants often starts early. Some young people may use inhalants as an easily accessible substitute for alcohol. Research suggests that chronic or long-term inhalant abusers are among the most difficult drug abuse patients to treat. Many suffer from **cognitive** impairment and other neurological dysfunction and may experience multiple psychological and social problems.

Pointers for Parents, Love: The Anti-Drug

Picture the scene: you take your daughter to the mall and she doesn't want to walk too close to you, or you drop off your son at practice and he leaps out of the car practically before an accident.

You love your kids and want what's best for them, but sometimes it can be hard to demonstrate how much you love them, particularly as they grow up and become more independent.

Research shows that one of the best ways you can help your kids avoid drug use is by spending time with them. Here are some helpful suggestions for knowing what's going on in your child's world when they seem to close every door on you:

Be a good role model for your kids. There is no such thing as 'do as I say, not as I do' when raising children. If you take drugs or abuse alcohol, your children are observing and learning from your behavior. On the other hand, if you are a living, day-to-day example of your value system, your children will learn and emulate the compassion, honesty, generosity, and openness that you want your children to have.

Be involved in your children's lives. According to behavioral scientist, Tony Biglan, Ph.D.:

'Create together time. Start a tradition or fun, weekly routine to do something with your child, such as going out for ice cream. Eat meals together as often as possible. Mealtime is a great opportunity to talk about the day's events, unwind, and reinforce a family bond. Studies show that kids whose families eat together at least five times a week are less likely to be involved with drugs and alcohol.

Try to be home after school. The 'danger zone' for drug use and other risky behavior is between 4 and 6 p.m. If you can, arrange to have flextime if it's available at your workplace. When your child will be with friends, make sure there is adult supervision.'

If Drug Addiction Is a Disease, Is There a Cure?

There is no cure for drug addiction, but it is a treatable disease; addicts can recover. Drug addiction therapy is a program of behavior change or modification that slowly retrains the brain. Like people with diabetes or heart disease, people in treatment for drug addiction learn behavioral changes and often take medications as part of their treatment regimen."

http://www.youngadultdrugetreatment.com/8/29/07

Alcoholism

I will give you four examples of alcoholic drinking and then the social issues along with the moral issues at the same time, in some cases the results will show defiant abuse to themselves and the effects it had on their families. Sometimes there are physical, mental, and sexual abuse cases.

There is another aspect to this universal problem; that relates to the civil law and personal rights, and the way I deal with **cognitive** identity and the **cognition** in relation to their home environment. Then as I deal with social and moral issues that becomes an obligation that has to do with the law of the city, country, State Laws. How they are involved in dealing with addictions, there are moral and scriptural views on the use of alcohol. In today's society we have all kinds of drugs.

Personal profile of the studies on addictions

We at Support outreach Services = **SOS Self Help Books & Links**.

First and for-most are the situations related to addictions, codependency and abuse, and how to deal the involvement and treatments. Those who live with the addiction and how they are unable to cope and deal with those addictions. First, let's deal with the symptoms; I will use websites that support the healing process as I deal with the depth of how to deal with those symptoms. There are people who are dealing with addiction and become codependents. I have dealt people who have been addicted for years, and I want to help you learn how they dealt with their a.

Second, I have put all these in a group category so you can identify with what you need to deal with and identify) and how they relate with these social disorders. There is a direct correlation with Co-dependencies and addictions/ and help people deal with alcoholism, and there addictive qualities, there is a common problem in all of them that is why I have put them together.

Third, because all of these need to go through the treatment process, support help, and therapy is practically the same in any of these addictions, and some address the moral and social problems.

Fourth, there is yet another aspect in some cases of alcoholism, etc., and that will result in health problems / illnesses, and in that case they are classified as a disease.

Fifth, I want to discuss the moral and social issues that practitioners, psychologists, and counselors are dealing with we have to live by the laws that govern these social issues. Morally it has to do with the rights of the individuals involved in alcoholism, etc. I believe there is a need to spend more time on the moral issues and treatment in our counseling, therapeutic analysis, and group sessions for the person and help the families involved, and to be able to understand their rights as individuals who want help.

This approach of dealing with alcohol is nothing new, and those who drink are not considered as an alcoholic, but the addiction is under law called alcoholism. Whether a person thinks of taking one drink of alcohol or wine is a moral issue to them that is a different issue. The laws of this country says it does not constitute drinking alcohol as breaking the law, and sad-to-say that is one of the reasons people have to live with alcoholism, etc. It has become a moral and social problem for centuries because of the laws of each country and every society deals with it differently.

Four personal examples of alcoholism by the author.

I want to continue by saying this part of the study and by pointing out family relations to drug use; I do believe there is a genetic tie to alcoholism and drug use. I have a study on "Children of Alcoholics" that proves there is a correlation to families in relation to alcohol and drug use and the genetic ties to children of alcoholics'.

I am going take another step in dealing with children of addictions.

Typically, a child living an alcoholic family leaves the children with many emotional and sometimes physiological problems described in these 7 emotions. Anger is possible the most common emotion children harbor in reaction to parental alcoholism. When children learn that expressed anger is wrong, expressed anger is often a put on with false smiles. Anger:

Fear and anxiety in COAs are afraid and terrified of what is happening at the time. Couple's with violence and psychological, physical, and sometimes sexual abuse, impending doom is the COA's silent companion. Many have been slapped, hit or thrown around more than once.

First, I can count on one hand the times I saw my father drink alcohol and my mother did not drink alcohol and her father and mother didn't either. I saw my dad drink a beer as a young man, never a mixed drink, he never got drunk. He would take a social beer with someone at home, and again never alone.

As he got older he never drank at all, his hobbies were hunting and fishing to get away and relax. She became a Christian my dad and mom never got addicted when they were young. I think this is where a lot of addictions starts and most teen addictions are addicted for life.

I am pretty sure my father grew up with a father who drank when he was young my dad's family problems left him with stomach problems they started as a teenager, and mom said it made him sick to drank alcohol and it also left him with emotional problems as I look back on his life I don't think his mother or father were alcoholic parent's. That is the reason it does not show up in the four of us none of us drink or use drugs. My children don't use alcohol and my grandchildren are not addicted to drugs. I think this a good indication that those who are not into alcohol are more likely not to get into alcohol and drugs.

Second, example in point, one of my sister's married a young man whose father was an alcoholic, he grew up with an alcoholic parent his mother was a Christian, but his father did quit drinking the last few years of his life. He was one of those who would go on binges, when he took the first drink he could not stop, and his three children definitely bear the scars from an alcoholic parent and their children did to some degree. Their children are the second generation, who also bear the scars of an alcoholic grandfather. I think there are emotional scars that go back to alcoholic grandparents, and that each one of them has had to deal with it as grandchildren, their parents didn't drink, but it was worse for those who drank, and they have been addicted because of the genetic ties and became addicted at an early age, very symptomatic of an alcoholic in the family.

Third, example in point was my first real in counter with alcoholism. It starts with a business partner who had an alcohol problem, he liked to drink all day when I first met him, and that has given me some insight into an alcoholic, on a personal basis. He wanted a drink the first thing in the morning, but I did not drink I said no drinking during the day, and he would finish the day starting around 5: in the evening, he would drink until he would almost pass out, and then he would put himself to bed. He was divorced, but that had nothing to do with his drinking, it probably caused the divorce.

There may have been drinking and abuse in the marriage not any physical abuse, he was one of those who liked the taste and how it made him feel at the time. He was really no problem to deal with because in the day we would conduct business as usual. He would ask me if I thought he was an alcoholic, I would say "not in the strictest sense of the word", but "I thought it would be better if he didn't drink at all".

This is "Alcohol Anonymous" definition if a person can't hold a job he is not an alcoholic, he did not consider himself as an alcoholic, he said that was their definition of an alcoholic "someone who could not work and carry on a business or work". There is a much bigger problem with alcoholics and that has to do with their relationships; which they have a hard time having a good relationship. While I was with him he was at least not as dependent on alcohol in the day time, but need it to put him to sleep. In the afternoon he was starting to hurt. As I look back that was some kind of a victory for him not drinking all day and he felt good and felt better.

Fourth, example is similar in the fact that he was not belligerent or abusive, but very passive aggressive drinker. I was in the swimming pool business at the time, and I had worked with him at the power plant, he worked for a sub-contractor. He told me he wanted to build a swimming pool at his home, but for an unusual reason. He said "my wife has told me to quit drinking or she is going to leave me. I love her and told her I would quit" and she said, "she wanted a swimming pool". He also told me of his drinking experience which I thought was quite unusual, he said "I drink all day, I am happy and don't cause any one any problems, and if the house would burn I would put more wood on the fire" he was in a state of euphoria, he was tranquilized by the alcohol, and feeling no pain, nor was he capable of real feelings at the end of the day, I am sure that is what she didn't like about her husband who cared more for his liquor than her. He was unable to have real feelings.

Personal profiling of these four examples of alcoholism.

Let me conclude by profiling these **four examples**, the last two were very passive, but they had aggressive drinking problems, they were not as aggressive as the **second example** he was aggressive and verbally abusive when he got drunk, some become loud and obnoxious, and abusive some use foul language when confronted, and they are belligerent; there was fighting and arguing in the **second example**. There are two types of abuse, one which is being an alcoholic, and two is when they become abusive physically and mentally, as in last **three examples** they were all addicted to alcohol, but the main difference is in the **second example** there was abuse, he became abusive toward anyone who confronted him, and that made him mad. She was a Christian woman, she defiantly didn't believe in any kind of alcohol and the argument ensued when he was drinking, she did challenge him because it made her mad when he drank.

I met him on several occasions he was a real nice person when he was not drinking. There is never a good time to confront an alcoholic, when they are drunk. They have to want help, and that is why some kind of intervene is needed professionally, group therapy, and / or a church support is very helpful in giving them something to do as you will see in this study on how to deal with alcoholism.

Is alcoholism and drugs a social issue or a disease?

These are some of the common social disorders and any of these addictions can lead to an illness and the need for treatment, is it a social issue, and when it relate to some form of abuse. Abuse can show up in any part of a person's life and reflect in the inner person's actions and reactions. Even smoking, drugs, and taking medications could fit into this category of abuse, because they can cause an illness and even death in some cases. This can become a "mental issue" and in that case it needs to be treated as such!

The drinking alcohol can cause "physical" damage to the body functions and system, and can also destroy the brain cells that creates a mental imbalance and that affects the body chemistry that feeds the bodies system. People can get to where they can't cope for any number of reasons and they can become dependent on artificial help substances to cope.

There are all kinds support groups and organizations out there to help people. I feel Support Outreach Services = **SOS** has a <u>primary purpose</u> in helping people with addictions and that is to help them find <u>support, support information, encouragement,</u> and <u>guidance for them</u>. <u>This is a place to start</u>! I have had a lot of people come to our sessions <u>looking for help</u> and <u>we let them know the kind of help available,</u> but I find most people want an easy way to fix the problem, I found this to be very true in my life. I am the coordinator of a faith based group, "Community Support Outreach Group Session" in West Plains, Missouri.

How does a person deal with the impact of a problem or crisis? And, on the other hand how does a person react to the causes of addictions (some feel they deserve what happens to them), and that is a real problem, the important question is what effect is it going to have on their lives and family if they continue in the addiction.

This puts us as practitioners, counselors, and therapists on the front line, because we have a life to deal with that also includes the individual's family that is affected by the addiction. What is going to happen to those who have to face the issue of alcoholism and drugs? This does not take anything away <u>from their responsibility</u> as a person who tries to find solutions for themselves, we think this is the <u>key issue that has to be answered</u>.

Practitioners, counselors, and therapists have to look at the situation <u>seriously,</u> <u>honestly</u> and <u>objectively</u>; we try to find best treatment plan possible for the person and the individuals involved, dealing with the rights of the individual and doing the right thing for all parties involved.

First, is how their treatment is going affect their life, but, the second, should be the treatment of the person or persons involved, and how will it help them. There should be help for all parties involved, and that could consist of separate or combined help and counseling depending on the best solution for each individual and the personal needs of the individuals.

Talking and dealing with teens and young adults about addictions.

By the time students leave high school over 50 % percent have experimented with alcohol, and 14 percent become alcoholics.

Millions of Americans who have experimented with cocaine, fewer than 5 percent become addicted.

Teens and young adults who have used alcohol and drugs: more often young women don't drink to get drunk, and that leads to the risk of being seduced into sex.

Meyer Glints, acting chief of the *Etiology Research Section of the National Institute for Drug and Alcohol Abuse.*   {5}
"What are the problems with alcohol:
- High-crime in our neighhoods where drugs and alcohol are sold.
- When drug dealers are the local role models and economic successes.
    1) The dealers are the ones who become a high risk for addictions
- They have easy access to drugs and alcohol
- And peer cultures glamorize the effects of drugs and alcohol.
- They become habit forming, dependent, and are addictive

Using medications of sorts can become addictive too:
- Of course, there is need for health purposes
- They sooth their sadness and melancholy, and they do feel good for a while, but usually takes more and more to satisfy the need
    1) Leads to anxiety, anger, depression, and high levels of distress.
- They can become dependent, addicted, or it becomes a chemical fixation for help
- This can unlimitedly lead to substance abuse."

Haward Moss, et al., "Plasma GABA-like Activity in Response to Ethanol Challenge in Men at High Risk for Alcoholism,"

Biological Psychiatry **27 (6) (1990).** [30]

"A neuropsychological study of sons of alcoholics who at age twelve showed signs of:
- Anxiety such as heightened heart rate in response to stress
- As well as impulsive behaviors

The boys had a poor **frontal lobe function** in the **brain area**, which was limited in helping them, in controlling their anxiety and impulsiveness. Also, the **prefrontal lobes** handle **working memory**—the consequences, which hold many routes of action in the **brain area**—this could give some possibilities in the insight into alcoholism.

Even they themselves found an immediate threat from anxiety, which could lead to alcoholism.

- The craving for alcohol was a very strong influence toward alcoholism
- The genetic tie to those who have high levels of anxiety and to alcoholism

Two, is someone who has high levels of anxiety, impulsiveness, and boredom
- This pattern shows up as early as in infancy:
- They become restless, cranky, and hard to handle

This pattern also shows up in grade school:
- Fighting, hyperactive, and getting into trouble a lot
- Anti-social and personality disorders
- Impulsive and boredom
- They often feel unhappy for no reason
- Low levels of predication in school and social events

They may find two deficiencies in:
- One, Serotonin
- Two, MAO

While depression can drive some to drank,

- The metabolic effects of alcohol often simply worsen the depression after a short lift
- The alcoholic as an **emotional palliative** and can more offend than not, calm anxiety, but then depression sets in.

It takes entirely different class of drug to soothe people with depression—at least temporarily.

- The **feeling** of unhappiness puts people at a greater risk for addictions.
- Although, cocaine which provides a direct antidote to **feeling depressed**.

Another, thing about cocaine most people on cocaine are usually subject to depression. There is risk involved in that the next episode is usually much stronger.

Binge drinking among College and University students to the point of passing out.

Bingeing on beer to the point of passing out. One of the techniques:
- Attach a funnel to a garden hose, so that a can of beer can be downed in about ten seconds.
- One survey found that two fifths of males college students downed seven or more drinks at a time
- While 11 percent called themselves a "heavy drinker"
- Another term might be "alcoholics"
- About ½ of collage men and about 40 percent of women have at least two binge-drinking episodes in a month.

This kind of 'heavy drinking' on a continual bases will lead to adult drinking patterns. The emotions show up in anger and anxiety that is not uncommon:

About <u>one</u> in <u>six</u> show aggressive patterns of alcoholism. These are usually symptoms of a saver alcoholic parent, or the treat maybe inherited. While no one knows for sure how a pattern begins in life by the time the repressor reaches adulthood they are under duress.

Teen Drug Use and Teen Drinking also known as Substance Abuse amongst teens and even children. Pages 1 – 3 [31]

"With today's society, kids have access to many different substances that can be addictive and damaging. If you suspect your child is using drugs or drinking alcohol, please seek help for them as soon as possible. Drug testing is helpful, but not always accurate. Teen Drug use and Teen Drinking may escalate to addiction.

We get calls constantly, that a child is only smoking pot. Unfortunately in most cases, marijuana can lead to more severe drugs, and marijuana is considered an illegal drug by, 'The United Sates'. Smoking marijuana is damaging to the child's body, brain and behavior. Even though marijuana is not considered a narcotic, most teens are very hooked on it. Many teens that are on prescribed medications such as Ritalin, Adderall, Strattera, Concerta, Zoloft, Prozac etc. are more at risk when mixing these medications with street drugs. It is critical you speak with your child / teen ager about this and learn all the side effects. Educating your child on the potential harm may help them to understand the dangers involved in mixing prescription drugs with street drugs. Awareness is the first step to understanding.

Alcohol is not any different with today's teens. Like adults, some teens use the substances to escape their problems; however they don't realize that it is not an escape but rather a deep dark hole. Some teens use substances to 'fit in' with the rest of their peers – teen peer pressure. This is when a child really needs to know that they don't need to 'fit in' if it means hurting themselves. Using drug and alcohol is harming them. Especially if a teen is taking prescribed medication (refer to the above paragraph) teen drinking can be harmful. The combination can bring out the worst in a person. Communicating with your teen, as difficult as it can be, is one of the best tools we have. Even if you think they are not listening, we hope eventually they will hear you.

If your teen is experimenting with this, please step in and get proper help through local resources. If it has extended into an addiction, it is probably time for a Residential Placement. If you feel your child is only experimenting, it is wise to start precautions early. An informed parent is an educated parent. This can be your life jacket when and if you need the proper intervention.

Always be prepared, it can save you from rash decisions later.

A teen that is just starting to experiment with substance use or starting to become difficult; a solid short term self-growth program may be very beneficial for them. However keep in mind, if this behavior has been escalating over a length of time, the short term program may only serve as a temporary Band-Aid.

Drugs and Alcoholic usage is definitely a sign that your child needs help. Teen Drug Addiction and Teen Drinking is a serious problem in today's society; if you suspect your child is using substances, especially if they are on prescribed medications, start seeking local help. If the local resources become exhausted, and you are still experiencing difficulties, it may be time for the next step; Therapeutic Boarding School or Residential Treatment Center."

Copyright © 2001-2007 P.U.R.E. Inc.

To get Help, Call TOLL FREE: 1-800-730-7260

Local and International Callers please Call: 954-349-7260

P.U.R.E. does not provide legal advice and does not have an attorney on staff.

http://www.helpyourteens.com/teen_drug_use_and_teen_drinking.html
9/04/07

Teen Drinking Statics a Family Guide   **Pages 1- 2 [32]**

"Talking to your kids about drinking, alcohol, smoking, and other drugs can help keep them away from risky behavior.

How much are today's youth drinking? Well, we found out all about teen alcohol use. An excellent source of alcohol use data is the Substance Abuse and Mental Health Services Administration's National Household Survey on Drug Use and Health (NSDUH). Some of the most recent survey results are listed below.

'The percentage of 12- to 17-year-olds who reported talking at least once in the past year with their parents about the dangers of drug, tobacco, or alcohol use. Youths who reported having such conversations had lower rates of current drug, tobacco, or alcohol use than those who did not talk with their parents about substance abuse!

The percentage of 12- to 20-year-olds who reported drinking alcohol in the past month. 18.8 percent of underage drinkers were binge drinkers and 6 percent were heavy drinkers. To compare, if you just look at the number of high school kids who drank in the last month, the percentage increases to 43.3!

The percentage of 12- to 17-year-olds who have had five or more drinks on the same occasion on at least 1 day in the past 30 days. This is called 'binge drinking.' To compare, if you just look at the number of high school kids who binge drank in the last month, the percentage increases to 25.5!'

Want more teen drinking statistics? Another survey for high school students, the 2005 Youth Risk Behavior Surveillance Survey (YRBSS), is conducted by the Centers for Disease Control and Prevention. Below are just a few of the survey's findings:

73.2 percentage of high school students nationwide who have had one or more drinks of alcohol during their lifetime.

28.5 percentage of high school students nationwide who rode in a car driven by someone who had been drinking one or more times during the 30 days preceding the survey.

25.6 percentage of high school students who drank alcohol (more than a few sips) for the first time before the age of 13. <u>High school students are starting to drink earlier and earlier</u>. The frequency of having had their first drink before 13 is:

    19.3 percent for 12th graders

    20.5 percent for 11th graders
    26.2 percent for 10th graders
    33.9 percent for 9th graders

23.3 percentage of sexually active high school students nationwide who drank alcohol or used drugs before last sexual intercourse.

9.9 percentage of high school students nationwide who reported driving a car or other vehicle after drinking alcohol one or more times during the 30 days preceding the survey.'

    The percentages for some teenage drinking behaviors are down from the 2001 YRBSS study. Lifetime drinking is down to 74.3 from 78.2 in 2001. Binge drinking for 12- to 17-year-olds also dropped from 29.9 in 2001 to 25.5. Kids are much more likely to choose not to drink when they have a strong and supportive relationship with a parent or guardian. Even if it's an uncomfortable conversation the first time, future conversations get easier. Make sure your child clearly understands your family's rules about drinking."

http://www.family.samhsa.gov/talk'alcohol.aspx   9/05/07

Teen discipline, youth drug use, prevention Family Guide
                                      Pages 1 – 2 [33]

"Make clear, sensible rules for your child and enforce them with consistency and appropriate consequences. "When you do this, you help your child develop daily habits of self-discipline. Following these rules can help protect your child's physical safety and mental well-being, which can lower her risk for substance abuse problems. Some rules, such as 'Respect Your Elders,' apply to all ages, but many will vary depending on your child's age and level of development. This section offers tips on how to establish expectations for your child's behavior and how to respond when she * doesn't obey.

Preventing Kids From Breaking the Rules

    Most parents, teachers, and other authority figures deal with young people who occasionally break the rules. As kids move from childhood to their teen years, they may push limits, ignore advice, and question authority. You may wonder how to get them to stop, do as they're told, and act right.

Post-High School Parenting

Now that your teen has graduated, he might think he's all grown up and ready to take on the world. But he may still need help from you to make the right choices along the way.

Practice What You Preach

Whether you are an occasional user or just have a drink or two with dinner, your tobacco, alcohol, and illegal drug use affects your children.

Combating Parental Stress

Has your daily 'to-do' list gotten so long that it no longer fits on a single piece of paper? Or do you have so much to do that you don't even have time to make a to-do list? You're not alone. Parents today are working longer hours and commuting greater distances to and from work. Their days don't slow down when they get home. Kids' after-school schedules can be jam-packed, making life busy—and often stressful—for parents.

Gadgets and Gizmos and Games

Children and technology have a close relationship. Video game players, cell phones, iPod, DVD players, and computers are among the hi-tech gadgets and gizmos that many kids and teens own. Tech items help young people have fun, learn new skills, and stay in touch with family and friends.

Cheating: New Alarm About an Old Problem

Stealing answers or copying someone else's work—some students probably have cheated since schools started handing out grades. While cheating may be nothing new, it has become more common and often uses new technology. Parents and school officials face the hard question of what to do about dishonesty and the shortcuts to success that many students take.

Wiggly Alcohol Tempts Teens

Remember when your mother gave you jiggly, slippery gelatin

desserts? Most of us have fond memories of those brightly colored treats. But times have changed, and a different kind of gelatin may be offered to your child. This new twist on the old classic features an ingredient that is dangerous for young people—alcohol.

How Can I Protect My Teen from Underage Drinking?

Teens say that parents are the number one influence in their lives, and you have everything you need—right now—to help protect your teen from underage drinking. Don't wait for a better time; this is the best time!

Teens say that parents are the number one influence in their lives, and you have everything you need—right now—to help protect your teen from underage drinking. Don't wait for a better time; this is the best time!

Talk with your kids, listen to your kids.

Find out what they are thinking, and what they are feeling. Every day, know who they hang out with, what they do, and where they're going. Not only will it help you influence and keep track of your child, but you also can get to know each other better.

Teach your teen.

Discuss the effects of alcohol use and why alcohol is especially bad for young people. The more your child knows, the better informed he will be to make wise decisions about alcohol use.

Set the right example.

If you drink, limit your alcohol use, especially in front of your children. Kids learn most of their habits from parents and caregivers.

Be firm and consistent.

Make sure to set clear expectations and follow through on the rules you make. Enforce the consequences of breaking the rules the first time. Be fair.

Control your surroundings.

Account for any alcohol you have around the house, and store it away from your teen. You might be surprised to know that most teens get alcohol by buying it or getting it from home—if not your home, teens say they often drink at their friends' houses. That liquor cabinet in the dining room might stir up your child's curiosity, so keep its contents out of reach.

Teach media literacy.

Watch TV with them and talk about what they are seeing and hearing; tell them why some programs are not as good as others. Set guidelines and try to limit your child's contact with TV shows, music, and magazine ads that promote alcohol. Encourage your child to take part in other activities—reading, playing sports, and writing.

Keep your eyes open, notice the signs.

If something does not seem right, it probably isn't. If you aren't sure how to approach your child, get ideas or get help from your doctor, your child's teacher, a counselor, or another caring adult.

Be proactive.

Get involved not only in your kid's life but also in the lives of other kids, parents, and caregivers. Do as much as you can, when you can, to prevent underage drinking. Make use of available tools and find out about related laws and organizations so you can be part of the larger effort.

In addition, if you want new ideas on how to help your teen make healthy choices, you can look around for help:

Connect with other parents and caregivers to get ideas on how to prevent your teen from drinking alcohol.

Take advantage of activities and events in your community that can help your children lead alcohol-free lives.

Get support, create a network. Not only is it wise to get to know your kids and their friends, but also get to know their friends' parents, too. Urge them to get involved in prevention activities and to be available to give and get support.

Safe Riding, Safe Driving

Motor vehicle crashes are the number one killer of youth ages 15 to 20. If you're the parent of a teen, it's likely that drunk and drugged driving is at the top of your list of concerns for your child. Many teens know someone who has been involved in or affected by a car crash with an impaired driver— a driver who had been drinking alcohol or using another drug that lowers the ability to drive safely. Sadly, some of those drivers are young people.

The Latest Craze—Marijuana-Flavored Candy?

A new product on the market may make parents double check the candy bowl. It's marijuana-flavored candy, and it already could be in stores near you. It may look like a normal lollipop or candy bar, but it tastes like pot."

http://www.family.samhsa.gov/set/   9/05/07

US Department of Health and Human Services
Substance abuse and mental health services administration
Center for substance abuse prevention
Teen Smoking   Pages 1 -3 [34]

"The differences between subjective feelings of those who smoke and those who don't are shown in behavioral changes that are more apparent in teens than adults. Teens seem to be more abrasive when smoking or they feel like they are older and wiser when they smoke. Why do they smoke when we have seen billions of dollars spent on antismoking campaigns? The American Lung Association estimates that every minute four thousand eight hundred teens will take their first drag off a cigarette. Of those four thousand eight hundred, about two thousand will go on to be chain smokers. The fact that teen smoking rates are steadily increasing is disturbing. We are finding out that about 80% of adult smokers started smoking as teenagers.

We now see a lot of smokers giving each other rewards in social aspects such as conversations, companionships, and other common social contacts. Research has proven the fact that nicotine has the ability to suppress feelings, suppress appetite for food, is used as stimulation after sex, and is a good way to relax from troubles and feelings of insecurities. People that smoke go to designated areas and congregate around the one that has the light, even when the weather is sub-zero. There they are huddled up against each other in an area, taking in the last drag before the break is over, or they find some kind of shelter to smoke their cigarettes.

Teens like to act as if they are someone special or dangerous. By smoking they can act on those feelings. Because it is so forbidden it becomes more alluring to teens. The problem is that when they take that first puff, they can become addicted. The idea that they are breaking the law or going against their parents and schools is an addiction within itself. Kids like to get attention; it does not matter if it's good attention or bad attention. They crave attention and by smoking they get big attention. The other teens look at them in all kinds of ways and the adults get upset and don't know what to do.

Nicotine is considered the number one entrance drug into other substance abuse problems. Research shows that teens between 13 and 17 years of age who smoke daily are more likely to use other drug substances. The use of other drugs is part of the peer pressure that our children have to face. The earlier that our youth begin using tobacco, the more likely they will continue using into adulthood.

Why is tobacco so addicting? It is because nicotine acts as a stimulant, which is stimulating the mind, body, and spirit. When the body tolerance levels high then one ends up needing to use larger doses of nicotine to maintain a certain level of the physiological effect. When the body becomes accustomed to the presence of nicotine, it then requires the use of the chemical to help the body to function normally. This level of dependence is referred to as an addiction.

Here are some common experiences from teens who smoke.
- They tried their first cigarette in sixth or seventh grade
- They often do not perform well in school
- They feel like they are not a part of the school
- They become isolated from other students
- They can't perform as well at sports events
- They feel like they have little hope of going to college
- They feel like they need a job to support their smoking habit

- They are reported to school officials for skipping classes
- They start using other illegal substances
- They begin experimenting with alcohol and other drugs
- They experience pressure from home and school and use tobacco as a form of relief
- Teen smokers enjoy trying to hide their smoking

'This has made school more fun for some tobacco users. These types of behaviors get attention because the initiation of smoking is influenced by having a friend, particularly a best friend, who smokes. The risk factors do not apply because those who are young think that they are indispensable. The peers who use or have favorable attitudes toward tobacco use are more likely to use other illegal substances. On the other hand, if the teen becomes a member of a pro-social group, such as those participating in sports, cheerleading, or any club that promotes healthy living, the likelihood that the teen will attempt to stop smoking improves.

The amount of teens smoking cigarettes dropped about 28% in 2001. The following are some-reasons-why:

a) The increase of cost in the retail price of cigarettes has gone up 70%
b) The schools have implemented efforts to fight the use of tobacco (teen smoking).
c) There is an increase in youth exposure to both state and national mass media campaigns.
d) The truth on the effects of nicotine that are in tobacco products.

When tobacco companies lost the lawsuit that made them pay for anti-smoking ads, they raised the cost of cigarettes. Young people are having a harder time finding ways to smoke because smokers are paying top dollar for their cigarettes. We are also seeing teens speak out in the media and in person and they have been capturing the attention of their peers and changing attitudes about how un-cool and unhealthy teen smoking is.

The times are changing; what the public and science did not know twenty years ago is now coming to the surface. The fact is that smoking cigarettes can cause many health problems including emphysema, high blood pressure, and various forms of cancer. We are seeing people live longer and healthier lives and the old idea that smoking makes you cool and attractive is gone. This is the truth about cigarettes; they are loaded with harmful chemicals and the end result is that they are a dangerous drug that can seriously harm people."

References

Christen, Arden G. & Joan A. Christen, (1994), "Why is Cigarette Smoking So Addicting?" Health Values, Vol. 18, No.1, January/February.
Fibkins, William L., (1993), "Combating Student Tobacco Addiction in Secondary Schools," NASSP - Bulletin, December.
"Guidelines for School Health Program to Prevent Tobacco Use and Addiction," (1994), Journal of - School Health, Vol. 64, No. 9, November.
Lynch, Barbara S. & Richard J. Bonnie, (1994). Growing Up Tobacco Free. Washington D.C.,   National Academy Press.
Nelson-Simley, Kathleen & Laurel Erickson, (1995), "The Nebraska 'Network of Drug-Free Youth' - Program," Journal of School Health, Vol. 65, No. 2, February.
Peck, Diane DiGiacomo& Connie Acott, (1993), "The Colorado Tobacco-Free Schools and Communities Project," Journal of School Health, Vol. 63, No. 5, May.
http://www.teendrugabuse.us/teensmoking.html9/07/07

Out-Of-Date Neural Alarms

One drawback of such neural alarms is that the urgent message, the **amygdala sends is sometimes out-of-date or not relevant** in the world we live-in. The emotional memory the amygdala scans the experience, comparing what has happened in the past to the now. The response may be mild but close enough to alarm, the amygdala. A few spare elements of the situation may bring back old memories similar to some dangerous situation in the past. The trouble it may be charged with **emotional memories** that trigger this crisis response and can be equally out dated. The emotional brain and memories can go back to our childhood.

During this early period of life other brain structures, particularly the **hippocampus, which is circuital for narrative for memories, and the neocortex, seat of rational thought.**

In memory, the amygdala and hippocampus work hand and hand; each stores and retrieve information independently. The early childhood can be triggered by wordless blueprints before an infants has words for their experiences, when these emotional memories are triggered in later life. It can be an emotional response to a past situation or event.

When emotions are fast and sloppy

At this point we going to use an illustration of amygdala in action. The direct route has vast advantages in brain activity, which is reckoned in thousandths of a second. The amygdala in a rat can begin a response to a perception in as little as twelve milliseconds-twelve thousandths of a second. The route from the thalamus to the neocortex to the amygdala takes about twice as long.

Some emotional mistakes that are based on feelings prior to the thought process are called "**precognitive emotions**", a reaction based on neural bits and pieces of sensory information that have not been fully sorted out and intergraded into a recognizable object. It's a very rare form of sensory information, something like a neural, *"name that tone"*, where instead of a snap judgment of the melody instead being based on just a few notes, a whole perception is grasped on such little information. If in the case of the amygdala senses a sensory pattern of importance emerging, it jumps to a conclusion, triggering its reactions before there is full confirming information-or any confirmation is reached.

Small wonder we have little insight into our more explosive emotions, especially when they still have a grip in our memory. The amygdala can and does act and react delirium of rag before the cortex knows what is going on because such raw emotion is triggered independent of, and prior to the thought process.

The emotional manager

The **prefrontal lobes** while the amygdala is at work in priming an anxious, impulsive reaction another part of the emotional brain allows for more fitting, corrective response. The **brains damper switch** for the amygdala and amygdala's surges appears to lie at **the other end of a major circuit to the neocortex, in the prefrontal lobes** just behind the forehead.

The **prefrontal cortex** seems to be at work when someone is fearful or enraged, but is stifled, when control the feelings are ordered to deal more effectively with a situation like drugs or smoking or when reappraisal calls for a completely different response, like a mother worried over the phone.

The **neocortex area of the brain brings a more analytical or appropriate response** to our emotional impulses, modulating the **amygdala** and other **limbic areas**.

Ordinarily the **prefrontal area** governs our emotional reactions from the start. **The largest sensory information comes from the thalamus**, remember, it does not go through the amygdala, but to the neocortex and its many centers for taking in and making sense of what is being perceived; that information and our response to it is coordinated by the prefrontal lobs. The seat of planning and organizing actions toward a goal, emotional impulse including emotional ones. In the neocortex a cascading series of circuits registers and analyzes that information, comprehends it through the prefrontal lobes, and then orchestrates a reaction. If in the process an emotional response is called for, the prefrontal lobes dictate it, working hand-in-hand with the amygdala and other circuits in the emotional brain.

This progress which allows for discernment in an emotional response to any situation. This is a standard arrangement, with the significant exception of emotional emergencies. When an emotion triggers within moments the prefrontal lobes perform what amounts to as risk/benefit ratio of myriad possible reactions, and which one of them is best.

The neocotex is slower because of the circuitry it is also more judicious and considerate, sense more thought precedes feeling.

Emotional hijacking presumably involves two dynamics, **triggering the amygdala** and failure to activate the **neocortex** process that usually keeps **emotional response** in balance. At these moments the **rational mind** is swamped by the **emotion**. One way the **prefrontal cortex** acts as an efficient manager of **emotion-weighing reactions** before acting it is by dampening the signals for a bad action sent out by the **amygdala** and other **limbic centers**. It is like a parent grabbing and asking a child properly (or wait) for what they want.

The "off switch", for depressing emotion seems to be the left prefrontal lobe. One of the tasks of the left frontal lob is to act as a neural thermostat, regulating unpleasant emotions. The right prefrontal lobes are a sat of negative feelings, while the left lobes keep those raw emotions in check, probably by inhibiting the right lobe. Those of the left prefrontal cortex were prone to catastrophic worries and fears; those with lesions on the right were "unduly cheerful"; during neurological exams they joked around and were so laid back they clearly did not care how well they did.

Harmonizing Emotions And Thoughts

The connections between **the amygdala (and related limbic structures)** and the **neocortex** are the hub of battles or cooperative treaties struck between head and heart, thought and feeling. This circuitry explains why emotion is so crucial to affective thoughts, both in making wise decisions and in simply allowing us to think clearly.

The emotion has power to disrupt the thinking process. Neuroscientists use the term "**working memory**", for the capacity of attention that holds the facts essential for completing a given task or problem whether it be the ideal features one seeks in a house while looking for another or eliminates of reasoning while taking a test.

The prefrontal cortex is the brain region responsible for **working memory**. But, circuits from the **limbic brain** to the **prefrontal lobes** means that the signals are **strong emotion**, anxiety, anger, and can create neural sabotaging the ability of the **prefrontal lobe** to maintain **working memory**. That is why when we are emotionally involved in bad behavior, we "**just can't think straight**", and why continual emotional desires can create deficits in a person's intellectual abilities, crippling the capacity to learn and refuse to do something.

These deficits are more subtle not always decided by IQ testing and show up more in neuropsychological measures as well in a person's continual aggressive and impulsive behaviors. For example people who had above-average IQ scores were doing poorly in school via the neuropsychological tests something has impaired frontal cortex functioning. They were also impulsive, anxious, and often disruptive, in trouble suggesting a faulty prefrontal control over their limbic urges. Despite their intellectual potential these children have problems with academic failures, alcoholism and become drug addicts, but because they are not able to control their emotions. The emotional brain is quite separate from those cortical areas tested by IQ tests, but controls rage and compassion these emotional circuits are experienced throughout their childhood and into their adult life.

Teen Smoking   **Pages 1 – 2 [35]**

"Despite continued efforts to prevent children from obtaining tobacco, they continue to do so at an alarming rate. We hear a lot about such factors as peer pressure, advertising, and seeing celebrities smoking as contributing to higher rates of teen smoking. What can a parent and the community in which they live do to counteract these outside influences bombarding their teens?

What can a parent do?
A study in the December 2001 issue of the journal <u>PEDIATRICS</u> indicates that it may actually be parents who have the greatest influence on whether their teens will smoke. The study reported that

'adolescents who perceived strong parental disapproval of their smoking were less than half as likely to have higher smoking...levels compared with those who did not perceive strong parental disapproval.' By contrast, those teens who thought that their parents were getting more lenient over time were significantly more likely to progress to becoming established smokers.

What else can parents do? There is an effective No Smoking message for children at all stages of development. Ideally, all children should be provided a smoke-free environment, at home and in the community. Parents should access smoke-free restaurants and other facilities so that their children will grow up seeing few adults in their community smoking and will believe that they are entitled to a smoke free environment.

Very young children can understand that both smoking and secondhand smoke are harmful. Children at this age need to be taught to disapprove of the smoke, not the smoker.

School-age children are often concerned about environmental issues, and tobacco use can be presented in the context of pollution. Secondhand smoke is a prime source of indoor air pollution, and discarded cigarettes are a major source of litter.

As children begin to enter their early teen years, parents need to be certain that young teens do not have access to tobacco products at home. Studies show that when young teens begin to experiment with smoking, their first cigarettes are frequently obtained from parents, older siblings, and older relatives.

During the teen years parents need to repeat their strong disapproval of tobacco use. Although there is much concern about teen smoking, teens need to understand that most of their peers do **not** smoke and that they do not need to smoke to 'fit in'. Consequences for using tobacco need to be established and implemented, if necessary. Parents should support the schools, athletic associations, restaurants, and stores that have strict no-tobacco-use policies.

What can the community do?

The Needham Board of Health has been and will continue to be aggressive in tackling the public health issue of tobacco.

In 1993, the Needham Board of Health established the local Tobacco Control Program. This program was funded by the Massachusetts Department of Public Health and was supported by a statewide referendum. After ten successful years, the Tobacco Control Program was unfortunately eliminated due to drastic statewide budget cuts.

This leaves us with a choice. To continue to work aggressively and try to curb tobacco use among children, or yield to the tobacco industry.

The Needham Board of Health has passed regulations dealing with smoking in the workplace, restaurants and bars, and other public domains. Unfortunately, tobacco products continue to permeate the Middle School and High School. We feel strongly that raising the legal age to be sold tobacco products to the age of 21 by the year 2005 will go a long way in reducing the number of young people using tobacco. These decisions and new regulations have been researched thoroughly. The California Medical Association has submitted legislation to enact similar regulations in that state.

We need to show our children that most adults do not smoke, and that smoking is no longer something to do to look "grown-up". We need to raise our children to expect a smoke-free environment. Our future depends upon it."

http://www.town.needham.ma.us/both/BOHHealthMattersTeenSmoking.htm   9/07/07

Conclusion on teen addictions

NEW BEGINNINGS IV, ADDICTION TREATMENTS

Chapter 12

TREATMENTS FOR ADDICTIONS

There are treatments for addictions Alcoholism-Drugs-Pills Uppers Downers and other substances. These have been common social disorders in our society for hundreds of years.

How are you going deal with your addiction?

Alcoholism & Intoxication Treatment Act Ps 1 thou 7 of 23 [36]

UNIFORM ALCOHOLISM AND
INTOXICATION TREATMENT ACT
Drafted by the
NATIONAL CONFERENCE OF COMMISSIONERS
ON UNIFORM STATE LAWS
and by it
APPROVED AND RECOMMENDED FOR ENACTMENT
IN ALL THE STATES
at its
ANNUAL CONFERENCE
MEETING IN ITS EIGHTIETH YEAR
AT VAIL, COLORADO
AUGUST 21 28, 1971

WITH PREFATORY NOTE AND COMMENTS
UNIFORM ALCOHOLISM AND
INTOXICATION TREATMENT ACT

The Committee which acted for the National Conference of Commissioners on Uniform State Laws in preparing the Uniform Alcoholism and Intoxication
Treatment Act was as follows:

ALLAN D. VESTAL, College of Law, University of Iowa, Iowa City, Iowa, Chairman

RICHARD E. DAY, College of Law, Ohio State University, Columbus, Ohio

HOWARD G. KULP, JR., 518 Market Street, Camden, New Jersey

JEREMIAH MARSH, Suite 2100, 160 North LaSalle Street, Chicago, Illinois

THOMAS NEEDHAM, 403 South Main Street, Providence, Rhode Island

DON J. McCLENAHAN, 312 Simplot Building, Boise, Idaho, Chairman, Section

UNIFORM ALCOHOLISM AND
INTOXICATION TREATMENT ACT
Drafted by the
NATIONAL CONFERENCE OF COMMISSIONERS
ON UNIFORM STATE LAWS
and by it
APPROVED AND RECOMMENDED FOR ENACTMENT
IN ALL THE STATES
at its
ANNUAL CONFERENCE
MEETING IN ITS EIGHTIETH YEAR
AT VAIL, COLORADO
AUGUST 21 28, 1971
WITH PREFATORY NOTE AND COMMENTS

UNIFORM ALCOHOLISM AND
INTOXICATION TREATMENT ACT

The Committee which acted for the National Conference of Commissioners on Uniform State Laws in preparing the Uniform Alcoholism and Intoxication Treatment Act was as follows:

ALLAN D. VESTAL, College of Law, University of Iowa, Iowa City, Iowa, Chairman

RICHARD E. DAY, College of Law, Ohio State University, Columbus, Ohio

HOWARD G. KULP, JR., 518 Market Street, Camden, New Jersey

JEREMIAH MARSH, Suite 2100, 160 North LaSalle Street, Chicago, Illinois

THOMAS NEEDHAM, 403 South Main Street, Providence, Rhode Island

DON J. McCLENAHAN, 312 Simplot Building, Boise, Idaho, Chairman, Section D,

  Ex Officio

Copies of all Uniform and Model Acts and other printed matter issued by the Conference may be obtained from:

NATIONAL CONFERENCE OF COMMISSIONERS
ON UNIFORM STATE LAWS
1155 East Sixtieth Street

Chicago, Illinois 60637

UNIFORM ALCOHOLISM AND
INTOXICATION TREATMENT ACT

PREFATORY NOTE

"The Uniform Alcoholism and Intoxication Treatment Act was prepared in response to the Nation's changing attitudes toward alcoholism and alcohol abuse. Although the World Health Organization and the American Medical Association recognized alcoholism as a disease in the 1950's, it was not until the mid-1960's that significant changes began to take place in society's view and treatment of the alcoholic and public inebriate.

During the past five years, dramatic changes in attitude and approach have come about initially as the result of court decisions, then the recommendations of governmental and private commissions, and finally legislative reform. The first landmark decisions, Easter v.

District of Columbia, 361 F.2d 50 (D.C. Cir. 1966) (en banc), and Driver v. Hinnant, 356 F. 2d 761 (4th Cir. 1966), held that because alcoholism is an illness, a homeless alcoholic could not avoid being drunk in public and therefore could not be punished for his public intoxication. Although the U.S. Supreme Court, in Powell v. Texas, 392 U.S. 514 (1968), declined to extend this holding to include an alcoholic who has a home and family, a majority of the court indicated that the punishment of a homeless alcoholic for public intoxication would violate the Eighth Amendment to the U.S. Constitution. The most important aspect of that decision was the unanimous recognition that current facilities, procedures, and legislative responses to the problem had been wholly inadequate.

In 1967 three authoritative commissions, the U.S. and the D.C. Crime Commissions and the Cooperative Commission on the Study of Alcoholism, found that the criminal law was an ineffective, inhumane, and costly device for the prevention and control of alcoholism or public drunkenness.

All recommended that a public health approach be substituted for current criminal procedures. Another major effort to change public policy toward alcoholism and the treatment of public intoxication came in 1969 when the American Bar Association and American Medical Association, which earlier had collaborated on new model legislation based on the Crime Commission Reports, released a 'Joint Statement of Principles Concerning Alcoholism' in which they urged State governments to adopt new comprehensive legislation in which alcoholism would be viewed as an illness and public intoxication would no longer be handled as a criminal offense.

The first jurisdiction to begin active legislative consideration of these new proposals was the District of Columbia, where Congress enacted the District of Columbia Alcoholism Rehabilitation Act in 1968 (Public Law 90-452). Hawaii, Maryland, North Dakota, Florida, and other States have also reformed their laws governing alcoholism and intoxication in the past four years.

The growing awareness and concern with the treatment of alcoholism and public intoxication also brought a Federal response. In 1968, Congress passed the Alcoholic Rehabilitation Act of 1968 (Public Law 90-574) the first Federal law dealing specifically with the treatment of alcoholism on a national basis. Congress declared in that Act that 'the handling of chronic alcoholics within the system of criminal justice perpetuates and aggravates the broad problem of alcoholism whereas treating it as a health problem permits early detection and prevention of alcoholism and effective treatment and rehabilitation, relieves police and other law enforcement agencies of an inappropriate burden that impedes their important work, and better serves the interests of the public.' In 1970, this Federal initiative in the field was substantially expanded with the enactment of the Comprehensive Alcohol Abuse and Alcoholism Prevention, Treatment, and Rehabilitation Act of 1970
(Public Law 91-616), and the establishment of the National Institute on Alcohol Abuse and Alcoholism.

The Uniform Alcoholism and Intoxication Treatment Act is designed to provide States with the legal framework within which to approach alcoholism and public intoxication from a health standpoint, as recommended by the courts, commissions, and professional organizations. The Act draws heavily upon the authoritative recommendations of the U.S. and D.C. Crime Commissions, on the recent District of Columbia and State statutes, and on model laws drafted by both the Joint Committee of the American Bar Association and the
American Medical Association and the Legislative Drafting Research Fund of Columbia University.

UNIFORM ALCOHOLISM AND INTOXICATION TREATMENT ACT

SECTION 1. [Declaration of Policy] It is the policy of this State that alcoholics and intoxicated persons may not be subjected to criminal prosecution because of their consumption of alcoholic beverages but rather should be afforded a continuum of treatment in order that they may lead normal lives as productive members of society.

Comment

This section is intended to preclude the handling of drunkenness under any of a wide variety of petty criminal offense statutes, such as loitering, vagrancy, disturbing the peace, and so forth. As the Crime Commissions pointed out, drunkenness by itself does not constitute disorderly conduct. The normal manifestations of intoxication staggering, lying down, sleeping on a park bench, lying unconscious in the gutter, begging, singing, etc. will therefore be handled under the civil provisions of this Act and not under the criminal law. See District of Columbia v. Greenwell, 96 Daily Wash.L.Reptr. 2133 (D.C.Ct.Gen.Sess. December 31, 1968).

SECTION 2. [Definitions] For the purposes of this Act:
(1) 'alcoholic' means a person who habitually lacks self-control as to the use of alcoholic beverages, or uses alcoholic beverages to the extent that his health is substantially impaired or endangered or his social or economic function is substantially disrupted;
(2) 'approved private treatment facility' means a private agency meeting the standards prescribed in Section 9(a) and approved under Section 9(c);
(3) 'approved public treatment facility' means a treatment agency operating under the direction and control of the division or providing treatment under this Act through a contract with the division under Section 8(g) and meeting the standards prescribed in Section 9(a) and approved under Section 9(c);
(4) 'commissioner' means the commissioner [or ....] of the department;
(5) 'department' means [the state department of health or mandate
(6) 'director' means the director of the division of alcoholism;
(7) 'division' means the division of alcoholism within the c department established under

Section 3;

(8) 'emergency service patrol' means a patrol established under Section 17;

(9) 'incapacitated by alcohol' means that a person, as a result of the use of alcohol, is unconscious or has his judgment otherwise so impaired that he is incapable of realizing and making a rational decision with respect to his need for treatment;

(10) 'incompetent person' means a person who has been adjudged incompetent by [the appropriate state court];

(11) 'intoxicated person' means a person whose mental or physical functioning is substantially impaired as a result of the use of alcohol;

(12) 'treatment' means the broad range of emergency, outpatient, intermediate, and inpatient services and care, including diagnostic evaluation, medical, psychiatric, psychological, and social service care, vocational rehabilitation and career counseling, which may be extended to alcoholics and intoxicated persons.

Comment

The term 'alcoholic' is defined in two alternative ways for two different purposes. The first alternative is a relatively narrow definition based on lack of self-control regarding the use of alcoholic beverages. Lack of self-control may be manifested either by the inability to abstain from drinking for any significant time period, or by the ability to remain sober between drinking episodes but an inability to refrain from drinking to intoxication whenever drinking an alcoholic beverage. This relatively narrow definition has been the basis for the court decisions holding an alcoholic not criminally responsible for his intoxication.

The second alternative definition adopts the World Health Organization's broad approach, that alcoholism can be defined as the use of alcoholic beverages to the extent that health or economic or social functioning are substantially impaired. The purpose of this broad definition is to make as large a group as possible eligible for treatment for alcoholism and related problems. Encouraging early treatment for drinking problems will ultimately lead to prevention. This broad definition of alcoholism is useful in making voluntary treatment available to as large a group as possible, but would be wholly inappropriate to define those alcoholics who justify civil commitment for involuntary treatment.

The Act defines 'treatment' broadly to include a wide range of types and kinds of services to reflect the fact that there is no single or uniform method of treatment that will be effective for all alcoholics. The Act provides a flexible approach with a variety of kinds of medical, social, rehabilitative, and psychological services according to the individual's particular needs."

(…) pages 8 thou 23
http://www.law.upenn.edu/library/ulc/fnact99/1970s/uaita71.txt
1/26/06

Mental Help Net – Perspective – Vol. 4, No 2– The Morality of Alcoholism   **Pages 1 -2 of 1-6**
Perspectives - Vol. 4, No. 2 - The Morality of Alcoholism –
                                           Page 1 of 2 [37]

Gary S. Stofle
This article is based upon ideas originally presented at the 1985 NASW Professional Symposium: "The People, Yes!" on November 9, 1985.
http://www.mentalhelp.net/poc/view_doc.php?type+doc&id+381
                                                        1/26/06

Alcohol Research & Health: The effects of parental exposure on Executive Functions   **Pages 1 of 5** [38]

"There is evidence from various researches that indicates that people who have been exposed to alcohol prenatally may exhibit impairments regarding their performance of relatively complex and normal tasks. These tasks include tests designed to measure executive functioning (EF)--the ability to plan and **guide behavior** to achieve a goal in an efficient manner. (EF) can be categorized into two domains, **cognition-based (EF)** and emotion-related (EF). People prenatally exposed to alcohol show impaired performance on tests assessing both domains. Moreover, one **cognition-based** and two emotion-related measures of EF appear to be reliable and stable predictors of **behavioral problems** in alcohol-affected people. A deficit in flexible recruitment of brain regions to do complex tasks may underlie the EF deficits in people prenatally exposed to alcohol. KEY WORDS: prenatal alcohol exposure; **cognitive and memory disorder**; brain damage; brain function; emotion; mood and affect disturbance; **behavioral problem**.

The term 'executive functioning' (EF) generally refers to **cognitive functions** involved in planning and **guiding behavior** in order to achieve a goal in an efficient manner. Impairments in EF have been found in patients with a wide range of neurodevelopmental disorders, including autism, attention deficit disorder, early treated phenylketonuria (PKU),

(1) Fragile X Syndrome (Pennington et al. 1996). Studies found that children who had been exposed to alcohol prenatally may also be impaired on tasks measuring competencies associated with EF (Kodituwakku et al. 1995; Mattson et al. 1999) as well as on other **cognitive functions** (e.g., visual processing and memory functions). This article explores the relationship between prenatal alcohol exposure and deficits in EF. It first describes the **cognitive skills** subsumed under EF. It then summarizes the existing literature on EF in people who have been exposed prenatally to alcohol

(2) and discusses the usefulness of EF performance in defining a neurobehavioral profile related to prenatal alcohol exposure.

EXECUTIVE FUNCTIONING

The concept of EF refers to deliberate, or effortful, actions that involve various abilities, such as holding and manipulating information "in the head" (i.e. working memory) and focusing on one task at a time (i.e., inhibiting task-irrelevant habitual responses). Such deliberate actions can be contrasted with involuntary, or automatic, actions (for a more detailed discussion of this distinction, see the sidebar).

EF can further be divided into two categories. The original concept of EF referred to **cognition-based actions**, and researchers and clinicians have used a variety of **cognitive tests** requiring deliberate attention to formally assess this type of EF. Such tests measure problem solving, conceptual set shifting (described in the following paragraph), and rapid generation of verbal or nonverbal responses. Subsequently, some scientists broadened the definition of EF to include another form of action selection that has been called emotion-related (Rolls et al. 1994), or affective (Dias et al. 1996) EF. Action selection at this level is based on rewards and punishments (i.e., positive and negative reinforcement) obtained in the past in similar situations. This emotion-related EF can be assessed using tests that measure the ability to modify behavior in response to changing reinforcement conditions.

Assessing Cognition-Based and Emotion-Related EF

The distinction between **cognition-based and emotion-related EF** can be further illustrated by comparing two tests commonly used to assess EF. The Wisconsin Card Sorting.

Test (WCST) is used to evaluate cognition-based EF. In this test, the subject is asked to sort cards by a given dimension (e.g., the cards' color) and then to shift attention to sorting them by a different dimension (e.g., the cards' form) according to the examiners feedback. Thus, the WCST measures the subject's ability to shift attention across different dimensions, a process formally known as conceptual, or extra-dimensional, set shifting.

Emotion-related EF can be assessed using the Visual Discrimination Reversal Test. In this test, the subject is required to learn stimulus--reward associations and to adjust responses when those associations are reversed.

For example, the subject may be shown two images that appear one at a time on a computer screen. The subject then receives a reward (e.g., a pleasant sound) for responding to one of the images and a negative response (e.g., an unpleasant sound) for responding to the other image. Once the subject has learned this routine, the pattern of reinforcement changes without warning so that the rewarding image becomes no rewarding and vice versa. The examiner then determines how quickly the subject adjusts to this reversal. Because this test measures the shifting of responses to two stimuli that vary in only one dimension (e.g., the pattern of the image), this type of response adjustment is called intra-dimensional set shifting. (Because the test measures the reversal of response-reward associations, some investigators also have used the term affective shifts.)

Brain Regions Involved in EF

The brain regions that control EF can be identified by determining whether patients with damage in specific brain areas (regardless of whether that damage is alcohol related) show impaired performance on tasks assessing EF. Such analyses indicated that **cognition-based EF** and **emotion-related EF** are controlled by different brain areas. For example, Damasio (1994) reported that patients with damage in the orbitofrontal cortex (see figure 1) performed poorly on an emotion-related decision-making task but completed the **WCST, which assesses cognition-based EF**, with ease. Similarly, Rolls and colleagues (1994) found that patients with or biro frontal damage were impaired in the Visual Discrimination Reversal Test, which assesses emotion-related EF, yet exhibited normal performance on cognition-based EF tasks. Furthermore, both Damasio (1994) and Rolls and colleagues (1994) found that the performance of patients with orbitofrontal damage on these emotion-related tasks was associated with the patients' social and other behavioral problems--that is, patients with greater impairment on those tasks exhibited greater social and other problems.

Animal studies have indicated that **cognition-based EF** may be controlled by brain areas in the lateral prefrontal cortex (see figure 1). Thus, lesions in the **lateral prefrontal cortex** but not in the **or bito frontal cortex** impaired the performance of monkeys on a test of extra-dimensional set shifting that was an analogue of the WCST (Dias et al. 1996). In contrast, monkeys with orbitofrontal lesions but not monkeys with lateral prefrontal lesions were impaired in performing intra-dimensional shifts in a Visual Discrimination Reversal Test.

COGNITION-BASED EF IN PEOPLE PRENATALLY EXPOSED TO ALCOHOL

Research has demonstrated that prenatal alcohol exposure can lead to brain damage in various regions. Moreover, alcohol-affected people exhibit a variety of behavioral and cognitive impairments. Given that the developmental outcome of alcohol-affected people is dependent on a wide range of variables (e.g., the amount and frequency of alcohol exposure, maternal age, and the parents' education) it is difficult to determine a threshold of alcohol consumption for such adverse effects. Some researchers have obtained evidence, however, that seven standard drinks (3) per week may be the threshold for most sensitive behavioral measures, although this threshold does not apply to all women and babies (Jacobson and Jacobson 1994). Although moderate alcohol exposure (i.e., 7.0 to 13.9 drinks per week) may produce impairments of EF, no relationship has been found between the number of abnormal physical features associated with heavy prenatal alcohol exposure and the degree of EF deficits in affected people. In other words, people with full-blown fetal alcohol syndrome (FAS)--the most severe consequence of prenatal alcohol exposure--and alcohol-exposed people without FAS both exhibit EF deficits to the same degree (Kodituwakku et al. 2001).

This section presents research on the performance of alcohol-affected people in tests assessing cognition-based EF. These tests use a range of tasks that involve holding and manipulating **cognitive (or emotionally insignificant) information in working memory, such as**

tests of cognitive planning and strategy development, conceptual set shifting, rapid generation of verbal or nonverbal responses according to specific rules, and the ability to solve new problems quickly and accurately (i.e., fluid intelligence)." (…)

NEURAL CORRELATES OF EF DEFICITS IN ALCOHOL-EXPOSED PEOPLE

Neuropathological and neuroimaging studies have found evidence of structural brain damage in people with substantial prenatal alcohol exposure. For example, autopsy studies of children with FAS have found a wide range of neuropathology, including the absence or imperfect development of the corpus callosum (see figure 1) and disorganization of various cortical regions (Clarren 1986). Neuroimaging studies using magnetic resonance imaging (MRI) also revealed abnormalities in several brain regions of alcohol-exposed children, specifically in the basal ganglia, the corpus callosum, and parts of the cerebellum (Roebuck et al. 1998; for more information, see the article by Mattson and colleagues, pp. 185-191, in this issue).

However, these analyses detected no gross abnormalities in the frontal lobes of alcohol-affected children, which would have been expected based on studies linking EF deficits to brain damage in non-alcohol-exposed people. Accordingly, it remains unclear what brain abnormalities account for the deficits in EF in people with prenatal alcohol exposure.

Functional neuroimaging techniques (e.g., functional MRI), which can assess the activity of different brain areas while the subject performs various tasks, have shown that the brain recruits multiple regions to perform complex tasks that alcohol-exposed people find challenging (Carpenter et al. 2000). Accordingly, one can hypothesize that the EF deficits in alcohol-affected people likely are associated with a deficit in the efficient recruitment of brain regions required to do a task. The finding that alcohol-exposed infants process information slowly (Jacobson 1998) is consistent with this hypothesis. Abnormalities in specific brain regions, such as the basal ganglia, and in the connectivity among brain areas may contribute to such inefficient recruitment, as has been suggested for other mental disorders.

For example, abnormal connectivity among brain regions has been proposed as a possible mechanism underlying frontal lobe dysfunction in patients with schizophrenia (Weinberger and Berman 1996). Neuroimaging studies of alcohol-exposed people have revealed evidence for disproportionately reduced white matter volumes (Archibald et al. 2001) and abnormalities of the corpus callosum, suggesting that the neural infrastructure required for information processing is compromised." (…)

REFERENCES
ARCHIBALD, S.L; GAMST, A; RILEY, E.P.; MATTSON, S.N.; AND JERNIGAN, T.L. Brain dysmorphology in individuals with severe prenatal alcohol exposure. Developmental Medicine and Child Neuorology 43:148-152, 2001.

BENTON, A.L. Differential behavioral effects in frontal lobe disease. Neuropsychologia 6:56-60, 1968.

CARMICHAEL-OLSON, H.; FELDMAN, J.J.; STREISSGUTH, A.P.; SAMPSON, P.D.; AND BOOKSTEIN, F.L. Neuropsychological deficits in adolescents with fetal alcohol syndrome: Clinical findings. Alcoholism: Clinical and Experimental Research 22:1998-2012, 1998.

CARPENTER, P.A.; JUST, M.A.; AND REICHLE, E.D. Working memory and executive function: Evidence from neuroimaging. Current Opinion in Neurobiology 10:195-199, 2000.

CLARREN, S.K. Neuropathology in fetal alcohol syndrome. In: West, J.R., ed. Alcohol and Brain Development. New York: Oxford, 1986.
COLES, C.D.; PLATZMAN, K.A.; RASKIND-HOOD, C.L.; BROWN, R.; FALEK, A.; AND SMITH, I.E. A comparison of children affected by

prenatal alcohol exposure and attention deficit, hyperactivity disorder. Alcoholism: Clinical and Experimental Research 21:150-161, 1997.

DAMASIO, A.R. Descartes Error: Emotion, Reason, and the Human Brain. New York: G.P. Putnam's Sons, 1994.

DIAS, R; ROBBINS, T.W.; AND ROBERTS, A.C. Dissociation in the prefrontal cortex of affective and attentional shifts. Nature 380:69-72, 1996.

DUNCAN, J.; SEITZ, R.; KOLODNY, J.; ET AL. A neural basis for general intelligence. Science 289:457-460, 2000.

JACOBSON, S. Specificity of neurobehavioral outcomes associated with prenatal alcohol exposure. Alcoholism: Clinical and Experimental Research 22:313-320, 1998.

JACOBSON, J.L., AND JACOBSON, S.W. Prenatal Alcohol Exposure and Neurobehavioral Development: Where is the thresold? Alcohol Health & Research World 18(1):30-36, 1994.

KELLY, S.A.; DAY, N.; AND STREISSGUTH, A.P. Effects of prenatal alcohol exposure on social behavior in humans and other species. Neurotoxicology and Teratology 22:143-149, 2000.

KODITUWAKKU, P.W.; HANDMAKER, N.S.; CUTLER, S.K.; WEATHERSBY, E.K.; AND
HANDMAKER, S.D. Specific impairments in self-regulation in children exposed to alcohol prenatally. Alcoholism: Clinical and Experimental Research 19:1558-1564, 1995.

KODITUWAKKU, P.W.; MAY, P.A.; CLERICUZIO, C.L.; AND WEERS, D. Emotion-related learning in individuals prenatally exposed to alcohol: An investigation of the relation between set shifting, extinction of responses, and behavior. Neuropsychologia, 39:699-708, 2001.

KOPERA-FRYE, K.; DEHAENE, S.; AND STREISSGUTH, A.P. Impairments of number processing induced by prenatal alcohol exposure. Neuropsychologia 34:1187-1196, 1996.

MATTSON, S.N.; GOODMAN, A.M.; CAINE, C.; DELIS, D.C.; AND RILEY, E.P. Executive functioning in children with heavy prenatal alcohol exposure. Alcoholism: Clinical and Experimental Research 23:1808-1815, 1999.

PENNINGTON, B.F.; BENNETTO, L.; MCALEER, O; AND ROBERTS, R.J. Executive function and working memory: Theoretical and measurement issues. In: Lyon, G.R., and Krasnegor, N.A., eds. Attention, Memory, and Executive Function. Baltimore, MD: Paul Brooke Publishing Co., 1996.

ROEBUCK, T.M.; MATTSON, S.N.; AND RILEY, E.P. A review of the neuroanatomical findings in children with fetal alcohol syndrome or prenatal exposure to alcohol. Alcoholism: Clinical and Experimental Research 22:339-344, 1998.

ROLLS, E.T.; HORNAK, D.W.; AND McGRATH, J. Emotion-related learning in patients with social and emotional changes associated with frontal lobe damage. Journal of Neurology, Neurosurgery & Psychiatry 57:1518-1524, 1994.

SCHONFELD, A.M.; MATTSON, S.N.; LANG, A.R.; DELIS, D.C.; AND RILEY, E.P. Verbal and nonverbal fluency in children with heavy prenatal alcohol exposure. Journal of Studies on Alcohol 62:239-246, 2001.

SHALLICE, T., AND EVANS, M.D. The involvement of the frontal lobes in cognitive estimation. Cortex 14:294-303, 1978.

STREISSGUTH, A.P.; BOOSTEIN, F.L.; BARR, H.M.; PRESS, S.; AND SAMPSON, P.D. A fetal alcohol behavior scale. Alcoholism: Clinical and Experimental Research 22:325-333, 1998.

WEINBERGER, D.R., AND BERMAN, K.F. Prefrontal function in schizophrenia: Confounds and controversies. Philosophical Transactions of the Royal Society of London, Series B351:1433-1444, 1996.
http://www.findarticles.com/p/articles/mi_m0CXH/is_3_25/ai_83029493
2/1/06

Profile on "The disease of alcoholism":

Now let's look at some warning signs that have to with bad mental health and alcoholism.
Anxiety
1. Anxiety brings about a feeling of uneasiness.
2. Anxiety brings about fear.
3. Anxiety brings about a sense of insecurity.
4. Anxiety brings about apprehension that something bad is going to happen.
5. Anxiety brings about unpleasantness and escapism.
6. Anxiety may lead to using drugs and alcoholism.

Mental disorders / illness / disease and their treatment

Mental health covers a vast spectrum of a person's well-being if they are addicted, from minor areas to dealings alcoholism and substance abuse should they be considered as mental illness when they become serous to severe problems. Now let's look at some:

Symptoms – disorders may be treated or cured, and dealt with in many ways depending on the severity of the problem or situation. They can be frightening if a person doesn't know how to deal with those uncertain feelings that makes a person insecure about their predicament or situation. But, for the most part knowledge and understanding of one's addiction and makeup/background are the keys to opening the vast unknowns in a person's recovery.

This can lead to many different kinds of symptoms:
Substance abuse

1) When it affects a person's health, when a person becomes dependent on alcohol and drugs.
2) They usually have defensive behavior patterns.
3) They are usually helpless in controlling or quitting drugs.
4) In some cases shyness and self-consciousness aide in their dependence and codependences.
5) Another misconception is that the addiction makes them happy and self-confident.
6) Another down side is they are usually depressed and unhappy is the reason they need drugs.
7) Another downside is the dependency and it takes more and more all the time.
8) Last is the money it takes to support the habits of alcohol and drugs.

Substance abuse help

1) Treatment centers and programs.
   (a) It depends on the determination of the person and how bad the addiction is?
   (b) Will-power and personal well-being will help.
   (c) They must decide to quit the drugs or alcohol.
   (d) Most programs advocate admitting to the problem.
   (e) Self-awareness and admitting the need for help.
   It may involve personal counseling and/or group support.

ALCOHLISM　　　　　　　　　　　　　　　　Pages 1 - 31 [39]
Alcoholism December 2001

WHAT IS ALCOHOLISM?

"Alcoholism is a chronic, progressive, and often fatal disease. It is a primary disorder and not a symptom of other diseases or emotional problems. The chemistry of alcohol allows it to affect nearly every type of cell in the body, including those in the central nervous system. After prolonged exposure to alcohol, the brain adapts to the changes alcohol makes and becomes dependent on it. The severity of this disease is influenced by factors such as genetics, psychology,-culture,-and-response-to-physical-pain.

Signs of alcoholism or alcohol dependence include the following:

- The only indication of early alcoholism may be the unpleasant physical responses to withdrawal that occur during even brief periods of abstinence.
- Alcoholics have little or no control over the quantity they drink or the duration or frequency of their drinking.
- They are preoccupied with drinking, deny their own addiction, and continue to drink even though they are aware of the dangers.
- Over time, some people become tolerant to the effects of drinking and require more alcohol to become intoxicated, creating the illusion that they can 'hold their liquor.'
- They have blackouts after drinking and frequent hangovers that cause them to miss work and other normal activities.
- Alcoholics might drink alone and start early in the day.
- They periodically quit drinking or switch from hard liquor to beer or wine, but these periods rarely last.
- Severe alcoholics often have a history of accidents, marital and work instability, and alcohol-related health problems.
- Episodic violent and abusive incidents involving spouses and children and a history of unexplained or frequent accidents are often signs of drug or alcohol abuse.

Alcoholism can often have no clear line between problem drinking and alcoholism. Eventually alcohol dominates their thinking, emotions, and actions and becomes the primary means through which a person can deal with people, work, and life.

DEFINITION OF ALCOHOL USE AND ABUSE

In addition to alcohol dependence, experts are now defining alcohol use by levels of harm that it may be causing. This information is useful to determine possible interventions at earlier stages. The following categories of alcohol use and abuse use a definition of one drink as 12-oz of beer, 5 oz of wine, or 1.5 oz (a jigger) of 90-proof liquor.

Moderate Drinking. Moderate drinking, particularly red wine, appears to offer health benefits. Moderate drinking is defined as equal to or less than two drinks a day for men and equal to or less than one drink a day for-women.

Hazardous (Heavy) Drinking. Hazardous drinking puts people at risk for adverse health problems. People who are heavy drinkers consume the following:

- More than 14 drinks per week or 4 to 5 drinks at one sitting for men.
- More than seven drinks a week or three drinks at one sitting for women.
- Frequent intoxication in either gender.
- *Harmful Drinking.* Drinking is considered harmful when alcohol consumption has actually caused physical or psychological harm. This is determined by the following:
- There is clear evidence that alcohol is responsible for such harm.
- The nature of that harm can be identified.
- Alcohol consumption has persisted for at least a month or has occurred repeatedly for the past year.
- The individual is not alcohol dependent.

Alcohol Abuse. People with alcohol abuse have one or more of the following alcohol-related problems over a period of one year:

- Failure to fulfill work or personal obligations.
- Recurrent use in potentially dangerous situations.

- Problems with the law.
- Continued use in spite of harm being done to social or personal relationships.
- A 2001 study, 55% patients continued to meet this criteria after five years but only 3.5% developed dependency, the next stage.

Alcohol Dependence. People who are alcohol dependent have three or more of the following alcohol-related problems over a period of one year:
- Increased amounts of alcohol needed to produce an effect.
- Withdrawal symptoms or drinking alcohol to avoid these symptoms.
- Drinking more over a given period than intended.
- Unsuccessful attempts to quit or cut down.
- Giving up significant leisure or work activities.
- Continuing drinking in spite of the knowledge of its physical or psychological harm to oneself or others.
- One long-term study, two-thirds of these individuals continued to be dependent on alcohol after five years.

HOW IS ALCOHOLISM DIAGNOSED?
Barriers to a Diagnosis

Even when people with alcoholism experience withdrawal symptoms, they nearly always deny the problem, leaving it up to coworkers, friends, or relatives to recognize the symptoms and to take the first steps toward encouraging treatment. Denial, in fact, may be an important-warning-signal-for-alcoholism.

Family members cannot always rely on a physician to make an initial diagnosis. Although 15% to 30% of people who are hospitalized suffer from alcoholism or alcohol dependence, physicians often fail to screen for these problem. In addition, doctors themselves often cannot recognize the symptoms. In one study, alcohol problems were detected by the physician in less than half of patients who had them. Even when physicians identify an alcohol problem, however, they are frequently reluctant to confront the patient with a diagnosis that might lead to treatment for addiction.

(...)

Personal Intervention. The best approaches for motivating a patient to seek treatment are interventional group meetings between people with alcoholism and their friends and family members who have been affected by the alcoholic behavior. Using this approach, each person affected offers a compassionate but direct and honest report describing specifically how he or she has been hurt by their loved one's or friend's alcoholism.

The family and friends should express their affection for the patient and their intentions for supporting the patient through recovery, but they must strongly and consistently demand that the patient seek treatment. Children may even be involved in this process, depending on their level of maturity and ability to handle the situation.
Employer Intervention. Employers can be particularly effective. Their approach should also be compassionate but strong, threatening the employee with loss of employment if he or she does not seek help. Some large companies provide access to inexpensive or free treatment programs for their workers.

Overall Treatment Goals

The ideal goals of long-term treatment by many physicians and organizations such as AA are total abstinence and replacement of the addictive patterns with satisfying, time-filling behaviors that can fill the void in daily activity which occurs when drinking has ceased. Patients who secure total abstinence have better survival rates, mental health, and marriages, and they are more responsible parents and employees than those who continue to drink or relapse.

Because abstinence is so difficult to attain, however, many professionals choose to treat alcoholism as a chronic disease. In other words, patients should expect and accept relapses, but should aim for as long as remission period as possible. Even reducing alcohol intake can lower the risk for alcohol-related medical problems.

Alcoholics Anonymous and other alcoholic treatment groups are greatly worried by treatment approaches that do not aim for strict abstinence, however. Many people with alcoholism are eager for any excuse to start drinking again. There is also no way to determine which people can stop after one drink and which ones cannot. At this time, seeking total abstinence is the only safe route.

Inpatient versus Outpatient Treatment

A number of treatment options now exist for alcoholism. It is first important to determine if in- or outpatient care would best benefit the individual. Inpatient care is performed in a general or psychiatric hospital or in a center dedicated to treatment of alcohol and other substance abuse. It is recommended for the following people:
Those with a coexisting medical or psychiatric disorder.
- Those who may harm themselves or others.
- Those who have not responded to conservative treatments.
- Those who have a disruptive home environment.

Many studies have reported better success rates with inpatient treatment of patients with alcoholism. Examples are the following:
- 'In one 1999 study, patients were hospitalized and treated for four weeks and compared to patients treated as outpatients for six weeks. At three months after treatment, inpatients had fewer complications and were less likely to return to drinking than outpatients. After six months to a year the differences were smaller.
- In another study, those in an inpatient group had significantly fewer prehospitalization and remained abstinent longer than people in two other outpatient groups (compulsory attendance at AA meetings or allowed to choose their own treatment option, including none at all).

Other studies, however, have shown no difference in results between inpatient and outpatient programs. Given the ambiguity in results and high expense of inpatient treatment, then, most care providers do not choose inpatient treatment for alcoholics who are not a threat to others.'

Inpatient Treatment Options. A typical inpatient regimen may include the following stages:

- A physical and psychiatric work-up for any physical or mental disorders.
- Detoxification.
- Treatment with medications.
- Psychotherapy or cognitive-behavioral therapy.
- An introduction to Alcoholics Anonymous (AA).

Outpatient Treatment Options. People with mild to moderate withdrawal symptoms are usually treated as outpatients. Treatments are similar to those in inpatient situations and include the following:

- Psychotherapy or counseling.
- Medications that target brain chemicals involved in addiction.
- Social support groups such as Alcoholics Anonymous.
- Studies are suggesting that cognitive therapies may be very effective for selected people.
- Even brief intervention by a family doctor can be helpful for reducing alcohol intake in many heavy drinkers.
- Because people with alcoholism are very likely to also be smokers, one study suggested that quitting smoking at the same time might even promote alcohol abstinence.
- After-care employs services that help alcoholics maintain sobriety. For example, in some cities, sober-living houses provide residences for people who are trying to stay sober. They do not offer formal treatment services, but the people living there offer each other support and maintain an abstinent environment.
-

Factors that Predict Success or Failure after Treatment

'A 2001 analysis of studies reported that 25% of people were continuously abstinent following treatment, and another 10% used alcohol moderately and without problems. And even among the remaining group, alcohol consumption was reduced by an average of 87%. Most studies strongly suggest that intensive and prolonged treatment is important for successful recovery, whether the patient is treated within or outside a treatment center. Certain factors play a role in success or failure:

- Patients from low-income groups tend to have worse results in general. Their difficulties are often intensified by lack of insurance, low self-esteem, and minimal social support.

In patients who have private insurance the factors predicting success differ from lower-income groups and appear to be gender related:

- The factors that tended to keep more women in treatment were unemployment, marriage, and higher incomes. Women who dropped out tended to have more severe psychiatric problems. African American women were also less likely to stay in treatment than non-African Americans.
- Factors that kept men in treatment were older age, pressure from the employer, and abstinence as a goal. Dropping out was associated with the opposite factors.'

(...)

WHAT IS THE TREATMENT FOR ALCOHOL WITHDRAWAL?

Symptoms of Withdrawal

When an alcoholic stops drinking, withdrawal symptoms begin within six to 48 hours and peak about 24 to 35 hours after the last drink. During this period the inhibition of brain activity caused by alcohol is abruptly reversed. Stress hormones are over-produced and the central nervous system becomes over-excited. Depending on severity, withdrawal symptoms may include the following:

- Fever.
- Rapid heartbeat.
- Changes in blood pressure either higher or lower.
- Extremely aggressive behavior.
- Hallucinations and other mental disturbances.
- Seizures occur in about 10% of adults during withdrawal, and in about 60% of these patients, the seizures are multiple. The time between the first and last seizure is usually six hours or less.
- About 5% of alcoholic patients experience delirium tremens, which usually develops two to four days after the last drink.

Although it is not clear if older people with alcoholism are at a higher risk for more severe symptoms than younger patients, several studies have indicated that they may suffer more complications during withdrawal, including delirium, falls, and a decreased ability to perform normal activities.

(...)

WHAT ARE THE PSYCHOTHERAPY TREATMENTS FOR ALCOHOLISM?
Choose a Psychotherapeutic Approach

The two standard forms of therapy for alcoholism are the following:

- Cognitive-behavioral therapy
- Interactional group psychotherapy based on the Alcoholics Anonymous (AA) 12-step program.

In one study, all treatment approaches were, on average, equally effective as long as the individual program was competently administered. One 2001 study reported that, in general, AA had a better abstinence rate than cognitive-behavioral therapy; AA was also less expensive.

Specific people, however, may do better with one program than another:

- In one study, people with fewer psychiatric problem did best with the AA approach. This confirms an earlier study in which researchers' categorized alcoholics as either Type A or Type B. Type A individuals became alcoholic at a later age, had less severe symptoms or fewer psychiatric problems, and had a better outlook on life than those with Type B. The people in the Type A group did well with the 12-step approach. They did not do as well with cognitive-behavioral therapy.

- Type B people became alcoholic at an early age, had a high family risk for alcoholism, more severe symptoms, and a negative outlook on life. This group tended to do better with cognitive-behavioral therapy.

This difference in response to the two forms of treatments held up after two years.

Interactional Group Psychotherapy (Alcoholics Anonymous)

Alcoholics Anonymous (AA), founded in 1935, is an excellent example of interactional group psychotherapy and remains the most well-known program for helping people with alcoholism. It offers a very strong support network using group meetings open seven days a week in locations all over the world. A buddy system, group understanding of alcoholism, and forgiveness for relapses are AA's standard methods for building self-worth and alleviating feelings-of-isolation.

AA's 12-step approach to recovery includes a spiritual component that might deter people who lack religious convictions. [*See Box* The 12 Steps of Alcoholics Anonymous.] Prayer and meditation, however, have been known to be of great value in the healing process of many diseases, even in people with no particular religious assignation. AA emphasizes that the 'higher power' component of its program need not refer to any specific belief system. Associated membership programs, Al-Anon and Alateen, offer help for family members and friends.

The 12 Steps of Alcoholics Anonymous

1. We admit we were powerless over alcohol - that our lives have become unmanageable.
2. We have come to believe that a Power greater than ourselves could restore us to sanity.
3. We have made a decision to turn our will and our lives over to the care of God, as we understand what this Power is.
4. We have made a searching and fearless moral inventory of ourselves.
5. We have admitted to God, to ourselves and to another human being the exact nature of our wrongs.
6. We are entirely ready to have God remove all these defects of character.
7. We have humbly asked God to remove our shortcomings.

Cognitive-Behavioral Therapy

Cognitive-behavioral therapy uses a structured teaching approach and may be better than AA for severe alcoholism. People with alcoholism are given instruction and homework assignments intended to improve their ability to cope with basic living situations, control their behavior, and change the way they think about drinking. The following are examples of approaches:

- 'Patients might write a history of their drinking experiences and describe what they consider to be risky situations.
- They are then assigned activities to help them cope when exposed to 'cues,' places or circumstances that trigger their desire to drink.
- Patients may also be given tasks that are designed to replace drinking. An interesting and successful example of such a program was one that enlisted patients in a softball team; this gave them the opportunity to practice coping skills, develop supportive relationships, and engage in healthy alternative activities.'

In one study of patients with both depression and alcoholism, cognitive therapy achieved 47% abstinence rates after six months compared to only 13% abstinence in patients who received standard treatments and relaxation techniques. It may be especially effective when used in combination with opioid antagonists, such as naltrexone. (...)

Treating Sleep Disturbances

Nearly all patients who are alcohol dependent suffer from insomnia and sleep problems, including having less sleep, taking longer to fall asleep, and experiencing less deep sleep. Such problems can last months to years after abstinence. There is some evidence that they are important factors in relapse. Medications for inducing sleep are not recommended in people with alcoholism. Available therapies include sleep hygiene, bright light therapy, meditation, relaxation methods, and other nondrug approaches."

WHERE ELSE CAN HELP BE OBTAINED FOR ALCOHOLISM?

Alcoholics Anonymous, World Services, Inc., P.O. Box 459, New York,

NY 10163. Call (212-870-3400) or on the Internet (http://www.alcoholics-anonymous.org/)

Al-Anon Family Group Headquarters, Inc., 1600 Corporate Landing Pkwy, Virginia Beach, VA 23454-5617
For meetings Call (800-344-2666) in the US, or (800-443-4525) in Canada.
For literature Call (800-356-9996) in the US, or (800-714-7498) in Canada
or on the Internet (http://www.Al-Anon-Alateen.org/)

Al-Anon was started by the wife of the founder of Alcoholics Anonymous to help families of alcoholics. They provide meetings and educational material established along the lines of those of AA. Also available through Al-Anon is Alateen, a support fellowship for adolescents affected by people with alcoholism. This group is not for teenagers with drinking problems.

National Institute on Alcohol Abuse and Alcoholism, 6000 Executive Boulevard - Willco Building, Bethesda, MD 20892-7003. On the Internet (http://www.niaaa.nih.gov/)

National Clearinghouse of Alcohol and Drug Information, PO Box 2345, Rockville, MD 20847-2345. Call (800-729-6686) or on the Internet (http://www.health.org/)
Offers many publications on alcohol and substance abuse.

Hazelden Foundation, PO Box 11, CO3, Center City, MN 55012-0011. Call (800-257-7810) or
(651-257-4010) from outside the US or on the Internet (http://www.hazelden.org/)
Maintains chemical dependency treatment centers. Also provides educational materials for adults and adolescents. Their web site is very useful.

National Council on Alcoholism, 20 Exchange Place, Suite 2902, New York, NY 10005. Call (800-NCA-CALL) or (212-269-7797) or on the Internet (http://www.ncadd.org/)
Their 800 number is a hotline that requires a touch-tone phone. A recorded message provides local numbers for counseling, help, and information after the caller keys in their zip code.

National Organization on Fetal Alcohol Syndrome, 216 G Street North East, Washington, DC 20002. Call (202-785-4585) or on the Internet (http://www.nofas.org/)

American Academy of Addiction Psychiatry, 7301 Mission Road, Suite 252, Prairie Village, KS 66208. Call (913-262-6161) or on the Internet (http://www.aaap.org) ``

On the Internet:
Web of Addictions (http://www.well.com/user/woa/) has good links and keeps up with current research.

Recovery (http://www.recovery.org/aa/) is a private web site with good links to other sites on alcoholism.

ABOUT WELL-CONNECTED

Well-Connected reports are written and updated by experienced medical writers and reviewed and edited by the in-house editors and a board of physicians, who have faculty positions at Harvard Medical School and Massachusetts General Hospital, Neither Harvard Medical School or Massachusetts General Hospital, as Institutions, review or endorse this content. The reports are distinguished from other information sources available to patients and health care consumers by their quality, detail of information, and currency. These reports are not intended as a substitute for medical professional help or advice but are to be used only as an aid in understanding current medical knowledge. A physician should always be consulted for any health problem or medical condition. The reports may not be copied without the express permission of the publisher.

Board of Editors
Harvey Simon, MD, Editor-in-Chief, Associate Professor of Medicine, Harvard Medical School; Physician, Massachusetts General Hospital

Stephen A. Cannistra, MD, Oncology, Associate Professor of Medicine, Harvard Medical School; Director, Gynecologic Medical Oncology, Beth Israel Deaconess Medical Center

Masha J. Etkin, MD, PhD, Gynecology, Harvard Medical School; Physician, Massachusetts General Hospital
John E. Godine, MD, PhD, Metabolism, Harvard Medical School; Associate Physician, Massachusetts General Hospital

Edwin Huang, MD, Gynecology, Harvard Medical School; Physician, Massachusetts General Hospital

Daniel Heller, MD, Pediatrics, Harvard Medical School; Associate Pediatrician, Massachusetts General Hospital; Active Staff, Children's Hospital

Paul C. Shellito, MD, Surgery, Harvard Medical School; Associate Visiting Surgeon, Massachusetts General Hospital

Theodore A. Stern, MD, Psychiatry, Harvard Medical School; Psychiatrist and Chief, Psychiatric Consultation Service, Massachusetts General Hospital
Nidus Information Services
Cynthia Chevins, Publisher
Bruce Carlson, Business Development Manager
Carol Peckham, Editorial Director

Lea Kling, Update Editor

© 2001 Nidus Information Services, Inc., 41 East 11th Street, 11th Floor, New York, NY 10003 or email office@well-connected.com or on the Internet at www.well-connected.com.
http://www.reutershealth.com/wellconnected/doc56.html   1/26/06

Is there a protective genes against alcoholism   Pages 1 -2 [40]

Contact: Hanno Also, M.D., Ph.D.
hannu.alho@ktl.fi
358-9-4744-8123 (Finland)
National Public Health Institute
Addle Contact: Valero Kiianmaa, Ph.D.
kalervo.kiianmaa@ktl.fi
358-9-4744-8111 (Finland)
National Public Health Institute
Alcoholism: Clinical & Experimental Research

"Is there a protective gene against alcoholism?

- Neuropeptides are peptides that are found in neural tissue.
- Previous research found that a gene variant of the neuropeptide Y (NPY) was linked with higher average alcohol consumption.
- A new study has found a higher prevalence of the NPY variant among social drinkers than among alcoholics.
- Researchers speculate the NPY variant may retard instead of predispose the transition to alcoholism.

Numerous studies have demonstrated that genetic factors can at least partially determine vulnerability to alcohol dependence. It remains unclear, however, which genes are involved and what their roles are. Neuropeptides are peptides that are found in neural tissue. An earlier study found that a gene variant of the neuropeptide Y (NPY) was associated with a 34 percent higher average alcohol consumption among the non-alcoholic population examined. Research published in the October issue of *Alcoholism: Clinical & Experimental Research* investigates if the Leu (7) / Pro (7) genetic polymorphism of NPY is associated with an increased susceptibility to alcoholism.

We were surprised to find an association between the NPY polymorphism and alcoholism that was contrary to our expectations, ö said Hannu Alho, a senior scientist in addiction medicine at the National Public Health Institute in Finland, and lead author of the study. Alho and his colleagues found that the carrier status of the Pro(7) amino acid substitution in the signal peptide of NPY was associated with a *decreased* risk of both Type I and Type II alcoholism. Alcoholism has two distinct subgroups: Type I is late in onset, exhibited by both genders, and associated with anxiety; Type II is characterized by heavy drinking at an early age, antisocial behavior, male predominance, and thought to have a much larger genetic than environmental influence. The researchers also found a higher prevalence of the variant in the social drinkers who served as controls. They speculate that the genetic polymorphism producing the Pro(7) substitution of NPY might not predispose to alcoholism, but instead retard the transition to alcoholism. ôNPY is well characterized as a neuromodulator in the central nervous system,ö explained Alho. ôThe best known effects of NPY are stimulation of feeding among animals, and activation of a Ĺfat-splittingĺ enzyme called lipase which increases energy storage in adipose (or fatty) tissue. Central administration of NPY in mice reduces anxiety, whereas NPY-deficient mice score high on measures of anxiety. In the normal variant of the NPY gene, one Leucine (Leu) amino acid is substituted by Proline (Pro) at position seven in the coding region of the gene. Normally it is the Leu/Leu type, but after this mutation it is the Leu/Pro type. We do not completely understand the impact of the Pro mutation on the NPY function. However, contrary to the previous observations, we did not find an association between alcoholism and this Pro mutation. Our finding may indicate that this Pro type is not associated with alcoholism, or our finding may be a coincidence because our study sample was not very large.ö

Study participants consisted of two groups: 122 alcoholics (101 male, 21 female), and 59 social drinkers (34 male, 25 female) who served as controls. The alcoholics were further divided into two groups, based on psychiatric evaluation of their alcoholism as Type 1 or 2. DNA was extracted from saliva samples and NPY genotypes determined.

"It has long been observed that alcoholism runs in families," said KalervoKiianmaa, head of the Alcohol Research Centre at the Finnish National Public Health Institute. "But a well-established observation does not provide compelling evidence for a genetic or an environmental influence. The first solid evidence for a potential genetic influence came from now-famous twin and adoption studies. The adoption studies by Goodwin and colleagues, for example, helped delineate the specific genetic influence. What researchers know as the Swedish Adoption studies provided strong support for the clinical impression that there are several types of alcoholism, and offered the additional insight that genetic factors might exert a greater influence in some types of alcoholism than in others." These and other studies, said Kiianmaa, have helped establish that for a substantial number of alcoholic patients, there is a genetic predisposition to develop alcohol dependence.

"In contrast to a large number of so-called genetic disorders such as cystic fibrosis, sickle cell anemia or Huntington's chorea," Kiianmaa observed, "the development of alcoholism depends on the interaction of genetically determined predisposing factors with environmentally determined precipitating factors. While the search for genes that predispose individuals to develop alcoholism is a compelling endeavor, there are a number of caveats which must be heeded."

Both Alho and Kiianmaa commented on the complexity of alcoholism as a disorder with a number of characteristic features common to complex diseases. Both cautioned against becoming overly excited about 'a protective gene' until additional studies are carried out.

"The role of neuropeptide Y in alcohol self-administration behavior and alcoholism is far from clear," said Kiianmaa. "The results obtained from different types of studies, including the present one, seem to be varying, even conflicting, and a clear picture does not emerge from them.

Therefore, anything said on the role of neuropeptide Y in alcoholism would be highly speculative. A lot of new work needs be done to clarify the situation.ö

Co-authors of the *Alcoholism: Clinical & Experimental Research* paper included: ErkkiIlveskoski, Olli A. Kajander, TarjaKunnas and Pekka J. Karhunen of the Department of Forensic Medicine in the Medical School at the University of Tempere; TerhoLehtimńki of the Laboratory of Atherosclerosis Genetics in the Department of Clinical Chemistry, Centre for Laboratory Medicine at the Tampere University Hospital; PekkaHeinńlń of the Department of Mental Health and Alcohol Research at the National Public Health Institute of Finland; and MattiVirkkunen of the Department of Psychiatry at Helsinki University Central Hospital. The study was funded by the Tampere University Hospital Medical Research Fund, the Finnish Foundation of Alcohol Research, the Y. Jahnsson Foundation, the Elli and ElviOksanen Fund, the Pirkanmaa Region Fund of the Finnish Cultural Foundation, and the JuhoVainio Foundation."
http://www.eurekalert.org/pub_releases/2001-10/ace-ita101101.php

1/31/06

Alcohol & Illicit Drugs   Pages 1 of 2 thou 7 [41]

Overview

"Alcoholism is a chronic, progressive and often-fatal disease. The condition involves a preoccupation with alcohol and impaired control over alcohol intake. You may continue to abuse alcohol despite serious adverse health, personal, work-related and financial consequences. Alcoholism involves physical dependence on the drug alcohol, but genetic, psychological and social factors contribute to an addiction.

You may have a problem with alcohol but not all the characteristics of alcoholism. Instead you may demonstrate 'alcohol abuse.' This means you engage in excessive drinking that results in health or social problems, but you aren't dependent on alcohol and haven't fully lost control over the use of alcohol.

According to the National Council on Alcoholism and Drug Dependence, about 14 million Americans abuse alcohol. Each year more than 100,000 Americans die of alcohol-related causes. Alcoholism is one of the most common preventable causes of death among Americans.

Alcoholism and alcohol abuse cause major social, economic and public health problems in the United States. The annual cost of lost productivity and health expenses related to alcoholism is more than $150 billion.

Signs and Symptoms

Most alcoholics deny that they have a drinking problem. Other signs of alcoholism and alcohol abuse include:
- Drinking alone or in secret
- Not remembering conversations or commitments
- Making a ritual of having drinks before, with or after dinner and becoming annoyed when this ritual is disturbed or questioned
- Losing interest in activities and hobbies that used to bring pleasure
- Irritability as usual drinking time nears, especially if alcohol isn't available
- Keeping alcohol in unlikely places at home, at work or in the car
- Gulping drinks, ordering doubles, becoming intoxicated intentionally to feel good or drinking to feel normal
- Having legal problems or problems with relationships, employment or finances.

Causes

Alcohol addiction Ś physical dependence on alcohol Ś occurs over time as drinking alcohol alters the balance of some chemicals in your brain, causing a strong desire for more alcohol. These chemicals include gamma-aminobutyric acid (GABA), which inhibits impulsiveness; glutamate, which excites the nervous system; norepinephrine, which is released in response to stress; and dopamine, serotonin and opioid peptides, which are responsible for pleasurable feelings. Excessive, long-term drinking can deplete or increase the levels of some of these chemicals, causing the body to crave alcohol to restore good feelings or to avoid negative feelings.

To develop alcohol addiction, other factors that lead to excessive drinking contribute to the addiction process. These include:

- **Genetics.** Your genetic makeup doesn't cause alcoholism. But, if you have an imbalance of brain chemicals, you may be more predisposed to alcoholism.
- **Emotional state.** High levels of stress, anxiety or emotional pain can lead some people to drink alcohol to block out the turmoil.
- **Psychological factors.** Having friends or a close partner who drinks regularly but who may not abuse alcohol could lead to excessive drinking on your part. It may be difficult for you to distance yourself from these 'enablers' or at least from their drinking habits.
- **Social and cultural factors.** The glamorous way that drinking alcohol is portrayed in advertising and in the entertainment media sends many people messages that it's OK to drink excessively.

(…)

http://www.hopenetworks.org/Overview_Alcoholism.html 1/31/06

Alcoholism codependency and addictions

Finally, addictions are perhaps the most misunderstood phenomena and that is in the treatment of addictions as I have tried to profile different aspects of alcoholism and drug addictions. Lot of what I have profiled on alcoholism is in a direct relation to the effects of drugs. It does seem to be a prevalent issue in today's society with varying types of recovery plans and how they deal with the responsibility, treatment, and cure for an alcoholism and the drug addiction it has affected almost every culture.

Most cultures seem to suffer with the effects of drugs and alcoholism and qualifying them as social disorders, the question is it a sin, to that extent I will give different views of these addictions in our society. Addictions can take on many forms and affects the person or persons, and it affects, society looks at in different ways. Almost, any common function in a person's life has the potential to becoming an addiction.

More often than not they are merely normal human pleasures taken one step too far, such as sex, over eating, or it could be over anything. But, once an activity in a person's life takes on an addictive quality it brings a certain danger to the physical, mental health and of course the well-being of the person, family, and the security for themselves and those around them.

Ventral Tegmental area, located in the mesencephalic part of the brain, there is a compact group of dopamine-secreting neurons whose axioms end in the nucleus (mesolimbic dopaminergic pathway). The spontaneous firing or the electrical stimulation of neurons belonging to that region that produces pleasurable sensations, feeling good. For people who are addicted could relate to their genetics, if a person can reduction of D2 (dopamine) receptors in the accumbens nucleus. Sooner or later a person becomes incapable of obtaining any degree of gratification from the common pleasures of life and also when a person is addicted.

Thus, they seek a typical avenues of escape which increases thenoxions "pleasurable" alternatives like alcoholism, cocaine addictions, impulsive gambling, and compulsion for sweet food. Certain brainstem structures, like the nuclei of the cranial nerves, stimulated by impulses coming from the cortex and the striatum (a subcortical formation), are responsible for the physiognomic: expressions of anger, joy, sadness, tenderness etc. This can cause them to worry, but their worries are self-perpetuating an endless loop of highly-ridden thoughts. Oddly enough it becomes an addiction, a habit that they can't shake. The limbic brain offers a sensation of rewards instead of anticipated wrong doing, the psychological frame work of the brain gets the credit for trying to prevent the danger if a person is not able to deal with the *need which leads to anxiety*.

The **frontal lobe function** in the **brain area** which limits in helping them in controlling their anxiety and impulsiveness. Also, the **prefrontal lobes** handle **working memory**—the consequences for what is happening, which holds the many routes of action in the **brain area**—this could give them some possibilities into the insight into alcoholism.

Even they themselves found a temporary relief from anxiety, which leads to why people use alcohol for relief from their problems and drugs for the most part are not a temporary relief.

- The craving for alcohol is a very strong influence toward alcoholism

The genetic tie to those who have high levels of anxiety use alcohol for the uforura that lasts for a while, but it brings someone who has high levels of anxiety, impulsiveness, and boredom when they are not drinking.

- This pattern can show up as early as in infancy when the parent is an alcoholic:
- They become restless, cranky, and hard to handle
- Fighting, hyperactive, and getting into trouble
- Anti-social and personality disorders
- They often feel unhappy for no reason
- Low levels of predication in school and social events

While depression can drive some to drank,

The metabolic effects of alcohol and drugs often simply worsen the depression after a short lift.

The alcoholic and drug addiction as an **emotional palliative**, can calm anxiety for a while, but than for depression sets in again.

It takes entirely different class of drug to soothe people with depression—at least temporarily.

The **feeling** of unhappiness puts people at a greater risk for addictions. Although, cocaine provides a temporary antidote to **feeling depressed**. Another thing about cocaine most people on cocaine are usually subject to depression. There is a risk involved in that the next episode usually takes a stronger dose.

Treatment for drug abuse in many cases can be **brain-based**, the **feeling** that drives them to "self-medication"—though drinking or drugs. The emotional make is much broader in scope and must include other reactions from within. The emotional balance for instance relates to hyper active/overreacting such as ADHD in children. The genetics plays a role in addictions / patterns show up in the hormonal make of the sex of a person, the social environment within which a person lives.

One of the indications is when the addiction takes precedence over all else in their life, and (he or she) (will invariably neglected the norms and balances, and usually it is out of control, and eventually it destroys and consumes anything that comes between them and any objective in (his or her) compulsive desire).

Addictions are better understood today than ever before, although there still remains a mystery on many levels of treatment and cures. At one time addictions were viewed as a sin or sins, a lack of will power, or a weakness of the human spirit and there is certainly that element I have tried to cover in this study.

Addiction to drugs is now traditionally viewed as a disease, but today most of the concentration is on drug presentation and the trafficking of drugs is viewed in light of the treatment process.

Another thing has changed in recent years a deeper understanding of both the physiology and psychology aspects has certainly helped in the understanding of these addictions as a diseases, I have pointed out the person has to take personal responsibility at some point.

But, perhaps the greatest change has come through the influence of the self-help groups such as; "Alcoholics Anonymous" "AAA meetings" which began in the 1930's when a small group of alcoholics formed a self-diagnosis defining alcoholism as a physiological and psychological "disease."

This approach has influenced the way alcoholism is treated and looked on in America, and it has also been translated to other compulsive cognitive behaviors of a person it can change how to deal with drug addictions, over eating disorders, and many other behaviors and patterns.

The identification is the moral fiber in treating addictions this has decreased the issue of it being a sin by definition: "it is a sin against the body." Therefore, I believe if that is a true statement, we still cannot ignore there is still a need to take up the moral issue in most cases, and how it should be dealt with as a person and how they see themselves, the effects of alcoholism has had it effects on the family of the alcoholic. They must understand their **personal responsibility** to the morality of **abuse** individually and in respect to the family.

Defiantly there can only be help for the individual when they are willing to accept help, and when they are an unwilling person they are going to rebel against any treatment.

A Profile addiction "a principle method for dealing with addictions".
By Dr. B. R. Laken {5}

I would like to conclude with a story told by Dr. B. R. Laken, he told this as a true story in one of his sermons.

A man came to him and said he wanted to quit smoking; in the sermon he identified the man as a farmer. "He said the man who came to him said he couldn't quit smoking, I have tried everything and nothing has worked, Dr. Laken said pray about it, the man came back to Dr.

Laken in a few days and said it didn't work, Dr. Laken said pray every day and it still didn't work," finally the farmer said "the only way he could quit smoking, when he was plowing a field one day he would get to the end of each row and he would pray, God help me make it through the this row and he did it at the end of each roll", by the end of the day he got victory over smoking.

There were some very good principles used in this illustration of the farmer.

1) He was persistent and didn't give up.
2) God is always a good answer to any problem or addiction.
3) He used good sound therapeutic principles, reputation of the same principles that work, when he needed help.
4) Whether its prayer or some other good methods of distracting the desire.

It is called delaying gratification by some psychological terms. Whatever, method a person uses, if he or she is consistent it helps them break the chain or pattern, and it is not good when it causes another problem or addiction to overcome the problem. The ultimate goal is breaking the problem or addiction; no dependency, and that will lead to living a happier and healthier life.

My hope is that a person can build on this last study and conquer some of their problems or addictions and continue to build on their personal victories, my hope is that this study has helped a person deal with the inner personal conflicts in a realistic way.

Self-Expression,
1) Personal profile of the human spirit
2) The human will
3) There are always different points of view and even arguments About dealing with the heart and mind-set!

I want to draw some parallels form this term, "surviving".

This happened in my life. For many years I lived under this kind of influence, and believe me I know a little about this kind of survival, feeling that I might not make it through the day. Another (Feeling bad about myself – thinking I must be a bad person for all of this to have happened to me.)

It was the personal victories and believing in myself that changed my life and thinking it will get better, but it didn't until I did something about it, then I became a much happier person. I think in all of this I am the same person I had always been, but people knew I was I struggling. I was always confident in my abilities and that show-up in certain aspects of my life.

So you see there is a need to do something about those problem areas weather its worth it's dealing with is up to *you*. I think I'm much better off for dealing with those issues in my life. I am able to go on with life. For one thing I have a better attitude, positive about my decisions, and trust my judgment now.

There were numerous health problems to deal with and live through since 1985. Again my life could have been shaken because of the personal health problems. I could have even been a cripple today if I had given into them, walking with cane, or even worse I could have lost my health and quality life.

I would like to tell you how I dealt with my health problems. I think that you will see a lot of turmoil at different times. I have overcome these obstacles and situations. I see people that have given into their health problems I have not told you all about myself as I am now; I fought for my healthy every day and have not given up on my health.

NEW BEGINNINGS V, HEATH & FITNESS PROGRAM & WORKOUT

Chapter 13

MY SECRETS TO A
HEALTHY HEART & FITNESS!
(Means: Rehabilitation & Maintenance)
It starts with Health-Awareness!

(There are 2 free booklets I & II)

My hope is I will be able to answer some of your particular questions about how I dealt with my health problems.
First, I profiled my problems and how I sought answers!
I looked up and read about my health problems in the "Mayo Clinic Health Book";
1996 Edition
The "American Heart Association web site"; [42]
www.americanheathassociation.org 3/27/00

Our objective is to present the need for good health!
1. What is the Cardiovascular System & Workout?
Definition: What is the Cardiovascular System? Heart, Lungs and Blood Vessels.
2. What is an exercise Program?
3. How do we deal with our Emotional Balance and Stress?
4. And then good diet? Etc., Etc.,
Almost everyone can participate regardless of their (Ability!)
I present the methods that helped me!
About 78 % of us don't get enough exercise!
1 out every 5 are disabled person!

Here are some EXCUSES! WHY?
People don't have a Health & Fitness Program?
♦ I'm healthy; I don't need a health & fitness program.

- I don't need it or I'm too busy right now.
- I'm disabled and my health is too bad.
- People have all kinds of Excuses.

Health Problems!
- There are millions of people that have some form of Arthritis and Arthritic conditions.
- There are 10's of millions that suffer with High Blood Pressure, Heart problems and Hypertension.
- Millions of others are Handicapped, Disabilities and Diseases.

NO GUARANTEE'S – JUST AN HONEST VIEW!
There are three parts of the body system that interact with the psychology of the brain and mind.

1) The Adrenalin, Thyroid, and Pituitary Glands Sucrets Chemicals into the body's energy and nerve system.

2) The central nerve system reacts to the chemical processes in the body, usually creating a balance or imbalance in a person's health, and mental well-being.

3) The Brain is the "Head Quarter" that interlocks these glands, systems, and that go through the central nervous system, and to be able to control your health and well-being as a person.

Again, when we look at our health there are physiological aspects in terms of the **brain works with body**, if any one or all of these glands there needs to be a balance, we can only speculate that the **limbic circuitry** would send *alarm* signals in response to cues of a feared illness, from the brain to the body, but the **prefrontal cortex** and *related zones* would have to learn a new and a more healthier response.

There is a great deal of truth that fear has anything to do with person's health, overcoming fear has a lot to do with the healing process because *every system has a warning system that goes through the brain.* When a person unlocks the *blocking functions to the brain* anything is possible at that point-in-time. I am going to give a personal example out of my life to prove this point.

There was a point in my life when I had major health problems, now that I have addressed them it should take away some of the fear, right.

Resolving this paradox by concluding that when fear and anxiety is expressed; when chronic fear of a health problem happens a person is more likely to have more problems when they are dealing with their health. An occasional display of anger is not dangerous to *your* health, but it is not a good sign if a person can't keep it in check, it can be bad if happens too often it can affect a person's mental-well-being, but the real problem is when things up-set a person it can affect a person's health.

I have tried to be careful when it comes to changes in the life system. The use of "our good judgment guidelines". Being wise and prudent in dealing with my life situations and concerning my health problems as well? There are people who deal *their* mental well-being, and if *you* want more details on how my life was changed. Read my autobiography **"Facing the real me, Run John Run, the real world and me. The hurt and pain, and the real cry for help**." There is some good information on my health and how I dealt with it and what happened. *My* first book "SOS LIFE ENHANCEMENT I compare it to looking at yourself in a mirror. *"Now that I've made a decision, what are the next steps in my life"*? If *you* want to know more about my health and fitness program I have "Tips on Health Awareness" (Booklet I). Then (Booklet II) "My Secretes to Healthy Heart and Fitness" has more details on how this program works. "The No-Non-Sense Workout" and "The Cardiovascular Workout", fits into my workout routine and program.

We are going to look at my health and the need for fitness, and then how behavior patterns fit in. I hope *you* will see a need for an exercise program in your life, and *you* have already seen how a fitness program saved my life, and saved me from a fate worse than death itself and being a cripple.

At the age of 56, in 1995 was the beginning of my Health & Fitness Program in my life.

I have gone through some of my personal experiences and the most important thing that happened is how I dealt with my health. It does give me special insight into the value of health and a fitness program. In conclusion my closing arguments for using these methods and principles, how they worked in my personal life and I hope they will inspiration and encourage you. In my report from the Social Security the doctor gave me ten years to live. After ten years of heart problems I thought I was going to have a heart attack, the doctor was almost right. If I hadn't done something about my health and started a fitness program I would not have the health I have today.

A preview of those **5 Steps** in my health history. (Booklets I& II)
When I followed the Steps **in this fitness program** *you* **will see my success and how my health turned around over the years to no medications.**

SOS Health-Awareness.

Steps 1 in (Booklet I)

My Health Journal!
How I dealt with my health!

Our Body and the Internal-system itself!
Our Life-system could be telling us something.
In my case I call it The Real Cry for Help!
What does a Workout & Fitness Mean?
What is a Health & Fitness Program about?

To Your Health -♥

1 out of **5** are Handicapped or Disabled
78% or 1 out 4 Do Not Exercise!

Who needs an Exercise Program?
✓ **Excuses are the No. 1 Hindrance!**
✓ **No Excuses! (NOW)**
Documentation & Vital Information: on my health!
My Personal Life, Health Profiles,
Evaluations & Studies.

NO BAND-AID APPROACH:
The Cardiovascular System & Body
Stress & Stress-relief

QUESTIONS, everyone needs to answer if possible.
A simple 2 minute Check Up Survey
(MY SECRETS TO GOODHEATHY

SOS Health-Awareness (Means: Rehabilitation & Maintenance of the BODY)
NO GUARANTEE'S – JUST AN HONEST VIEW!

Steps 2- 4 in (Booklet II)
HEALTHY HEART & FITNESS!
1. Total workout program
2. Total exercise program
3. Total health program
4. Proper-breathing techniques
   (Beginners N-N-S workout)

"The No-Non-Sense"
> Workout (100 point rewards)
> Tips on Why, When, & How to
> Start & Finish a Workout!
> Support & Workshops!
> How to Maintain a Healthy Heart
> & Exercise Program."

The biological clock is ticking!
www.sosselfhelpbooks.info

How does the power of positive thinking work in your health?

One of the most potent antidotes is seeing things differently, in a positive light. It is only natural to feel bad when a person is sick, but the point is not letting it go too far.

However stepping back and thinking about something maybe a great way to get back on track look at things in a positive light is another antidote to health-awareness.

By the same token cancer patients no matter how bad the condition, were in better frame of mind when they were able to think of someone who was worse off than they were, "what seemed bad didn't seem so bad." Those that compared themselves with people who were healthy "were the most depressed."

Another effective way of dealing with your health when depression feeds on ***rumination*** and ***preoccupations*** with one's self, helping others lifts a person's spirit, and helps them empathize with others in pain.

In some cancer treatment centers they accentuate on the positive approach to healing. My aim is to clarify the different views and present them in a positive manner leaving no doubt as to where I stand regarding all of these arguments about good health, each profile and data presented has some degree of truth as I see it, and how good health practices plays a role in treating *your* health.

Finding ways to deal with your health!

The things to I watched for as I dealt with the warning signs in my health, and how I saw the alarms going off.

I have spent a lot of time studying and researching ways that make sense, and to be able to pass them on is my goal. That is the reason for telling *you* about my health problems.

I have spent five years working on my master' degree in counseling and doctorate – PH-D in psychology I am clinical psychologist and do counseling, and trying to understand what makes me tick. I find that I'm more at peace with myself, I eat properly, learned proper exercise techniques and to be psychically healthier.

I have dedicated my life to life serving and helping others. My hope is these two booklets on health will be a part of the finished work on how people can improve their life. If for no other reason than to know that they can live a healthier life, I want to *thank you* for coming along to see what can happened. If I've done that my heart goes out to you and this journey has been worth it. Maybe I'll inspire *you* to do something *you* have always wanted to do. The main thing is for *you* to find *yourself* and a joy and peace in *your* life. This was my very first taught when I started writing. I remember back when I was in the first grade the very first book we read was "Run Dick run and Dick said run Jane run. The teaching method was to read it over and over again. That is the same methods I use in our **SOS Self-help books** on cognitive behavior studies you may think I get the point.

The title of that book has a lot to do with the basic principles in our counseling. Let me take it another step by setting up the title of these three self-help books.

What is this story line and how does the conception of this story come about. It is very interesting oddly enough. Let me say this I never thought at any time I would be writing about my life experiences, or presenting my studies. In and about 1987 or 88 there was a special time in my life. It was kind of like a flash back so to speak or in this case it was a flash forward. At the time I had no idea of what was going to happen I thought I was going to a heart attack. In May of 1996 I knew what I was going to do, and then how am I going to do it? I knew back in 87 or 88 that I was going to be doing some studies, but I didn't know how to go about writing books, all I knew I was supposed to do something. I stated by writing about my family.

I have a business background and a full time professional occupation at that time. I have worked hard and have had some real successes, but a long with some disappointments, failures and there were some life treating health problems to deal with. Each sequence of events leads to another then another.

I like to think of it as unwinding a ball of yearn it seems to be getting smaller and I am getting older. I hope you can enjoy and understand the seriousness of these events and how they relate to each other. I am going the long way around to get to the total picture. So please stay with me as I have lived a very healthy life, but abnormal at the same time. What am I saying my life has not changed up to this point; I have had a lot of fun being me. The reason for telling my story is to show you by example how not to do things in your life. There are some lessons to be learned or at least I think I have learned some real lessons.

How I over overcoming bitterness in my life!
This is one of the biggest killers in a person's life, and that is not the worst part it is a dreaded killer. A person doesn't usually realize how much damage has been done. The evidence is how it destroys a person's joy, happiness, and brings out the negativism in *them*. They don't have any fun because they have been robbed of their real joy. How can all this happen?

The movie industry uses this in many of their plots revenge for hurting someone in their family, country, or themselves in some way. They go out to revenge a death and in some cases a kidnapping, but the whole plot is about revenge and getting even. Oh how sweet it seems in the movies, but there is a paradox in the Bible that says "turn the other cheek". In real life situations the same thing happens when someone hurts their child or family, they want revenge, and for them to be tried and convicted. (A closer look at it makes them feel better, and if there is closer look, but if not they feel justice has been done.) I see that in news events where a person feels better when justice is severed.

I think I could have used that kind of help earlier in my life. I was looking for help, but didn't know where to look or what I was looking for. When I found things that helped I decided to create **SOS self-help books**. I am passing on things that have help me, and hope it will be of help. Everybody comes to a point at different times thinking they need a change. When a person wants a change for one reason or another, what are they going to do about those changes is very important. The problem is in some cases it never gets past the thinking stage. A person doesn't always make the right decisions, and even worse that they don't always have the right motives.

"WHY"? A person may need help.

Principles of Restoration
- **Hope**
- **Success**
- **Fulfillment**
- **The Human-well and Spirit**

Let's look at **restoration & maintenance,** sometimes all it takes is a minor adjustment, some minor reconstruction, or it may take a major over haul job. The rehabilitation of a person's life or situation is very important.

It can be a lot like rebuilding a car, or the human body. Sometimes the damage is too much, and a person may have to have major reconstruction or an operation. A heart may fall under such reconstruction, but if it is a car a person may buy a new car, or rebuild and start over. However, the body is much different when major damage has been done what will it take to restore the injury or illness. Then in most cases *you* check with a doctor to see what needs to be done, the important thing is how far are *you* willing to go to rehabilitate the injury or illness. Regardless what *you* do, you have to redefine *your* life and set new goals.

SUPPORT GROUPS

CARE PARTNERS

Chapter 14

SUPPORT OUTREACH SERVICES

Mission Statement

- **SOS** studies tries to bridge the **G.A.P.** in a person's life. (**G**uidance **A**nswers **P**assion)
- Being Loyal, Faithful & Responsible!
- Caring and sharing in a person's life!
- **SOS** self-help books and information has a PRIMARY GOAL to serve and Help People, *Help Themselves!*
- A dedicated effort to **Profiles / Evaluations, Analysis, & Assessments**!
- A commitment to good health and fitness!
- Complete Confidentially!
- As an independent organization we're a (neutral party)!

I believe there are bridges to be built and crossed, and **GAPS** to be filled, what are we looking for and how do we find the missing **(LINKS)**?

In this study I have looked at my life through a telescope and used it as a magnifying glass. There are some real lessons I had to learn. My life is not a textbook, but how I felt at the time. Not so much whether it was right or wrong, but what I learned did help me.

Support Services

I would like for you and others to become a part of **S**upport **O**utreach Services. We are a support service and programs that offer anyone a chance to participate as a support partner.

Our information network we have my life story, plus our study guides, and newsletters and other materials.

(Please look at our "Services and Programs"; you will want to be a part of your life)?

MARRIAGE – FAMILY & ADDICTIONS

We hope some of these services and study guides you will want in your home or library.

Check out Support Outreach Services = **Processing Center.**

INFORMATION NETWORK

Most of OUR SERVICES ARE FREE. When *you* order our books, the study materials and DVD's there is an expense our basic plan for ordering our materials depends on the material.

Outreach Services
News Letters.

Our news letters are a vital link "**SOS Life Line News**" young people and young adults News. We will have information pertaining to teens and college age young people. We will have information that adults can identify with whether they are single or married, and whatever *your* relationship you have with your children.

It is an independent processing center our newsletter has: "SOS LIFE LINE", "Gems for Jams" a community service bulletin board, but really it is much more than that. Here *you* can share those special thoughts, poems, words of wisdom that have helped *you*. This could be something *you* have written yourself, or someone else may has written (Give credit to the author). The main idea is to get people to share something personal out of their life. This will give us a chance to access a wealth of information, and this information will be shared with others. We would like to hear about the experiences in *your* life, and maybe *you* would like to share *your* experiences with someone else. This is a wonderful program for *you* and my hope is *you* are going to enjoy having this as a part of *your* life. There is one of two ways to share, or we have our web site www.sosselfhelpbooks.info we may choose to use your personal experiences in our News Letter, **SOS LIFE LINE**.

The next step is to get *you* to participate. There are no specials because all of our services are based on helping others. We do not use PRESSUER TACTICS.

My hope is you will want to be a part of OUR HELP NETWORK. So that we can fill the different needs in a person's life. I have wonderful Pastor's and churches that are a part of our network.

There is a real need for the right kind of help and support in a person's life today. There are inspirational speakers and you can get a list of our programs and services. *You* can pick and choose the subjects and information that are of interest to *you* or *your organization*.

There are no membership fees or meeting to attend. We have OUR COMMUNICATION NETWORK set up for *you*. I feel that the age we live in has given us some of the best avenues available to communicate. The phone, internet, and our newsletters are our way of meeting with *you*. Then *you* can share with us and or a care partner out there. We will have conferences and seminars from time to time that you can attend if you like. Then we will present subjects from our books and speakers.

INTERNET ACCESS. drbarrettphd@yahoo.com

Here is our access to the internet. www.sosslfhepbooks.info

We hope you along with some of the Churches and organizations

Stop or Continue: {6}

I want you to feel a part our programs, because our evaluations are done by a neutral party.

LIST OF CONFERENCE & SEMNIAR SUBJECTS.

My life story *"Facing the real me, Run John Run, the real world and me. The hurt and pain, and the real cry for help"*.
(Book).
Study guide "Leader Ship Training on Group Sessions

SOS LIFE ENHANCEMENT,
Who are you, behavior identification and **behavior modification**; **Evaluations** "now that you have made a decision, what are the next steps in your life."

I believe everyone needs a check-up at some time in their life or when you feel the need for encouragement, or something to inspire you, or when you want to know more about yourself.

"SOS SELF IMPROVEMENT"
SELF-ACTUALIZATION - Image, Esteem, Worth & Discipline = Self-Identity Pride/Vanity, Self-Control, Self-Discipline, & Motivation.

"SOS NEW BEGINNINHGS."
Analytical Study dealing with personal situations require a good understanding of what a person is going through in Relationships, Marriage and Family. I deal with Divorce, Single Parenting, and Blended Families.

SOS Health & Fitness Program and "The No Non Cents workout". (Booklets 1 & 2).

SOS Bible Lessons, 1. Biblical Principals to live by: Bible Lessons to Study by and then different Bible subjects / IV)
How to pray, intercessory prayer, and Spiritual Warfare
(Booklets on Different Bible Subjects).

- A. My Testimony – Christian Principles
- B. Person to person – A look at the Person!
  PART 1 *Who am I*: Who is that person inside of me?
  PART 2 *What am I*: What is the person inside dealing with?
  PART 3 *Where am I going*: Where is the person inside going?
- C. Restoration of a life – "Dealing with the person inside".
- D. Conflict of the Ages – *Who and What is Man*: Where does Man fit in?
- E. Controversy of Sin – Biblical principles to live by: Where does God fit in?

Care Partner Survey?

Name _____

Care-Supporter, Survey P_Sv-1B: (Talent – Time – Finances)
Yes No

____ ____ A. Would you like to be a Care-Supporter, helping **SOS**?
____ ____   Helping with our Newsletter?
____ ____   Computer: Layouts ____ Programming ____
____ ____   Computer: Up-dating Addresses ____ Mailing list ____
____ ____   Doing research?
____ ____   Writing letters?
____ ____   Addressing envelopes?
____ ____   Miscellaneous tasks?

How much time minutes ____ hours ____ per month?

____ ____ B. What is your talent, or gift in helping others

_____

____ ____   How much time in minutes ____ hours ____ per month?
____ ____ C. Would you be willing donate, an amount per month $____
____ ____ D. Are you a Christian?
____ ____   If so, what denomination do you prefer

_____

____ ____   Are you member of a church; if so what church (optional)

_____

____ ____ E. Your testimony & burden (optional)

_____

____ ____ F. Would you like to be a Care-Prayer-Supporter, our motto is standing in the G.A.P. **for others?** **G**od **A**nswers **P**rayer.

We want you to agree with us that the information, you gave is true and honest to the best of your knowledge. We need your signature and date to verify surveys

We need YOUR PERMISSION: Please sign one or both lines:
If we can use this information in our survey sign here:

Name_____ Date_____

If *you* would like us to help us in some way, you sign here:
Name_____ Date_____
Thank you, the end of personal information survey

The most important thing I want *you* to know now that you become a part of support services. The purpose is to bring people together from all walks of life, share their experiences and help each other. Another way you can help is by sharing information with each other, and we have a network to make this information available.

OUR SERVICES
1. Common Ground – A personal encounter, "One to One".
2. The Panic Button – Is Our Message Line.
3. Independent Processing Center for Materials – Help and Study Guides, Books, Booklets.
4. Decision Materials – 1. Our life story, 2. Our study guides, 3. Our health & fitness programs.
5. Support Center (A) Support Partner (B) Support Group (C) Support Information (D)

Group Identities
6. Help Network – Communication Network – Information Network.
7. Life Enhancement Evaluations, Assessments, and Analysis.
8. Web site & email access.

Bible Studies etc.
I'm not here to argue doctrinal issues with anyone. You may want to add these books to *your* studies, and there will be separate books and booklets on Biblical Principles with **cognitive behavior** studies they are based on principles that anyone can use in their life. It is a separate study and very important as we look at **human behaviors** from the Biblical point of view. These studies have helped me, and the principles I use can help *you*. I want *you* to keep in mind that there are three different studies.

The IV-A, Biblical Principles to live by, sires IV-B, Bible Lessons IV-C. On prayer and how to pray). *You* can order any one or all depending on what *you* want to help *you*.

I went through a lot to find the real me in the real world. Some of it was fun at times, and there were some real tragedies to deal with. This always brings out the best and worst, the flaws show up in a person's character. This also brought about a very wide range of **cognition emotional** studies, and I had to deal them. I was not happy, and didn't seem to fit in anywhere! But now I feel much better about myself?

Thank you for being so patient with me. I feel we have come a long way; I have so much more to accomplish. My hope is *you* have enjoyed our time together in this study. I certainly have enjoyed sharing my thoughts with *you*. I have dealt with these case studies honestly and in a very kind and gentle way. Now *you* can see why I am so excited about these programs and information. Please feel free to contact us for whatever reason and let me know how *you* feel. If our studies have helped *you*, we would like to know what *you* think of our studies and the services we have to offer.

There is enough information to get *you* started off on the right track. Remember it took years for me to sort all this out in my life, and *you* can go at *your* own speed. I hope *you* have not missed anything along the way.

I have divided our studies into chapters with different kinds of help, because everybody has different needs.

"Personal-Attention" There are several alternatives out there Support Outreach Services and programs are one of them pulse our study guides.

There is an expense in producing these books, booklets and video's.
MY TESTIMONY & OUR INTRODUCTION BOOKLET.
MY BOOKS
YOU CAN GET ANY OF OUR BOOKS, BOOKLETS AND VIDEO'S THAT YOU WANT. Anything above that will enable us to help someone else.
Directory Service.

Our directory is one of our ways to help others I hope *your* organization or church will want to be a part of our directory, because it is unique and assists all of us in several ways. It will have various listings, and they can be very important in a person's life.

Support **O**utreach **S**ervices SOS LLC is a non-profit organization. We are not supported by any government agency, Church or denomination. We are supported by our directory, conferences, donations, and book sales. When you help us, we will share the results of our studies and surveys and keep you up to date through our newsletters. I hope you will want to help us in some way, but if you can't we will be glad to help. Only what *you* feel in your heart is all we expect from *you*.

Third Ad Listings

A comprehensive coverage of *your* Organization, Counseling Service or Church, Ministries, these services may be just what some person needs in their life. There are a lot of Christian services out there. What would *you* like for people to know about *you* and what *you* 'reorganization has to offer? It could be a business or service that meets the needs in *your* community and what would *you* like for people to know about *your* services.

(SOS) Directory & Referral Service!   {7}

　　___ ___   Our Directory, has Ads! & Listings!

　　___ ___   Businesses, Counselors, Clubs, Support Groups, and Service Organizations

　　___ ___   List of Churches, Classes, and Ministries

　　___ ___ Independent Services and Ministries

Dr. John Barrett PH-D, Program Coordinator.
Support outreach Services = **SOS LLC**

HOW TO REACH Support Outreach Services.

I would love to hear from you regardless of your need: Call or Write.
Support **O**utreach Services
　1122 W Cass Ave.

West Plains, Mo. 65775

A person needs to do something that allows *them* a chance to rebuild mentally as well as physically. I think if a person rebuilds physically this can give *them* a mental edge at the same time. Having this part of *their* life under control is good, but not a prerequisite if they are **climbing a mountain**. I am going to deal with my self-image, esteem, and self-worth in "SOS SELF IMPROVEMENT" book understanding one's self places a value and responsibility on *your* life and having that delicate balance of self-esteem. Of course too much ego or not enough ego is a real problem; the same is true in having too much pride and boasting about yourself at the same time. The "*Bible says pride comes before a fall*" there needs to be humility at the same time, consider your self-worth. If a person looks at *themselves* real CLOSE they will find some flaws and it can get them down on *themselves* as person.

What is (he or she) like on the inside is the real question? Have you been honest with *yourself* and others? The person that counts is the person on the inside, because (he or she) is the only one that can set *you* free or give *you* peace of mind. God can't do that if you don't let Him, or unless *you have kept things in your heart*. If you are not happy with *yourself*, *you* are not going to be happy regardless of what *you* do whether you are rich or poor. It is not going to make any difference even if you give to the poor, *and you* can even go to Church.

This could be the stepping stone it takes to turn *your* life around. I found this principle to be very true in my life. This is a major step in the healing process is renewing and remodeling the old person. My hope is *you* will end with a new *you*, old problems become a new way of thinking. I believe in talking openly in ways that deal with the healing process. I believe with proper guidance and help *you* will feel better about yourself. Just talking about *your* problems will not bring about healing in *your* life. Some good may come out of talking it may give you a better understanding, dedication and discipline.

You have to want help, and a plan of action in *your* life. People can use any of our **S**upport **O**utreach **S**ervices and Programs to help you.

Most of the time *people* get out of life what *they* put into it. **SOS** study guides will provide the right kind of help and guidance, but it is up to *you*. Most of the time if we can deal with the mind and the soul this will provide healing, because they go hand in hand. The mind sets the tone in the way *you* are going to deal with the healing process. It is very, very important to have the right attitude.

One, is by my personal experiences, personal profiles, illustrations, axioms, and research.

Two, I feel it is very important for *you* to be able to see what is going on in *your* life.

Three, I want *you* to enhance *your* life with some of these wonderful studies and programs.

THE PERSON

There is a conflict from within and I did not given up from the very outset.
Focus on helping yourself and don't let others discourage you.
No one wants to be told what to do.
You may think that is what I'm trying to do!

- There are patterns in a person's life and health-system and some can be changed.
- If you are not careful they will become a down-hill-spiral.
- I had to deal with these forces and it wasn't easy.

First and for most is the decision!
Second is carrying out the decision
Third was the exercise needed and then a workout program!

    1) *You* have to make a conscious effort on your part.
    2) *You* have to be motivated by *your* decision.
    3) *You* have to maintain good work ethics and habits.
    4) *You* need Dedication, Determination and Discipline.

Appendix *i*
RESUME of my Masters of Arts, & PH-D Studies

Here are the courses in relation to my **Masters Art Degree, Psychology & Christian Counseling**– completed April, 13th. 2008:

I. Marriage and Family Counseling: A Christian Approach to Counseling Couples

    ISBed by: Inter Varsity Press N: 0-8308-1769-7

    By: Everett L. Worthington, Jr.

    Published by: Inter Varsity Press

    Based on the Book:

    ISBN: 0-8308-1769-7

II. Emotional Intelligence. Book: Emotional Intelligence - Author: Daniel Goleman

    Published: Bantam Books

III. Psychology & Human Development. Based on the Book: PSYCHOLOGY, 5th Edition

    BY: Henry Gleitman, Alan J. Fridlund and Daniel Reisberg

    ISBN #: 0393973646

    Published by: W.W. Norton & Company, Inc.

IV. Counseling for problems and self-control. Divine Discipline, How to Develop and Maintain Self Control

    Author: Ronda Harrington Kelly

    Publisher: Pelican Publishing Company (July 1992)

    ISBN-10: 0882898922 - **ISBN-13:** 978-0882898926

V. Counseling in relation to self-esteem and the humanistic view. Based on the Book: THE BIBLICAL VIEW OF SELF-ESTEEM, SELF-LOVE AND SELF-IMAGE By: Jay E. Adams

    ISBN#:0890815534

HARVEST HOUSE PUBLISHERS 1-541-684-8900. Or Amazon.com

VI. WKSP04 - Workshop Topics:
    Walking Through the Fires of Conflict
    Counseling for Today
    Life Coaching
    Leadership/Time Management
    Christian Counseling
VII. PCC 589 Helping the Helpers Conference
VIII. WKSP0ST - Workshop 2005
IX. Thesis = Masters Thesis
    Support Outreach Services = SOS

I. Support * Links / Help & Healing topics? Support? Guidance
  A. Support Help and Healing –Bridging the GAPS is Guidance Answers Passion Support;
  B. Mentoring, Coaching, and Counseling
  C. Personal & Support Groups
II. Outreach * Common-Ground (*in home tools*) & Personal Profiles.
    Matching profiles / (seminars & Conferences) & Group Sessions

Louisiana Baptist University; Masters of Art in Psychology and Christian Counseling
                May 13, 2005:

PH-D course studies
Personal Life Experience Profiles:
Attached Pages / LCCOU 600, 601, 609, 610, & 611
Class Curriculum Studies
    1. PCC 622 COUNSELING ADULT CHILDREN OF ALCOHOLIICS –
  Based on the Book: WORKING WITH CHILDREN OF ALCOHOLICS
      Second Edition BY: Bryan E. Robinson & J. Lyn Rhoden
          ISBN# 0-7619-0757-2 (Paperback)
          ISBN# 0-7619-0756-4 (Hardbound)
        Published by: SAGE Publications Ltd.
    2. PCC 624 COUNSELING BEFORE MARRIAGE –

Based on the Book: Marriage Counseling: A Christian Approach to Counseling Couples
ISBN: 0-8308-1769-7
By: Everett L. Worthington, Jr. Published by: Inter Varsity Press

3. PCC 630 CONFLICT MANAGEMENT AND COUNSELING
4. PCC 632 BIBICAL COUNSELING THRAPIES –
   Based on the Book: COMPETENT TO COUNSEL
   ISBN#: 0310511402
   By: Jay E. Adams
   Published by: Zondervan Publishing House800-727-3480
   STUDY OF NOUTHETIC COUNSELING I

May 1/2007
Doctorate Dissertation is = Life Enhancement ABC's
Professor and adviser: Dr. Mark Crook, at Louisiana Baptist University

I believe in Personal Responsibility, Recovery, Restoration, Reconciliation
Rehabilitation & Preventive Maintenance!
Mentally - Emotionally – Physically

"I'm proud to an America"!
www.supportoutreach.info
Link to! SOS Intro-Booklet
Link to! Support Helping-Healing = Personal care & talking with someone one to one
Link to! outreach Common-Ground Matching Profiles + Conferences & Retreats
Link to! Services Studies & Information, Surveys & Evaluations, Health-Awareness
(Rehabilitation & Maintenance) = Health-Awareness & Fitness.
Link to! Email drbarrettphd@yahoo.com**&**web site www.sosselfhelpbooks.info

Appendix *ii*

Definitions:
Merriam – Webster Unabridged   P. 139
Assessments

1. **Physiology:** *Noun*
Latin *physiology is* natural science
   1 a :a branch of biology that deals with the functions and activities of life or of living matter (as organs, tissues, or cells) and of the physical and chemical phenomena involved – compare anatomy.
   2 :the organic process and phenomena of an organism or any of its parts or of a particular bodily process
Referenced from Merriam-Webster Collegiate.com
Merriam-Webster's Collegiate Dictionary Eleventh Edition / (date 2/15/04)
   http://unabridged.merriam-webster.com/cgi-bin/unabridged
                                                                    2/3/07

Family Genogram
Genetic & Temperament Analysis   P. 16 - 24

Questionnaires
Questionnaire I on Your Marriage Relationship   P. 27
Questionnaire II *Creating the Love Formula Analysis Form*
                                                    P. 62 - 64
Questionnaire III How do you feel about your job/school, spouse, friends, relatives, and especially your abilities   P. 84 - 87
Questionnaire VI What is the acid test in a relationship and marriage, it is "LOVE"   P. 114 - 115
Assessment of your LOVE"
P. 84Questionnaire V SOS study guide principles in marriage"! (+5 to -5)   P. 117
Questionnaire VI Questions to (ask each other):   P. 144
Questionnaire VII

How to maintain a good relationship is being able to communicate with each other?   P. 147 - 157
Know your communications' Skills Quiz: P. 107 - 110
Questionnaire VIII Normal and abnormal is defined by good and poor emotional control: P. 158
Questionnaire IX 14 Critical Situations?   P. 269 - 270

Appendix *iii*
Web References

Bing Image Research's
Advice Marriage Relationship, Inspirational quotes   Page 1 of 3
[1] P. 30 - 33

Why Teens Have Sex   Pages 1 & 2 [2] P. 36 - 43
Sex Smarts for Teens   Pages 1 – 3 [3] P. 44 - 49
Fact Sheet-Living Together Before Marriage Pages 1 – 3   [4] P. 49 - 53

Women Aged 15 – 29 Are Increasingly Having First Child Before Marriage   Page 1of 3[5] P. 53 - 55
Teen marriages   Pages 1 – 2 [6] P. 55 - 56
The Love Formula – Find Mr. or Ms. Right – Relationship
                                Pages 1 – 5 [7] P. 56 - 58
Recipe for a Happy Marriage: Fact or Fiction Pages 1-5   [8]
                                P. 60 - 65
Marriage ABCs Product Reviews Articles Forums Help
                                Pages 1-2 [9] P. 70–76
Newlyweds' 5 Biggest Pitfalls   Pages 1 - 2 [10] P. 96 - 97
Marriage ABCs Product Reviews Articles Forums Help.
                                Pages 1 - 2 [11] P. 106 - 113
Increasing Intimacy in Marriage   Pages 1 - 1 [12] P. 120 - 121
Overcoming Sexual Addiction in Marriage
                                Pages 1 -2 [13] P. 170 - 196
Divorce Rate: Divorce Rate in America Page 1 of 1 [14]
                                P. 201 - 202
The 10 Most Common Causes of Divorce / Marriage and Separation Advice   Page 1-5 [15]P. 211- 212
Recipe for a happy marriage Fact or Fiction Page 1 - 5 [16]
                                P. 214 - 219
Healing Your Heart After Divorce Pages 1 - 2 [17] P. 219 - 223
DivorceCare: Divorce Recovery Support Groups
                                Page 1 of 1 [18] P. 241 - 242
Parenting-solutions/kids-first   Pages 1 – 2 [19] P. 243 - 244

Children of Divorce   Pages 1 -5 [20] P. 354 - 256
Children of divorced parents are more likely to end their own marriage. Main Category: **Psychology / Psychiatry News**
                               Pages 1 - 5 [21] P. 256 - 265
Helping Children Adjust to Divorce   Pages 1 – 7 [22] P. 265 - 268
A Stepparent's Role   Pages 1 – 2 [23] P. 278 - 288
Step-parents   Pages 1 – 3 [24] P. 291 - 295
Parents On A step-Parents   Pages 1 – 2 [25] P. 295 - 298
Blended families # 1   Pages 1 – 3 [26] P. 298 - 301
Drugs, Brain, and Behavior – The Science of Addiction – Addictions Pages 1 -4 [27]P. 305 - 310
Treatment for Young Adults Troubled Teen Drug Use and Alcohol Rehab   Page 1 of 1 [28]P. 319 – 332
Teen Drug Use and Teen Drinking also known as Substance Abuse amongst teens and even children. Pages 1 – 3 [29] P. 332 – 336
Teen Drinking Statics a Family Guide   Pages 1- 2 [30] P. 346 – 348
Teen discipline, youth drug use, prevention Family Guide
                               Pages 1 – 2 [31] P. 348 - 350
Teen Smoking   Pages 1 – 2 [32] P. 350 - 352
US Department of Health and Human Services
Substance abuse and mental health services administration
Center for substance abuse prevention &Alcoholism & Intoxication Treatment Act   Pages 1 - 3 [33] P. 352 – 356
Mental Help Net – Perspective – Vol. 4, No 2– The Morality of Alcoholism   Pages 1 -2 of 1-6 [34] P. 356 - 360
Alcohol Research & Health: The effects of parental exposure on Executive Functions   Pages 1 of 5 [35] P. 360 - 363
ALCOHLISM   Pages 1 - 31[36] P. 366 - 374
Is there a protective genes against alcoholism Pages 1 -2 [37]
                               P. 374
Alcohol & Illicit Drugs Pages 1 of 2 thou 7 [38]P. 374 - 383
Is there a protective genes against alcoholism Pages 1 -2 [39]

P. 385 - 404

Alcoholism December 2001 - WHAT IS ALCOHOLISM?
Pages 1 – 2 [40] P. 405 – 409

The "American Heart Association web site"; Page 1 [41]
P. 410 - 412

Appendix *iiii*

By John O'Donohue
In out-of-the-way places of the heart,
Unconditional love that supersedes all else
Quotes & Poems   {1}

First, let's look at the Stages in the marriage relationship. {2}
P. 93

Demonstration Chart I: {3} **P. 116**
Evaluation of the marriage relationship, the <u>Life line</u> Age + Stage

Fifteen Ways to Say, "I'm Sorry."   {4}**P. 151**

Meyer Glantz, acting chief of the *Etiology Research Section of the*
A Profile addiction "a principle method for dealing with
Addictions". By Dr. B. R. Laken   {5} **P. 310**
National Institute for Drug and Alcohol Abuse.   {6}**P. 438**
(SOS) Directory & Referral Service!   {7}**P. 444**

Appendix *iiii*
Bible References

Mark 3:25 (KJV)	**P. 56**
Matt. 5:41-42 & Luke 6:27-29	**P. 58**
Gen 2:24 (KJV)	**P 60**
John 8:7-11;	**P. 117**
1 Corinthians 7:1-40(KJV)	**P. 119 - 122**
Proverbs 5:15-19; I Corinthians *7:2-5*	**P. 123**
I John 1:7-10 (KJV)	**P. 148**
Matt. 22:37-40; John 13:34-35; John 13:9-13; John 15:12-17; I Cor. Chapter 13;	**P. 149**
Rom. 13:8-10; Eph. 3:18-19	**P. 149**
Philippians 4:6-7 & Eph. 5:23	**P. 149**

www.ingramcontent.com/pod-product-compliance
Lightning Source LLC
Chambersburg PA
CBHW071646090426
42738CB00009B/1437